D1195165

HITLER'S
STORMTROOPERS

HITLER'S
STORMTROOPERS
THE SA, THE NAZIS' BROWNSHIRTS,
1922 – 1945

Jean-Denis Lepage

Frontline Books

HITLER'S STORMTROOPERS:
The SA, The Nazis' Brownshirts, 1922-1945

This edition published in 2016 by Frontline Books,
an imprint of Pen & Sword Books Ltd,
47 Church Street, Barnsley, S. Yorkshire, S70 2AS
www.frontline-books.com

ISBN: 978-1-84832-425-1

CIP data records for this title are available from the British Library

For more information on our books, please visit
www.frontline-books.com
email info@frontline-books.com
or write to us at the above address.

Printed and bound by CPI Group (UK) Ltd, Croydon, CR0 4YY
Typeset in 10.5/12.5 point Palatino

Contents

Acknowledgements   ix
Introduction   xi
List of Abbreviations   xv

PART 1: THE NATIONALSOZIALISTISCHE DEUTSCHE ARBEITERPARTEI (NSDAP)

Chapter 1: ORIGINS OF THE NSDAP
    The German Workers' Party (DAP)   1
    The National Socialist German Worker's Party (NSDAP)   2
    The Putsch of November 1923   3
    Hitler in Prison   5

Chapter 2: THE ROAD TO POWER
    The Period 1925–9   6
    The 1929 Crisis   7
    The 'Seizure' of Power   9

Chapter 3: THE NAZI IDEOLOGY
    Mein Kampf   11
    The Nazi Programme   11
    Racism and Anti-Semitism   14
    Totalitarianism   18
    Greater Germany   19
    Socialism   19
    War   21
    Nazism and Religion   22
    Blut und Boden   23
    Propaganda   24
    The Leader Principle   25

Chapter 4: MEMBERS OF THE NSDAP

    Membership   28

    Role and Indoctrination of the Members   30

    Salute and Oath   33

    Commemorative Days   35

Chapter 5: ORGANISATION OF THE NSDAP

    Units   39

    Ranks   41

    Party and Associated Organisations   41

    Rivalry at the Top   42

    USCHLA   44

Chapter 6: NSDAP REGALIA AND UNIFORMS

    Regalia   46

    The Swastika and *Hoheitszeichen*   46

    Daggers   49

    The *Reichszeugmeisterei*   51

    Uniforms   53

    NSDAP Anthem   57

PART 2: ORIGINS AND GROWTH OF THE *STURMABTEILUNG*

Chapter 7: THE *FREIKORPS*

    The Men of the *Freikorps*   61

    The *Freikorps'* Role in Post-war Germany   65

    A Threatening Force   66

Chapter 8: ORIGINS OF THE SA

    Gymnastic Association   73

    The *Sturmabteilung*   76

    Hermann Göring   78

    Ernst Röhm   82

Chapter 9: DEVELOPMENT OF THE SA

    Growth of the SA   89

    The *Frontbann*   92

    Conflict between Hitler and Röhm   85

    Franz-Felix Pfeffer von Salomon   98

    New Generations of SA   102

    Political Education   104

    The Return of Röhm   106

    Röhm's Clique   107

    Röhm's Reforms   109

Chapter 10: THE ROLE OF THE SA BEFORE 1933
    Propaganda and Hooliganism   114
    Battles against the Communists   119
    The Boxheimer Papers   125
    The Nature of SA Violence before 1933   126
    SA Martyrs   130

PART 3: THE ORGANISATION OF THE SA

Chapter 11: A MILITARY ORGANISATION
    The Number of SA Men   135
    Ranks   136
    Units   138
    Finances   141

Chapter 12: UNIFORMS AND FLAGS
    Early Uniforms   144
    The Grey Uniform   144
    Brown Shirts   145
    Flags and Banners   156

Chapter 13: *SONDEREINHEITEN* (SPECIAL UNITS)
    Introduction   162
    The Hitler Youth   177
    SA Reserve   180

Chapter 14: OTHER EUROPEAN FASCIST PARTIES AND THEIR MILITIAS
    Introduction   182
    Italy   183
    Great Britain   185
    United States of America   187
    France   187
    Denmark   195
    Norway   195
    Sweden   195
    Switzerland   195
    The Netherlands   197
    Belgium   198
    Hungary   200

PART 4: ZENITH AND FALL OF THE SA

Chapter 15: THE SA AFTER THE SEIZURE OF POWER
    Auxiliary Police (Hilfspolizei)   205

Early Concentration Camps 212
The SA: A Threat to Hitler's Regime 215

Chapter 16: THE LURKING RIVALS: THE SS
The Creation of the SS 218
Heinrich Himmler 223
Differences between the SA and the SS 225

Chapter 17: THE CRISIS OF 1934
Röhm's 'Second Revolution' 229
The SA and the German Army 233
Hitler's Hesitation 237
The Purge of 29–30 June 1934 240
Other Victims of the Purge 245
Hitler's Triumph 248
Business as Usual 251

Chapter 18: THE SA UNTIL 1945
Viktor Lutze 253
Re-organisation of the SA 254
SA Resentment 262
The Army After June 1934 268

Chapter 19: AFTERMATH 273

Chronology 277
Bibliography 289
Index 293

Acknowledgements

The author wishes to thank Jeannette à Stuling,
Simone and Bernard Luquet-Lepage, Willem Wiese,
Eltjo-Jakob de Lang and Ben Marcato, Jan à Stuling,
Michèle Clermont, Véronique Janty, Alex Dekker, Monique Brinks,
Peter De Laet and Siepje Kronenberg.

Introduction

By the end of the First World War much of Europe lay in ruins. Millions were dead, millions more had been maimed. Germany was in chaos, a country torn by revolution, civil war and starvation.

In 1919 in Paris, a peace conference was held to determine the fate of the world. Germany played the part of the accused. In the most humiliating way the Germans were forced to sign an admission of their war guilt. Substantial border territories were taken from them such as Eupen-Malmedy (by Belgium), Alsace-Lorraine (by France), Upper Silesia, Posen and West Prussia (by Poland) and a part of Schleswig (by Denmark). Danzig became a free city with no land access to Germany. All Germany's African colonies fell to the victors. On the verge of starvation Germany was ordered to hand over cattle, horses and the remnants of her merchant fleet. The defeated German army was reduced to 100,000 regular soldiers, forbidden the use of heavy weapons, and forced to renounce conscription. Enormous war reparations were demanded, the left bank of the Rhine was to be occupied for a period of fifteen years, and the French occupied the industrial Ruhr.

The defunct Second Reich – replaced by a democracy called the Weimar Republic which was to last from 1919 to 1933 – remained for several years the powerless toy of the victors. Many officers and soldiers of the disbanded army were not able to grasp, after all they had gone through, after all the sacrifices and the initial victories, that the war had indeed been lost. The 'stab-in-the-back' legend was born, and the myth grew of betrayal by the Social Democrats and the Jews. The humiliated German national feeling, trampled and crippled by the Treaty of Versailles, developed into vehement nationalism. The harshness of the

Treaty created a climate ideal for the growth of radical right-wing and nationalist parties. In Munich, a demagogue by the name of Adolf Hitler had already created the Nazi Party (NSDAP, the National-Socialist German Workers Party). Backed up by a paramilitary militia (SA stormtroopers) and various Bavarian right-wing movements, Hitler prepared a putsch against the Social Democrat government in 1923 in Munich. This amateurish and ill-prepared attempt failed. Hitler was arrested and imprisoned, but the Nazi movement was not wiped out. When Hitler was released from his short stay in prison, he began his political activity in earnest and re-created his party in 1925.

The Weimar Republic was marked by honest attempts at reconstruction, the creation of order, freedom and the assurance of a future for the nation. This was a difficult task as the short-sighted victorious nations only added fuel to Hitler's fire. The German people were working like slaves for nothing, since the hard-earned results of their production disappeared abroad as reparations. The modest achievements of Weimar were wiped out by the world economic crisis triggered by the Wall Street Crash of 1929. The Republic plunged into a catastrophic situation characterised by unemployment, bankruptcy, galloping inflation and general misery, which resulted in uncontrolled nationalism.

The Nazis exploited this collective frustration, persuading the poor exploited mass of proletarians and the ruined middle class that the Jews, the Democrats and the 'Reds' were to blame for everything. Hitler promised work, bread, freedom and a glorious future.

For the Nazis, Germany's only hope was to achieve equal status once more, strengthening her defences and ridding herself of all alien elements – by becoming truly and genuinely German again. Hitler's party grew at an amazing rate and – being the largest in the Reichstag – became a serious threat to the Weimar Republic. Success was largely due to the support of the conservatives, nationalists, landowners, militarists, petty bourgeois and rich German capitalists and industrialists who were alarmed at the increasing Communist threat. On 30 January 1933 President Hindenburg handed over the reins of government to Adolf Hitler who soon established a totalitarian dictatorship.

The *Sturmabteilung der NSDAP* (SA, assault battalion of the Nazi Party) – created in August 1920 – were strong-arm squads intended to protect the Nazis' meetings, to provoke disturbances, to break up other parties' meetings, and to beat up political opponents as part of a deliberate campaign of intimidation. After 1925 the name *Braunhemden* (Brownshirts) was also given to them because of the colour of their uniforms. Under the leadership of Hitler's close political associate, Ernst Röhm, this militia grew to become a huge and radical paramilitary force.

This book intends to answer several questions concerning Hitler's SA private militia organised within the Nazi Party. How did the SA become a national movement? Who was its chief Ernst Röhm? What was the relationship between Röhm and Hitler? What role did the SA play in providing Hitler with the keys to power? After the *Machtergreifung*, the 'seizure' of power by the Nazi on 30 January 1933, what was the function of the Brownshirts? Why did the brutal and scandalous Ernst Röhm stand in Hitler's way? What became of the SA after the bloody purge of June 1934?

To have a good understanding of what the SA was, it is important to know where the organisation originated from, what ideas it stood for and what methods it used. The first part of this book therefore deals with the Nazi Party, its origin, growth, organisation, and ideology. And as Nazism put the emphasis on display, attention is also paid to uniforms, flags and regalia.

The materials that are presented in this book were gleaned from various sources, but the SA is much less well known than Hitler's other militia, the infamous *Schutzstaffeln* (SS). In-depth studies of the SA are rare, publications are difficult to obtain, and some contain limited or incomplete information. There are very few reliable biographical works on Ernst Röhm, and it is only relatively recently that historians have come to appreciate the full extent of Röhm's contribution to the rise of Hitler. It is the author's hope that this book will go some way towards filling that gap. The aim of this book is both simple and ambitious: to bring some light historically and technically on the period 1919 to 1934 and to give a general overview of Hitler's SA, a reference for the professional and amateur historian.

The information in this book is true and complete to the best of the author's knowledge. But if any of reader of this work should detect factual or historical errors, or would like to share additional information with me for a future revision of this book, I encourage them to contact me at the publisher's address.

Of course, the author has no truck with any attempt at apologising for Nazism, or justifying Nazi crimes, or encouraging any form of neo-Nazism. On the contrary, this book is intended to be a historical and technical presentation of what Hitler's SA was, how it was organised and how it worked without forgetting all the sufferings, misery and death the Nazi regime brought to millions of people.

Jean-Denis Lepage
Groningen, The Netherlands

Abbreviations

AF	*Action Française*
AV	*Amerikadeutscher Volksbund* (German-American League)
AVV-VVK	*Alles Voor Vlaanderen-Vlaanderen Voor Kristus* ('All for Flanders, Flanders for Christ')
BDM	*Bund Deutscher Mädel* (League of German Maidens)
BUF	British Union of Fascists
CSAR	see OSARN
CV	*Central Verein deutscher Bürger jüdischen Glaubens* (Central Association for German citizens of Jewish confession)
DAF	*Deutsche Arbeit Front* (German Labour Front)
DAP	*Deutsche Arbeiterpartei* (German Workers' Party)
DLV	*Deutsche Luftsportverband* (German Air Sport League)
EME	*Ebredo Magyarok Egyesulete* (Association of Awakening Hungarians)
FJK	*SA Feldjägerkorps*
FONG	Friends of the New Germany (USA)
HJ	*Hitler Jugend* (Hitler Youth)
KWHK	*Kriegwinterhilfswerk* (Wartime Winter Relief Organisation)

KZ	*Konzentrationlager* (concentration camp)
LSSAH	*Leibstandarte-SS Adolf Hitler* (SS Bodyguard Adolf Hitler)
LVF	*Légion des Volontaires Français contre le Bolchevisme* (Legion of French Volunteers against Bolshevism)
MJP	*Mouvement des Jeunesses Patriotes* (Movement of Patriotic Youth [French])
MOVE	*Magyar Orszagos Vedero Egyesulet* (Association of Hungarian National Defence)
MSA	*Motor Sturmabteilung* (SA motorised units)
MVSN	*Milizia Volontaria per la Sigurezza Nazionale* (Volunteer Militia for National Security [Italian])
NS	*Nasjonal Samling* (National Union [Norwegian])
NSAB	*Nationalsozialistische Arztebund* (National Socialist Doctors' League)
NSB	*Nationaal-Socialistische Bewering* (National Socialist Movement [Dutch])
NSDAP	*Nationalsozialistische Deutsche Arbeiterpartei* (National Socialist German Workers' Party)
NSD-DB	*Nationalsozialistische Deutsch Doktoren Bund* (National Socialist German Professors' League)
NSDStB	*Nationalsozialistische Deutsch Studenten Bund* (National Socialist German Students' League)
NSF	*Nationalsozialistische-Frauenschaft* (National Socialist Women's Organisation)
NSFK	*NS-Flieger Korps* (National Socialist Flying Corps)
NSJ	*Nationalsozialistische Juristenbund* (National Socialist Jurists' League)
NSKK	*Nationalsozialistische Kraftfahrer-Korps* (Nazi Motor Corps)
NSKV	*Nationalsozialistische Kriegsopfer Verzorgung* (National Socialist Organisation for Veterans and War Victims)
NSLB	*Nationalsozialistische Lehrerbund* (National Socialist Teachers' League)
NSRK	*Nationalsozialistische Reiter Korps* (National Socialist Cavalry Corps)

NSV	*Nationalsozialistische Volkswohlfahrte* (National Socialist People's Welfare Organisation)
OC	Organisation Consul
OKW	*Oberkommando der Wehrmacht* (Supreme Command of the German Armed Forces)
OSAF	*Oberste Sturmabteilung Führung* (Upper SA Command)
OSARN/CSAR	*Organisation secrète d'Action révolutionnaire nationale* (Secret Organisation of National Revolutionary Action)/*Comité Secret d'Action Révolutionnaire* (Secret Committee for Revolutionary Action) [French]
OT	*Organisation Todt*
PCF	*Parti Communiste Français* (French Communist Party)
PPF	*Parti Populaire Français* (French Popular Party)
PSF	*Parti Socialiste de France* (French Socialist Party)
PSN	*Parti Socialiste National* (National Socialist Party [French])
RAD	*Reicharbeitsdienst* (National Labour Service)
RAZ	*Reichsautozug Deutschland* (National Motor Squad Germany)
RNP	*Rassemblement National Populaire* (National Popular Union [French])
RSHA	*Reichssicherheitshauptamt* (SS State Central Security Office)
RuSHA	*Rasse-und Siedlungshauptamt* (SS Central Office for Race and Settlement)
RZM	*Reichszeugmeisterei* (National Quartermaster's Department)
SA	*Sturmabteilung* (Assault battalions)
SD	*Sicherheitsdienst* (Security Service)
SS	*Schutzstaffel* (Protection Squad)
SS-VT	*SS-Verfügungstruppen* (SS military units – forerunners of the *Waffen-SS*)
TeNo	*Technische Nothilfe* (Technical Emergency Service)

USCHLA	*Untersuchungs-und Schlichtungs-Ausschüsse* (USCHLA, Committee for Investigation and Arbitrage)
VGAD	*Verstärkter Grenzaufsichtsdienst* (Reinforced Border Surveillance Service)
VNV	*Vlaamsch Nationaal Verbond* (Flemish National League)
WHW	*Winterhilfswerk* (Winter Help League)
WuVHA	*Wirtschafts-und Verwaltungshauptamt* (SS Economic and Administrative Office)
ZVfD	*Zionistische Vereinigung für Deutschland* (Zionist Association for Germany)

Part 1

The National Sozialistische Deutsche Arbeiterpartei (NSDAP)

Chapter 1

Origins of the NSDAP

THE GERMAN WORKERS' PARTY (DAP)

In March 1918, a nationalist political group, the 'Committee for a Just Peace', was founded at Bremen in Northern Germany. The committee had a branch in Munich, headed by a worker named Anton Drexler. Drexler was a Bavarian idealist and nationalist, frustrated by his unfitness for military service. In January 1919, Drexler broke away from the Committee and created his own right-wing nationalist party, naming it the *Deutsche Arbeiterpartei* (DAP, German Workers' Party). The DAP was one of the numerous parties which sprang up in post-war Germany – and particularly in Bavaria – at a time of economic and political ferment when the nation's affairs were in a state of great instability and when violence was rampant. Bavaria is a German province with a history of particularism. Within the Second Reich (1871–1918), it was a kingdom which enjoyed political self-government, wide autonomy and its own army. Prussian hegemony provoked the resentment of many Bavarians, and the tragic costs of the First World War, followed by the defeat of 1918, the humiliation of the Treaty of Versailles and the turmoil of the post-war period were blamed on northern Protestant Prussian militarism.

The name of Drexler's party was misleading. The political goals of the DAP were vague, being at the same time modest and radical, patriotic and nationalist, anti-capitalist and anti-Semitic. It appealed not so much to the working class as to the discontented chauvinistic petty bourgeois with an emphasis on a profound hatred of the 'Jewish-Masonic conspiracy' and Socialism. What few members Drexler's party had came from the Munich railway yards, while others were craftsmen, skilled workers, white-collar workers, commercial employees, small shopkeepers, a few academics and demobilised soldiers who were finding it hard to re-establish themselves in civilian life. The whole thing – halfway between a secret society and a drinking club – was a manifestation of a vague lower-middle-class disquiet fed by the trauma of the lost war. Emotions and fears took the place of political analysis, simple slogans replaced a proper political programme, and hazy theories were calculated to win the respect of unsophisticated citizens. The DAP had little success and barely achieved local importance. Its murky existence was confined to the back rooms of several Munich beer halls.

THE NATIONAL SOCIALIST GERMAN WORKER'S PARTY (NSDAP)

In mid-1919, Major Konstantin Hierl and Captain Karl Mayer of the German Army ordered a not-yet demobilised soldier of Austrian birth called Adolf Hitler (1889–1945) to investigate counteracting Communist influence in Munich by making contact with ultra-rightist groups. Hitler's first encounter with Drexler's DAP therefore was largely fortuitous as he was a spy in the service of the Army. Hitler attended a DAP meeting and attracted Drexler's attention by making an impromptu speech against a Bavarian separatist. Invited to return, Hitler joined the DAP in September 1919. Rapidly he became a popular orator, and an influential member as the ready-made political group accorded with his own confused ideas about politics. Hitler was demobilised in March 1920 and became leader of the DAP in April 1920. The party was then re-named the *Nationalsozialistische Deutsche Arbeiterpartei* (NSDAP, National Socialist German Worker's Party). For convenience this was abbreviated to two pairs of letter, the acronym *Nazi* (short for national, pronounced na-tzi-o-nal). In February 1920, the small DAP had revealed its political programme in the form of twenty-five points. Drawn up by Drexler, Feder and Hitler, the 25-point programme remained official Party policy until the end of the Nazi movement in May 1945. Today it is no longer necessary to demonstrate that the Nazi's 'socialist demands' were purely demagogic. While the sincerity of Drexler and Feder is undoubted, there is every reason to doubt Hitler's. It is obvious that for him the first four points of the programme were all-important, and these highly instructive points were as follows.

- Union of all Germans in a *Großdeutschland* (Greater Germany) based on the right of self-determination.
- Revocation of the Treaty of Versailles.
- Land and territories to feed the German people and settle its surplus population (*Lebensraum* or 'living space').
- Restriction of citizenship to those of German blood.
- Jews to be denied membership of the German *Volk* ('nation').

In July 1921, after an internal quarrel, Anton Drexler was kicked upstairs as Honorary President, and from then on the ruthless, megalomaniacal and egocentric Hitler began to eliminate all opposition in order to obtain unlimited power within the party. Drexler left the NSDAP in 1924, and never participated in the Nazi movement again. A forgotten figure, he died in February 1942.

Under the energetic leadership of Hitler, the few members of the tiny NSDAP regarded themselves as revolutionaries. Soon they did not hesitate to employ violence. From the start, the ambitious Hitler thought big and wanted to turn the small and insignificant local Bavarian group into a national German movement.

THE PUTSCH OF NOVEMBER 1923

In the period 1922–3, the political situation of Germany worsened as the country faced a critical situation. As the Germans were unable to pay reparations as stipulated by the Treaty of Versailles, the French government refused any concessions and in January 1923 occupied the Ruhr, the industrial and mining heart of Germany. The occupation became a serious crisis and a trial of strength between the two nations. German opposition manifested itself passive resistance, strikes and sabotage, and the French reacted with fines, arrests, deportation and a few executions of extreme opponents and saboteurs. The occupation of the Ruhr resulted in the collapse in the value of the Reichsmark and, in July 1923, the nightmare of hyper-inflation, bringing the end of trade, bankrupt businesses, shortages of food and mass unemployment. This dealt a further blow to the standing of the Weimar Republic (named after the town where the democratic constitution had been drawn up in 1919). From Hitler's point of view, this situation appeared pre-revolutionary. Indeed, Nazism was a phenomenon, which throve only on disorder and insecurity and Hitler saw the opportunity to take advantage of the troubles to his own profit. His plan was to fight against the internal enemy, and once victory at home had been secured, the Nazis could then deal with Germany's foreign foes.

Gradually the idea of a violent putsch took form, and Hitler and the men around him performed astounding political contortions. Indeed an essential precondition of success was a common policy of all the Bavarian nationalist groups. For this purpose the so-called *Kampfbund* (Combat League) was created on 30 September 1923 in Nuremberg. There Hitler joined other patriotic nationalist leaders to celebrate German Day, which marked the anniversary of the Prussian victory over France in 1870. The league included several far-right nationalist parties and patriotic societies, notably the German National Socialist party in Bavaria, Adolf Hitler's NSDAP and its *Sturmabteilung* (SA), the Oberland League (an armed anti-communist paramilitary unit 4,000 strong led by Friedrich Weber) and the *Bund Reichskriegsflagge* (Imperial War Flag Society, also called the *Verband Reichskriegsflagge*, Imperial War Flag Union, another paramilitary organisation founded by Ernst Röhm in 1923). These men were armed fighters, practically all disgruntled nationalists, and many were tough and determined war veterans. Hitler was the *Kampfbund*'s political leader, while Hermann Kriebel led its militia. The purpose was to consolidate and streamline the ultra-nationalist agenda and also prepare the overthrow of the Weimar Republic. Though the Nazi Party was by no means the largest group, in a powerful speech Hitler pleaded for a free hand in the struggle against the Weimar Republic. Like a snake in the grass, Hitler weaved through the maze of conflicting purposes, allying himself with everyone, hardly bothering to keep his own Party informed of his shifting and often contradictory schemes. He managed to be entrusted with the leadership of the entire national movement in Southern Germany and decided to take power by force. On the evening of 8 November 1923, Hitler and his followers burst in on a political meeting in the Bürgerbräukeller – a large Munich beer hall – and arrested the Bavarian state commissioner and the head of the Bavarian armed forces. Pistol in hand, Hitler proclaimed the National Revolution.

The next morning Hitler, General Erich Ludendorff (1865–1937) – one of Germany greatest generals of the First World War – and some 9,000 Nazi followers marched to the centre of the city with the vague intention to seize power in Bavaria and sparking a revolution throughout Germany. The ill-prepared and badly executed coup, known as *Marsch auf die Feldherrnhalle* (or Munich Beer Hall putsch) was a humiliating fiasco. It failed because both the Bavarian army and the *Reichswehr* had refused at the last moment to endorse the extremist programme of Hitler and his associates. The Nazi putsch was bloodily repressed by troops who opened fire on the conspirators. Sixteen Nazis were killed, several more were wounded and most of the leaders – including Hitler – were arrested and put on trial.

HITLER IN PRISON

At his trial Hitler pleaded his own case –that he had acted for the ultimate good of the Fatherland – with such rhetorical effect that the judges were far from unanimous about his guilt. Whether willingly or as a result of intimidation, the judges were predisposed towards him and Hitler received the lowest penalty prescribed for conspiracy and high treason. The attitude of the judges throughout the Weimar Republic was one of leniency towards criminals who could be excused as patriots. Hitler was sentenced to a nominal five years' in prison, and the Nazi Party and the SA squads were banned. To maintain legality, the Party was briefly renamed the National Socialist Freedom Party and the SA continued under the name of *Frontbann*. Normally the failed putsch should have meant the end of Hitler's political career. In any normal democratic state, an act of armed treason forever excludes the chief perpetrator from further political life. Moreover, Hitler was a foreigner. But at that time Bavaria was not a normal state, and paradoxically Hitler's failed coup and trial served to turn his defeat into a triumph and helped him build a national reputation. Hitler enjoyed an easy and comfortable detention in the fortress of Landsberg. He was allowed free communication with the outside world, and was well fed. He received colleagues and supporters and began to dictate his book *Mein Kampf* to his faithful secretary/deputy Rudolf Heß. Under an amnesty he only spent just over a year in prison, from 11 November 1923 to 20 December 1924. Hitler emerged from Landsberg prison with the halo of a political martyr.

Chapter 2

The Road to Power

THE PERIOD 1925–9

Hitler's detention in Landsberg marked the end of the first period of his political career. When he started his political activities anew in early 1925, Hitler had become a wiser, if not a better, man. He had thought deeply, learned a lot and henceforth abandoned all ideas of violent revolution, as the police and the army were too strong to oppose. Instead he decided to observe 'legal' principles for political success, with unity under his sole leadership, vigorous opportunistic propaganda, gaining the support of the Army and making maximum use of the democratic means that were available. His ambitions were no longer centred on Munich and Bavaria but on Berlin. Of course, Hitler had no personal objection to the use of violence to secure his aims, rather approving of it than not. He had always employed and sanctioned it in the past and was quite prepared to do so in the future, but after the failed putsch it was his firm intention to gain power by the perfection of propaganda, by promising anything to everyone and ultimately by winning votes. For tactical reasons he would temporarily renounce or underplay some of his ideas and ambitions while emphasising others, but by then the foundations of his movement were laid and the course was set.

After prison in 1925, Hitler was forbidden to speak in public and the road to power was long and difficult. During the period 1925 to 1929, Germany made an astonishing recovery: the position of the Weimar Republic stabilised, the economy was partly restored, inflation was controlled, the number of unemployed decreased, social agitation was stemmed, and as a result radical and ultra-nationalist parties like the

NSDAP were in steep decline. However, the economic situation remained precarious as the supporting funds had been lent from the United States of America. Furthermore, the Weimar Republic was unpopular among the upper classes, conservatives and right-wing political groups. The Republic had been constituted as a democracy to uphold the provisions of the Versailles Treaty. It was a national German government based in and acting from Berlin but its powers were weakened by the continued existence of semi-autonomous governments in the States of Prussia, Saxony, Württemberg and Bavaria. The regional governments had the power to veto any rulings issued from Berlin. It was in this unstable situation that extremists of both Left and Right tried to increase their influence. Hitler called the founders of the Weimar Republic the 'November Criminals', those who had been instrumental in bringing about the defeat and surrender of 11 November 1918. In the Nazi point of view, the hated Weimar Republic stood for all the evils of 'Jewish' democracy, being held responsible for all the sufferings imposed upon the German people: the dishonour of peace, war reparations, the monetary system, the ruin of the country, emasculating pacifism, and the presence of French troops in the Ruhr .

Between 1925 and 1929, owing to Hitler's change of plan and methods, the NSDAP was no longer a provincial movement centred in Munich, but a party aiming to develop nationally, notably in northern Germany and Berlin. Its influence, unity and significance were rather limited, however. The party was prepared for a long uphill struggle, when suddenly Hitler was provided with another period of chaos.

THE 1929 CRISIS

The international crisis of 1929 worked like a detonator. The Wall Street Crash of October 1929 struck a blow at American business confidence and cut foreign lending. Much of the speculation had been done on credit so that financial institutions and investors now began to call in short-term foreign loans. As overall business activity declined, so did America imports. The outflow of US dollars to Europe was thus checked and then reversed. During the early 1930s the American recession worsened and the full effects of the crisis began to be felt in Europe. The fragile, artificial and uncertain German economy collapsed, with the contraction of trade and production, cessation of foreign loans, withdrawal of investment, prices collapse, falls in wages, bankruptcies, the forced sale of property, shops and farms, factories closing and large-scale unemployment (about six million jobless in 1930). The crisis had far-reaching consequences, affecting not only the working and middle classes, but also retired people who lost their savings, as well as peasants and farmers who were forced to sell their properties. Germany was stricken by a social, economic and political earthquake, and millions of hopeless people were no longer amenable to the arguments of reason.

The Nazi Party was never a political party in any proper sense of the term. It was a movement, a conspiracy to gain power, and to achieve this it needed active members and followers, money and votes. After the failed putsch of 1923, Hitler was opposed to the use of force at least on a level that would result in a direct clash with the army and the police, the powerful and constitutional forces of the State. Instead he intended to seize power by legal means, but the Nazi Party was not a parliamentary political organisation as its unequivocal aim was the overthrow of the Weimar Republic. Hitler always threatened the use of force, but he confined its use to opponents who had no such sanctions at their disposal. For the rest he relied upon the power of propaganda displaying hatred, passion and fanaticism in order to gain support from every section of German society, the possessors and the dispossessed alike. By spreading lies, using easy slogans, distorting facts, and interpreting the truth in their own interests, the Nazis inspired fantastic fears, extravagant hatreds and false hopes. They exploited the people's angry and desperate mood, blaming international Jewish capitalism and the Weimar Republic for the crushing crisis, and claimed that no one else but Hitler could restore order, national pride and wealth. Hitler had always said that the 'Republic of the November Criminals' would lead to disaster, and by the early 1930s many voters thought he was right. Cunningly using the framework of the democratic constitution, the NSDAP began to attract a mass of followers and achieved significant successes at the polls, combining the votes of disillusioned workers and the ruined middle classes.

The radicalisation of German politics was shown by the fact that an overwhelming number of voters – particularly the young – supported either the Nazis or the Communists: German voters were falling into the hands of the extremists. At the same time the German upper classes, confronted with economic stagnation and unable to rally the lower and middle classes behind their drab, middle-of-the-road parties, in desperation began to look to authoritarianism. It was thought that only a strong leader could hold society together and revive the economy. There were backstairs intrigues with the financial and industrial magnates, who feared the triumph of the Communist opposition. In the 1930 elections the Nazi Party made spectacular progress and it emerged as one the most popular political formations. For the first time since 1923 the Nazis were taken seriously. Negotiations with leading financiers, bankers and industrial and press tycoons led to a direct subsidy from industrialists such Emil Kirdorf and Baron Fritz Thyssen who now regarded Hitler as a possible bulwark against Communist revolution; they guaranteed the Nazi's debts and financed their election campaigns.

A point of interest is Hitler's nationality. By birth Hitler was an Austrian but having not fought in the Austrian army during the First World War he had lost it. Hitler did nothing to acquire German nationality in the 1920s. The champion of German ultra-nationalism was not even a German citizen. In 1930 a certain Doctor Frick suggested the stateless Hitler be appointed Gendarmerie Commissioner as this post, which was vacant, involved the obtaining of German nationality. This was rejected by Hitler who considered it ridiculous and far beneath his standing to become – even purely honorifically – a police superintendent. In early 1932, Göbbels suggested Hitler be appointed as Professor to the Technical High-School of Brunswick (this position too automatically included the obtaining of German nationality). But could a man who had not a single academic qualification be made a Professor? Finally the question of Hitler's nationality was solved by Hermann Göring who had the brilliant idea of having him appointed economic councillor to the Brunswick delegation in Berlin. Hitler became a (purely honorary) 'councillor' and officially a German citizen on 25 February 1932.

THE 'SEIZURE' OF POWER

After complicated and tortuous political moves in 1931–2, Hitler did not seize power, but was appointed to office in a political bargain. As brilliantly described by Alan Bullock in his 1952 book *Hitler, A Study in Tyranny*, the growth and the triumph of the Nazi Party were not fortuitous. 'Despite the relative mass support he had won, Hitler came to power as the result, neither of any irresistible revolutionary movement sweeping him to power, nor by SA terror and force, nor even of a popular victory at the polls, but as part of a shoddy political deal, the bad judgement of his temporary supporters and also because of the division of his political opponents. The politicians who supported Hitler and the businessmen who contributed to Nazi coffers believed that they would be able to tame him. Expecting to use him as their tool for their own purposes, they learned later to their dismay that instead he was skilful in using them. They learnt too late that he who sups with the Devil needs a very long spoon'.

January 30th 1933 was a landmark for Germany and the world when President Hindenburg – in a strictly constitutional fashion – appointed Hitler Chancellor (corresponding to the function of Prime Minister). Hitler never abandoned the cloak of legality – instead he turned the law inside out and made illegality legal. He broke the bonds which had been designed to restrain him and gradually became an all-powerful dictator. The Weimar Republic was never formally abrogated but within a few months, after having arbitrarily crushed all opposition, the cunning Hitler imposed a dictatorship, proclaimed himself *Führer* of Germany, and established a one-party state by an act of 14 July 1933. Disregarding conventional rules, he destroyed political freedom and the rule of law. He transformed the German economy and finances, abolished the separate states and made Germany for the first time a united nation. Unscrupulously he freed Germany from the restrictions of the Versailles Treaty and restored the armed forces. There was nothing original in Hitler's policy: his unique quality was the gift of translating commonplace thoughts into action.

The Nazi Party had some 27,000 paid-up members in 1925, 49,000 in 1926, 108,000 in 1928 and 178,000 by the end of 1929. The NSDAP had 210,000 members in March 1930 and 850,000 in January 1933. By September 1939 this had increased to more than 4 million with 150,000 officials, by January 1943 the NSDAP numbered 6.5 million, and 8.5 million in 1945. During the years of the struggle for power, the NSDAP had faced 40,000 court cases. By the end of 1932, its members could boast of prison sentences totalling 14,000 years and 1,500,000 marks in fines.

Chapter 3

The Nazi Ideology

Mein Kampf

During his short stay in prison in 1924, Hitler wrote his infamous book *Mein Kampf* ('My Struggle'), which became the 'Bible' of Nazism and a bestseller, making the author a wealthy man. About ten million copies were sold in Hitler's lifetime. *Mein Kampf*, written in a monotonous, turgid and convoluted style, is notorious for its grammatical inadequacies, its obscure dialectal idioms and its ill-phrased sentences. The book contains most of the central tenets of Hitler's ideology, such as the fixation on issues of race, ultra-nationalism, militarism, the need for 'regeneration', the glorification of violence, war and, as the title suggests, struggle. It also showed that Hitler's ambitions had moved on from national politics to world conquest. However, for him politics was purely pragmatic, and he declared later that large parts of his book were no longer valid when the situation changed. Hitler saw himself as a visionary with a mission, an infallible prophet, and an empire-builder who believed in his own inspiration. He was also a cunning opportunist, an ungrateful gang leader without scruples, a consummator actor, and a master manipulator of mass emotion. He deliberately exploited the irrational side of human nature, both in himself and others.

THE NAZI PROGRAMME

Nazi ideology was poor, indifferent, mediocre, crude and in many aspects simplistic. In fact it was negative, being 'against' or 'anti' in essence. It was indeed principally marked by anti-intellectualism, anti-individualism, anti-Semitism, anti-parliamentarism, anti-democracy, anti-liberal, anti-Marxism, anti-pacifism, anti-criticism and even anti-capitalism – only in theory, because Hitler had to compromise with the men who funded him and his party. The Nazis extolled brute force, discipline, arrogance, the absence of morale and scruples, fanaticism, nationalism, and above all xenophobia and racism.

The Nazi programme issued in the early 1920s never offered voters a well-defined programme of politics and economics. Rather it was a 'grand design', a *Weltanschauung* ('vision of the world'), a comprehensive view, an attitude toward life in general in which actions were determined by the practical reality of a given moment. The Nazi programme was indeed a loose framework in which arrogant individuals could seek their own places, and an ideal nebulous enough to fulfil everybody's expectations. Vagueness was a deliberate feature of Hitler's ideology. He achieved unprecedented personal power by systematically promising anything to everyone while doing secret deals with anyone who could be of some use to him, no matter how much difference there was between those secret promises and the official oratory in public.

What the Nazis proposed and promised was not particularly new or original. The twenty-five demands in the NSDAP programme were as follows:

1. The union of all Germans in a *Großdeutschland* (Greater Germany) based on the right of self-determination.
2. The revocation of the Treaty of Versailles.
3. Land and territories to feed the German people and settle its surplus population (*Lebensraum*, 'living space').
4. The restriction of state citizenship to those of German blood, no Jew to be a German.
5. Non-Germans in Germany to be only guests and subject to appropriate laws.
6. Official posts to be filled only according to character and qualification.
7. The livelihood of citizens to be the state's first duty.
8. Non-German immigration to be stopped.
9. Equal rights and duties for all citizens.
10. Each citizen must work for the general public good.
11. All income not earned by work to be confiscated by the state.

12. All war profits to be confiscated.
13. All large business trusts to be nationalised.
14. Profit-sharing in all large industries.
15. Adequate provision for old age.
16. Small businessmen and traders to be strengthened and large department stores to be handed over to them.
17. Reform of land ownership and end to land speculation.
18. Ruthless prosecution of serious criminals, and the death penalty for profiteers.
19. Materialist Roman law to be replaced with ancestral German traditions.
20. A thorough reconstruction of the national education system.
21. The state to assist motherhood and youth.
22. Abolition of the paid professional army, and the formation of a national conscript army.
23. Newspapers to be owned by Germans; non-Germans banned from working on them.
24. Religious freedom, except for religions, which endanger the German race.
25. A strong central government for the execution of effective legislation.

Nazi ideology was not only simplistic, it was also contradictory. The emphasis was on anti-Semitism, ultra-nationalism, the concept of Aryan racial supremacy, contempt for liberal democracy and the principle of unique leadership. Greatly influenced by Mussolini's Fascism, the Nazi programme was designed to appeal to everyone with a grievance of some kind. More than an intellectually-constructed doctrine, it was a flexible movement aiming at aggressive action. For many people, it was a kind of religion based on blind faith, on irrationality, and on exploitation of subconscious fears and primary instincts. The ideology was a jumble of vague generalisations and prejudiced ideas, a hotchpotch of various misappropriated philosophical principles lent from various theorists such as Darwin, Fichte, Jakob Grimm, E. M. Arndt, Treitschke, H. S. Chamberlain, Paul de Lagarde, Richard Wagner, Adolf Stöcker, Adam Muller, Rühle von Lilienstern, Hegel, Nietzsche, Hans F. K. Günther and many others. In addition, historical falsifications and a motley of 'scientific' facts were forged by Nazi 'philosophers' (notably Walther Darré and Alfred Rosenberg), and used to excuse brutality, ruthlessness, megalomania, a complete disregard for democracy and individual rights. The only goal was the absolute power of Hitler via the absolute hegemony of Germany.

RACISM AND ANTI-SEMITISM

The main characteristic, the pillar, the fundamental tenet of Nazi ideology was racism. This was not a unique view in the era of colonialism when the European culture and economy was based on the supposed superiority of the white race and the exploitation of the other 'inferior' African and Asian races. In the age of the 'Yellow Peril' and the 'White Man's Burden', European and North American cultures were already primed to accept the superiority of certain races over others. Of course the Nazis considered coloured people from Africa and Asia as inferior, as many white people did at that time in the USA and in Europe. What singled Nazism out from accepted European and North American racism was the inequality within the white race. Nazi racism was based on the belief that the superior race was that of the 'Germanic' Aryans. The Aryans were Proto-Indo-European people who established themselves in Iran and northern India between 2,000 and 1,000 years BC. The Aryans later moved into Europe and – supposedly – were the ancestors of the German people. Racist Nazi ideology was borrowed in large part from the work of the French diplomat and theorist Joseph Arthur, comte de Gobineau (1816–82). In his book *Essai sur l'inégalité des races humaines*, published in 1853, Gobineau – without any historical or scientific proof – made a link between the Germans and the Ancient Aryans, and proclaimed the superiority of the Germanic race. It should be noted, however, that Hitler did not always show great respect for the Germanic ancestors – at least in private. Culturally he often displayed a striking preference for the ancient peoples of the Mediterranean and especially Athens.

The supposed Germanic superiority had also been prepared for by a good deal of nonsense talk and absurd writing at the end of the nineteenth century. Some of the theories of these philosophers and thinkers were mixed together, resulting in the confused Nazi conception of human races. Nazi racial doctrine was seen by many as something which could be turned to good account, and often regarded as salvation from decadence. Hitler's ridiculous racial verbiage had three dimensions; it provided Germany with its purpose (expansion in the form of *Lebensraum*, living space), its social cohesion (the *Volksgemeinschaft*, the racial community) and its scapegoats (Jews, Gypsies, Slavs and foreigners). Without any historical or scientific proof, the Germans were declared the *Herrenvolk* (master people), made up of *Übermenschen* (supermen) who were regarded as biologically superior to everyone else and intended to rule the world. Other white people (e.g. south European Latins or Arabs) were graded as inferior but were tolerated. However, other white people (Jews, Gypsies and Slavs) were declared *Untermenschen* (sub-humans), and were denied membership of the human race. The most terrifying Nazi creed was indeed anti-Semitism. The driving force of Nazism was an existential fear, which was transmuted into violence and terror against real or imaginary enemies. The premise was that the structure of a successful society had to have 'racial purity' as its foundation. The fact that there was no such thing as racial purity in Germany, in Europe or anywhere else was no obstacle to forming Nazi ideology. It was built up from the hatred of the Jews. The term 'Jew' could never be defined in Semite racial features but only connected to the Judaic religion. Incidentally there is really no such thing as race, although race is often regarded as a genetic distinction, and refers to people with shared ancestry and shared genetic traits. Common ancestry is not required to be a Jew. Many Jews worldwide share common ancestry, but you can be a Jew without sharing this common ancestry, for example, by converting. Thus, although one could never become black or Asian, blacks and Asians can become Jews. Clearly Jews are not a race, and there is more to being Jewish than just a religion. Officially for the Nazis a Jew was someone whose parents and grandparents were of Jewish religion.

Citizenship in Nazi Germany was thus determined by such uncertain criteria as 'race' and 'blood'. As we have just seen, according to the Nazi 25-point programme, no Jew could be a German citizen. Non-Germans in Germany were considered as 'guests' and subjected to appropriate laws, and non-German immigration was to be stopped. For Hitler, the Jews were responsible for all the negative manifestations of modern life. They were a separate race, impossible to be assimilated. They were responsible for the defeat of 1918. They were associated with the malign, exploitative forces of capitalism, but also with the evils of Marxism and Communism. Hitler was convinced that Jewish capitalism and Jewish communism were partners. He firmly believed that both capitalism and communism were weapons created and used by the Jews. For him there was a Jewish world conspiracy aimed at taking power everywhere. The Jews were accused of infiltrating nations in order to subvert them internally. They were depicted as dangerous parasites contaminating the purity of German blood: they were referred to as octopuses, vipers, serpents, or noxious bacilli undermining the German community from within, spiders sucking the blood out of the German people, or rats trying to pollute them. For Hitler syphilis was the typical Jewish attribute, a quasi-asset of Jewry in general. In the new *völkisch* epoch the 'French disease' of old was now termed the 'Jewish disease'. The 'pure German *Herrenvolk*' was thus threatened with decay by the 'impure Jews'. So Jews had to be wiped out, exterminated, eradicated. Hitler identified the Jewish menace to German society, which he claimed to perceive, with the Communist threat of which many Germans were excessively afraid. The strong Aryans were to be strengthened at the expense of the usurping weak, the Jews. In other words regenerating Germany meant eradicating the Jews. At first there was neither plans nor blueprint nor agenda nor timetable for mass murder, but from the start the shocking message was clear and the ugly warning was there for those who wished to heed it. This criminal attitude became the new moral norm. It became the duty of the new elites, the Nazis and the SS, to make the dream of the new German state into a lasting reality. This goal, eradication of Jews by mass murder, was commensurate with 'unprecedented' brutality and was carried out, mainly after 1942, by industrial-scale extermination in the death camps run by the SS.

Of course the Nazi shared the widespread belief that coloured and Asian people were inferior but it is worth noting that Hitler gave his Japanese allies the title of 'Honorary Aryans'. Although the Japanese were of a different race, they were considered by Hitler to possess qualities similar enough to Germanic Nordic characteristics to warrant the designation. This ludicrous contradiction was mainly used to justify the German-Japanese agreement against Communism signed on 25 November 1936.

An amazing feature of the Nazi Party is how far short of 'Aryan' standard perfection most of its leaders fell. The men who claimed to a providential destiny as the saviours of the white Germanic Aryan race, and who caused the horrible death of millions of innocent victims for their 'racial inferiority' did not have the appearance of the ideal, heroic, fair-haired, blue-eyed, athletic and tall Germanic *Ubermensch* at all. Hitler's ancestry was quite unclear, his biological grandfather was unknown and only presumed, and his name was possibly of Czech/Slav origin. His stature was not particularly athletic, his hair was dark, and his general physical appearance was more Slavic than Germanic. Hitler was not an athlete, he never played sport or took exercise; he was lazy and moody, shy and awkward, distrustful and contemptuous, and there was something essentially insecure and ridiculous about him, as Charlie Chaplin brilliantly captured in his 1940 film, *The Great Dictator*. Hermann Göring had been a slim and handsome man and a glamorous pilot in the First World War, but later became fat and addicted to drugs, loot and luxury. *Reichsführer-SS* Heinrich Himmler was a dull bureaucrat with a bullet head, poor eyesight and bad health. Minister of Propaganda Josef Göbbels was short, thin, dark-haired and had a club foot, which left him with a pronounced limp and a serious inferiority complex. SA Chief Ernst Röhm was an ugly, short, fat homosexual. Hitler's secretary and NSDAP chief Martin Bormann was a short, fat, dark-haired man with limited intelligence. Robert Ley, Head of the German Labour Front (DAF), was a fat drunk with a psychologically unstable and socially insecure personality. The eccentric Rudolf Heß, Hitler's designated successor, was so deranged that even his fellow Nazi leaders noticed. The ruthless editor of the Nazi newspaper *Der Sturmer*, Julius Streicher, was clinically insane – but apparently that was not a handicap in the Nazi movement. Had the times not been so unstable in Germany these men would probably have remained a bunch of emotionally-crippled misfits, impotently acting out their delusions on the fringes of politics.

As a matter of fact, the Jews in Germany, as one can easily imagine, were no threat at all. On the contrary they were a minority, but a minority that had provided Germany with important artists, philosophers and businessmen as well as skilled and hardworking artisans and civil servants. In 1925 there were 564,379 *Glaubenjuden* (those of Jewish faith), representing about 0.9 per cent of the total population. In 1933 they were only 0.76 per cent. They were mostly living in the provinces of Prussia, Saxony, Bavaria, and Baden and in the largest German cities. In Berlin, for example, there were 173,000 Jews. On the whole German Jews were opposed to Marxism, and to ultra-nationalism, and only a few were Zionists. Zionism was created in the late nineteenth century by the journalist and writer Theodor Herzl (1860–1904), advocating the creation of a Jewish homeland and their own state (Israel) in Palestine. On the whole the Jewish community was perfectly integrated into German society. All able Jewish men had fought in the First World War and many had died for Germany, so they could not be accused of lacking patriotism. The German Jews had several organisations and associations intended to defend the community from anti-Semitism, discrimination and exclusion but also from the total assimilation that was regarded as loss of their cultural identity. The largest and most popular association was the *Central Verein deutscher Bürger jüdischen Glaubens* (CV, Central Association for German citizens of Jewish confession) founded in 1893. Other associations included the *Reichsbund jüdischer Frontsoldaten* (National League of Jewish Veterans), and the *Convent deutscher Studenten jüdischen Glaubens* (Union of German Jewish Students) dedicated to the defence of its members' patriotic honour. There was also the *Zionistische Vereinigung für Deutschland* (ZVfD, Zionist Association for Germany) with a youth movement, its own newspaper and a migration office.

TOTALITARIANISM

The Nazi ideology was contradictory, claiming in principle to be elitist but being in practice a mass movement. The supposed German superiority was thus totalitarian: it was not personal but collective, each citizen had to conform and work for the common good. The national interest was more important than individual rights and all personal freedoms were abolished: as a slogan said, 'Public need comes before private greed'. The individual human being became unimportant and the object of racial or national interest gave a new definition to the principle of *raison d'état*. National Socialism was profoundly racist and xenophobic and its ideology was totally regressive. It was the complete negation of freedom and the universal rights of man acquired and expressed by the US Constitution of 1787 and the French Revolution of 1789. Liberty was replaced by leadership and submission, Equality by racism, segregation, dominance and obedience, and Fraternity by racial supremacy and oppression. Nazism was the denial of the ideological consensus on which the entire international system was based.

A short-term Nazi aim was the recovery of national pride expressed by the slogan *Deutschland erwache* ('Germany wakes up'). Because the superior race had been humiliated in 1918, and because the post-war collapse had been caused, not by military defeat, but by a *Dolchstoß*, a 'stab in the back' by Socialists, democrats and Jews, and the Treaty of Versailles was merely a *Diktat* (an imposed treaty), which had to be renounced. There was a deep feeling of humiliation and hatred against the French and the Allies, but also against the 'November Criminals' who had betrayed the honour of both the German nation and army by signing the armistice of November 1918. The indignity of Versailles revived an aggressive nationalist chauvinism, which had manifested itself in Germany in the early nineteenth century. In fact the 'stab in the back' theory, widely exploited by the Nazis and believed by many (notably the Army, the Conservatives and Nationalists), was a lie. The truth, of course, was quite different. With the failure of the German Spring Offensives of 1918, the German armies were in a hopeless position, and on the brink of total collapse. The leading generals had gladly ceded political power to the civilian government just in time, in order to force it to bear the political burden of signing the Armistice, and accepting the harsh terms of the Treaty of Versailles.

GREATER GERMANY

An important aspect of Nazism was that all Germanic people had to be re-united in a great *Reich* (empire), called *Großdeutschland* (Greater Germany) to form a *Volksgemeinschaft* (national/racial pure community). However, the hypocritical and pragmatic Nazis respected the neutrality of Sweden throughout the war (for economic reasons), that of the German-speaking population of the Tyrol (to maintain friendly relations with Mussolini and Fascist Italy) and that of the large Swiss German-speaking community (for secret financial reasons and to maintain communications with Italy). The ideology glorified militarism and aimed at the building of a united order to prepare the German nation for fighting. The *Herrenvolk* needed more land for food production and for the settlement of the excess German population. These territories, *Lebensraum*, had to be taken in Eastern Europe from the unworthy and inferior Slavs. This justified a brutal crusade against 'Soviet-Jewish barbarism'. Hitler saw Greater Germany as a new Roman empire, a New Order extending firm rule over the subject races of Europe and Western Asia.

SOCIALISM

Hitler was not a Socialist. As a matter of fact he was bored by and indifferent to economic issues. National Socialism was supposed to combine two contradictory forces: nationalism, which became dominant, and socialism, which proved weak and ineffective. Politically the Nazis were 'socialist' only to gain working-class votes. However, in the lower ranks of the Nazi Party certain socialist trends were so inescapably apparent that for a long time they were a matter for serious concern on the part of influential industrialists and rich businessmen (whose financial support Hitler was eagerly trying to secure). The 'socialist' faction of the Nazi Party was represented by a prominent figure named Gregor Strasser, who was expelled in 1932 and murdered on Hitler's orders during the SA purge of June 1934. Gregor's brother Otto was also a leading member of the party's dissident left wing, and broke from the NSDAP due to disputes with the Hitlerite nationalist faction. Otto Strasser formed the Black Front, a group intended to split the Nazi Party and take it from the grasp of Hitler. This movement also functioned during his exile and the Second World War as a secret opposition group.

Although the Nazis used efficient Soviet-style techniques to manipulate crowds, and although both ideologies were awful dictatorships with catastrophic and criminal results in the end, Nazism was, however, fundamentally different from the Soviet Union's Communism. As a matter of fact, the Nazi ideology nourished a powerful hatred against the Socialism created by the 'Jew' Karl Marx (called Bolshevism after Lenin's radical communist doctrine of 1903). If economic realities were avoided in *Mein Kampf*, the orthodox Nazi view aimed at creating a hazy third way between decaying bourgeois democratic capitalism and the growing threat of radical communism. Hitler was indifferent to economic questions. Although 'all income not earned by work was to be confiscated' (at least officially in the Nazi 25-point programme), he respected private property, and accepted the role of liberal capitalism in modern society and economic life because he recognised these as foundations of the culture. He opposed only the abuses of capitalism, but not capitalism in principle. 'Small businesses must be strengthened and large retail firms are to be dismantled' was another point of the Nazi programme intended to obtain the votes and support of the middle class, but this never happened due to compromises with the big capitalists. German heavy industry magnates, lords of the coal, iron and steel industries, bankers, corporate lawyers, editors and publishing tycoons, but also small businessmen, middle-class shopkeepers and employees feared Communism more than anything else. Hitler was quick to realise that, and made the danger of Marxism and the evilly-disposed Jews the central themes of his campaign. By associating his racist and elitist ideology with the ideas of private property and individual initiative the cunning Hitler established a common interest with all those who feared Communism.

WAR

If Communism was to be shattered, the economy and industry – in Hitler's mind – had to be organised in the framework of a non-democratic regime, in other words controlled by his strong political power in order to serve his own megalomaniac and imperialist goals. Nazi ideology, no less than Nazi economics, was one of preparation for war. Both depended for their continued success upon the maintenance of a national spirit and a popular effort, which in the end found expression in aggressive action. Nazism was the crude application and institutionalisation at state level of the basic biologic principle of 'struggle for life' and the rule Might is Right. Only the strongest would survive: the weakest had no right to live. In that way Nazi ideology represented a complete break with traditional European civilisation based on Christian forgiveness, charity and love of one's fellow human beings. War, the belief in violence, the right of the strongest, racism and thus genocide were not corruptions of Nazism, they were its essence.

War was planned and prepared for as early as 1933 during the so-called period of *Gleichschaltung* – which can be translated as unification, regimentation and conformity. *Gleichschaltung* was the organisation of the German nation under the sole control of the Nazi Party. All other political parties were forbidden, institutions and government were Nazified, and trade unions were abolished in June 1933 and replaced with the *Deutsche Arbeit Front* (DAF, German Labour Front). Employers and employees were forced to join the DAF whose function was to conciliate disputes rather than advance social demands. Industry, trade and agriculture were subordinate to the preparation for war. The country was purged and organised hierarchically according to racial and leadership principles. People were forced to conform and opponents were arrested and detained without trial in the newly-created concentration camps. The Nazis demanded total involvement by creating numerous organisations, corporations, fronts, agencies and associations run or directly affiliated with the Party. The process of

Gleichschaltung concentrated effective political and military power in the hands of Hitler to a degree unknown in Germany since the days of Frederick the Great (1712–86). There were no checks and balances to his dictatorship: 'With us the Leader and the Idea are one,' Hitler said, 'and every party member has to do what the Leader orders. Our organisation is built on discipline'.

NAZISM AND RELIGION

Hitler was originally a Catholic but his party was profoundly atheist and his ideology was evidently not at home in any of the philosophies produced by the Judaeo-Christian faith. The religions of divine revelation remained inaccessible to the Nazis. They rejected the classical view of mankind, Judaeo-Christian Western civilisation and liberal democracy. The Nazi ideology was receptive to ideas about the coming of the biological age, of 'heroic vitality', of arrogant racism, as well as of the veneration of strength, force and war. However, being necessary for the people and being a strong and conservative element, the Church was tolerated as an instrument that could be useful to them. Alfred Rosenberg proposed replacing the Bible with *Mein Kampf* and the Christian cross with the swastika, and harsh pronouncements against the Church were made in private, but in public Hitler generally adopted a milder tone. Actually Hitler was rather bored by religion and religious issues. Prudently he held ambivalent views on the subject, and did not bind himself to any creed. In fact it suited him that Nazism was regarded by many Germans as a rampart against godless Soviet Bolshevism/Communism. However, there was no doubt that in the long term he would not tolerate religion within Nazi society. Officially there was religious freedom in Nazi Germany but two religions were outlawed and seen as enemies: firstly, Judaism was deemed to be a dangerous threat to the purity of the German race as we have just discussed. Secondly, Charles Taze Russell's Jehovah Witnesses, who were pacifists and rejected violence and military service.

Behind the official freedom of religion, in practice there was harassment, persecution and repression. On 20 July 1933 Hitler signed a concordat with Pope Pius XI (Achille Ratti, pope from 1922 until his death in 1939), which guaranteed the neutrality and the integrity of the Catholic Church. Coming to an understanding with the Protestant Churches was more difficult. The *Bekenntniskirche*, the Confessional

Church, worked to maintain the purity of the Evangelical faith, so the Protestants were brought into line by force. The Nazis launched the *Kirchenkampf*, a violent campaign directed by Martin Bormann against the various branches of the Protestant Churches. Many priests and pastors were harassed or dismissed, and some were even arrested and murdered in camps and prisons. Hitler's struggle with the churches ended with the outbreak of the Second World War, as it was feared it might impair the morale of German soldiers. Hitler was too shrewd a politician to come out openly against Christianity, but if Germany had won the war, it is likely that both the Catholic and Protestant faiths would have been annihilated, and replaced with a kind of Hitler personality cult.

BLUT UND BODEN

The anti-urban National Socialist theory of *Blut und Boden* (Blood and Soil, *Blubo* for short) was advocated by Nazi leaders such as Walther Darré (Minister of Food and Agriculture) and Alfred Rosenberg (in his own words responsible for the Nazi Party's 'intellectual and ideological education and training'). The *Blubo* theory held that the roots of national renewal were to be found in the native soil of Germany. Urban life was decried and traditional peasant virtues were extolled. Hitler (at least in public) cried out against the erosion of morals in the big cities and emphasised the importance of a healthy peasantry as a mainstay for the state. The Nazi programme originally included a wide reform of landownership and the end to land speculation but this too never happened, in order to gain the wealthy landowners' support. In agriculture Nazi policy proved inconsistent and far less successful than in industry. The Nazis prevented further division of lands and regulated farm production but the achievements were minor. Although agricultural production aimed at self-sufficiency, Germany still depended on food imports as late as 1938. In the end, *Blut und Boden* was simply another propaganda trick launched to gain the peasants' support. Germany was a modern urban industrial nation and had to remain so in order to produce weapons.

As for urbanism, the *Führer* and his architect Albert Speer (who portrayed himself as an apolitical artist and technocrat) had huge, megalomaniacal plans to re-build Berlin and the main cities of the Reich. Hitler and Speer favoured and developed a pompous gigantic neoclassic style, which was intended to impress and to glorify the regime for a thousand years. Indeed Nazi ideology was not exclusively anti-modernist in character. There were of course Nazi leaders who were anti-modern, mystical and agrarian utopianists like Walther Darré, Alfred Rosenberg and, to a certain extent, Heinrich Himmler. Others like Fritz Todt, Robert Ley, Albert Speer and Josef Göbbels were, like Hitler himself, rather modernist, rationalist and materialist, and pursued wholly modern ideas with technocratic efficiency. There were thus profound contradictions between the version of National Socialist ideology that was propagated, and the self-image and world-view of Hitler and other Nazi leaders. It is worth noting that Darré's Secretary of State Herbert Backe and Reinhard Heydrich (a high-ranking SS official) laughed together at the philosophical idiosyncrasies of their respective superiors, Darré and Himmler. In private Hitler, Göring and Göbbels mocked Rosenberg's peasant ancestral *Blubo* ideas and Himmler's mystical medieval knightly dreams.

PROPAGANDA

The whole Nazi ideology was intended to create a united, popular and authoritarian state illustrated by the slogan: *Ein Volk! Ein Reich! Ein Führer!* One People! One Empire! One Leader!

Hitler formulated this ideology, which was used to legitimise wars of conquest and genocide. Hitler cannot be called a 'patriot' (someone who loves his country and people) because he was only concerned with his own unquestioned power. In 1940 the exiled Otto Strasser published his conversations (and quarrels) with Hitler in the early years of the Nazi movement. In one of the conversations Strasser recalled how badly Hitler wanted power: 'Power, we must seize power!' And when Strasser objected that the programme of the NSDAP was too vague, Hitler thumped the table and screamed: 'Power first! Afterwards we can act as circumstances dictate!' The Nazi ideology combined both terror, with the SS Gestapo and concentration camps, with a firmly controlled, skilful and well-organised propaganda service, headed by Josef Göbbels. This organised impressive mass meetings, quasi-religious ceremonies and rallies. It used modern media such as posters with striking images and catchy slogans, it produced pictures, films, radio programmes, magazines and official NSDAP newspapers such as the *Völkischer Beobachter*, *Der Stürmer* and many other daily, weekly and monthly publications. Hitler was a gifted actor and Göbbels was a clever and practiced demagogue. Both had clearly understood how to unleash mass instincts, how to play on the passions and the fears of the ordinary, respectable, average German for their own ends. They manipulated their audiences emotionally, and gave expression and direction to fierce and primal passions. At their meetings they succeeded in fusing the assembled unemployed, workers, shopkeepers, housewives, petty bourgeois, the wealthy and students into a homogenous mob whose feelings and opinions they could mould as they pleased. Mass meetings were very important as Hitler wrote in *Mein Kampf*: 'Mass assemblies are necessary for the reason that, in attending, the individual who felt himself only on the point of joining our movement, now begins to feel isolated and in fear of being left alone as he acquires for the first time the picture of a great community which has a strengthening and encouraging effect on most people. Brigaded in a company or battalion, surrounded by his companions, he will march with a lighter heart to the attack than if he had to march alone. In the crowd he feels himself in some way thus sheltered'. The manipulative Göbbels could provide a 'spontaneous' cheering crowd at any moment. All media were to be German-owned, with all foreigners and Jews banned from employment by them. Propaganda also used lies, falsification and forgery. History, the educational system and culture were re-shaped and forged in order to fit Nazi ideology.

THE LEADER PRINCIPLE

The achievement of the angry, aggressive, and deranged Nazi aims was the task of the party led by its quasi-religious saviour, Adolf Hitler. The *Führer*'s will and authority were unquestionable and flew directly downwards to the nation according to the *Führerprinzip* (leader principle). This concept outlined that Germany was to be an authoritarian state with power emanating from the leader at the top: the will of the *Führer* was the highest law. Nazi Germany was a unitary state but its national and local administration was a maze. Hitler had no interest at all in establishing a fixed system of government. Since life was a permanent struggle for survival, Germany was not to be administrated but firmly led. Nazi rule was determined by three main principles: leadership, loyalty and racial character. However, behind its monolithic façade, the intricate and deceptive Nazi regime was in fact a caricature of a totalitarian state. It was based on a struggle for power between Party and State and between each Nazi organisation. It was a chaotic jumble of vested interests and political strings, spheres of authority and plenary powers, patronage and rivalry. It was ultimately an unrestricted and ruthless free-for-all. Appointment, power, function and length of tenure depended exclusively upon Hitler's mood and whim. Nothing was totally clear, definitive or long-lasting except the personal interest and will of the *Führer* who kept the centre of political power permanently shifting among his closest collaborators, thereby preventing the emergence of unwelcome rivals. This disorganised and uncontrolled situation existed at all levels along the chain of command. The hierarchy was composed of upper and lower leaders, all of whom had a place in the pecking order. There was intense rivalry for promotion to the party aristocracy, but a system of multiplicity, instinctive rather than deliberate, ensured that no subordinate could combine with his rivals to act against Hitler. It is therefore very difficult to shed light into the jungle of competing authorities and functions, which grew and constantly changed within the Nazi organisation under the impact of war and the movement's own dynamism. There was a deliberate contra- and juxtaposition of State and Party institutions with overlapping functions. Nazi rule has often been described as 'organised chaos' or 'confusion of powers' or a 'polycratic system' in which various personalities within the leadership and institutions struggled for power, influence and wealth.

Nazi propaganda created a larger-than-life image of the *Führer*, both as an idol endowed with superhuman qualities with revolutionary plans, and as a modest and simple man upholding traditional bourgeois virtues and guaranteeing peace – at least until 1939. The Hitler personality cult was designed deliberately to appeal to the diseased side of the human psyche, above all to the capacity for resentment. It struck a chord with the widespread disillusionment with the institutions, parties and leaders of the Weimar Republic, and the chameleon-like Hitler seemed to offer something different to each class of society and pulled them all together with the uniqueness of his own vision for the future. A cluster of myths was created around the *Führer*. In his daily life, Hitler was a simple man, a teetotaller, a vegetarian, and a non-smoker. This was emphasised but the propaganda also depicted him as an asexual bachelor, as a man without human ties of love and friendship, but a man with a divine mission using all his time and abilities for the good of Germany, and all his energy for the love of the Germans. This was intended to exemplify the German people's yearning for greatness through the image of the leader. The cult of the *Führer* was coolly calculated and artificially stage-managed. Most of those who propagated the Hitler myth were often themselves in its thrall, like Robert Ley, head of the DAF, the leader of the Hitler Youth movement Baldur von Schirach, as well as Joseph Göbbels, Minister for Public Enlightenment and Propaganda, and Rudolf Heß who spoke of his master and leader in biblical terms approaching hysteria. The Second World War added a new dimension to the worship of Hitler. Göbbels extolled the *Führer* as the greatest general, and most gifted strategist of all time, equal to Alexander the Great, Julius Caesar, Charlemagne. '*Hitler ist der Sieg!*' ('Hitler is Victory') was a popular slogan – at least before the setbacks of 1943 and the defeats of 1944–5.

Without any legal background or official declaration, Hitler being Chancellor and *Führer*, certainly not Kaiser, Nazi Germany was proclaimed by the propaganda the *drittes Reich* (Third Empire) The Third Reich (1933–45) followed the First Holy Roman Empire, which lasted from 962 until 1806, and the Second Prussian Reich ruled by the Hohenzollern dynasty from 1871 to 1918. The nostalgic imperial reference back to previous periods of German hegemony reflected the spurious version of German history applied by Hitler to the development of his totalitarian state. The same tendency was evident in Mussolini's Fascist Italy, which was intended to be a revival of the ancient glory of the Roman Empire.

Chapter 4

Members of the NSDAP

MEMBERSHIP

The NSDAP was composed of volunteer members, called *Parteigenosse* (Pg) or *Mitglieder der NSDAP*. There were three main conditions for membership: to be a *Reichsdeutsche* (German national); to be eighteen years old; and to have non-Jewish and non-Slav descent since 1800. Members of the party having joined before the *Machtergreifung* (or *Machtübernahme*, the seizure of power on 30 January 1933) were called *Alte Kämpfer* (old fighters). These happy few benefited from various rights and privileges, and were particularly honoured with a golden chevron worn on the upper right arm of their uniform, proudly showing their early commitment to the movement. Hitler often praised them for their services, giving the Old Fighters preference for jobs in the bureaucracy and granted them civil service status. Those who had been injured in street fights against the enemies of Nazism in the early *Kampfzeit* (the pre-1933 period of struggle) received the same benefits as disabled war veterans. With almost no exemptions, Hitler's familiars were *Alte Kämpfer*: Göring, Göbbels, Ley, Heß, Bormann, his chauffeur Julius Schreck, Max Amann the NSDAP publisher, Franz-Xavier Schwartz the party treasurer and Heinrich Hoffmann the court photographer. However, if Hitler continued to look back and often recalled the heroic and romantic early years of the *Kampfzeit*, his thirst for power prevented him to be totally loyal and grateful. Some of the Nazi leaders who held important positions before the seizure of power did not play a role in the Third Reich, such as the DAP founder Anton Drexler, and to the brothers Otto and Gregor Strasser. Otto Strasser quarrelled with Hitler in 1930 and left the party; his brother Gregor resigned his post in December 1932 and was shot on 30 June 1934. The mercurial career of the SA leader, Ernst Röhm ended in the same way. Ideologues and theorists who had some influence in the NSDAP before 1933, like Gottfried Feder and Alfred Rosenberg (both party members since 1919), did not play the role they had hoped in the Third Reich.

The Party was composed of active members who believed in Nazi values, fought to implement the aims of the NSDAP, and collaborated in the propagation of the doctrine and winning over new members. The best elements among the activists could be appointed as local organisers and individuals who were the most capable of helping to bring the movement to victory could be selected to become district leaders of the movement. But there was a majority of more or less passive 'followers' who more or less understood what Nazism was all about but who totally accepted it aims and methods. If many *Parteigenossen* were convinced National Socialists, the vast majority – particularly after the seizure of power in January 1933 – joined for opportunistic personal motives: to make a career, to profit from various advantages, for greed, or to become a local *Führer*, what the Germans call *mitlaufen* (freely translated as 'following' or 'just walking along' with the Nazis). The active Nazi senior leadership and propagandists did not bother too much about the personal worth of individual followers, not enquiring too deeply into their abilities, intelligence, personality, individual character or motivations. For reasons of expediency even turncoat Communists and Socialists joined the Nazi Party, where they were derisively known as 'Beefsteak Nazis' – 'brown on the outside and red on the inside'. *Septemberlings* was the contemptuous name given by Göbbels to new members who had joined the party after the election success of September 1930. Other terms used sarcastically to describe German late starters who hastened to join the Nazi Party in March 1933 after Hitler's accession to power were *Märzgefallene* ('Those Who Joined in March') and *Märzveichen* ('March violets').

Statistically speaking the typical Nazi voter in 1932 was a self-employed member of the middle class who lived in a small town. He (or she) had formerly voted for a party of the centre or for a regional party opposed to the power and influence of big industry and trade unions. The Nazi Party was ideologically anti-feminist but the Weimar Republic had granted women the right to vote. Before the seizure of power, women were thus special targets for the Nazis. Hitler always did his best to charm women, praising their qualities and always making great promises in order to gain their votes. However, after the seizure of power in 1933, came the true face of the 'macho' and misogynistic Nazi character. The payment of family allowances was used to get women out of the workplace, and they were strictly supervised and indoctrinated by various organisations such as the *Nationalsozialistische-Frauenschaft* (NSF, Women's Organisation), the *Bund Deutscher Mädel* (BDM, League of German Maidens, for girls aged 15 to 18, a part of the Hitler Youth movement) and the *Glaube und Schönheit* (Faith and Beauty) society. Motherhood, and motherhood only, was the highest aim for German girls and women. Families were encouraged to have at least four children.

Role and Indoctrination of the Members

The sole object of the party was to secure power by any means and when this was done, members were eager for authority, influence, position and wealth. The ordinary members and lowest ranks were volunteers who had their own jobs and offered their free time and holidays to the party. Higher ranks were permanent officials, paid by the NSDAP. All of them, whatever their motivations were or whatever rank they had in the hierarchy, were political agents actively spreading the Nazi creed and imposing it upon the community. Although *Mitglieder* were not official civil servants, they represented Hitler and propagated his will at home, in schools, in shops, in working places, everywhere at local, regional and national level. They participated in the streamlining *Gleichschaltung*, the total nazification of the country affecting the economy, labour, administration, national life, culture and education. Nazi followers, members and leaders were at war with Jews, Freemasons, Social Democrats, Communists, Gypsies, Jehovah's Witnesses, trade unionists and all other real or supposed enemies of the regime. Members were volunteers, but they had to be vigorously enthusiastic and completely committed. They watched over and spied on the entire German population. They worked closely with the local and special police services (notably the *Sicherheitsdienst* and Gestapo), which since 1936 were under the control of the dreaded SS. Party members and SS police were instruments of Nazi terror, which had the whole nation in its grip. However, terror, manipulation and brainwashing did not only come from party and police because the chaotic Nazi system – although it had many political police services and surveillance agencies – could not put a policeman behind every inhabitant. Consequently a large part of the German population connived and participated in the repression of Jews, suspects and nonconformists by aggressive pressure, denunciation, inquisition, harassment or simply by indifference, silence and passivity. Many intelligent, well-intentioned, educated, principled people became so caught up in Nazism, so captivated by Hitler's magnetism, or so afraid and terrorized, or so greedy and avid to have their share in the new system, that they could accept everything: the secret police, concentration camps, the nonsensical rhetoric of Aryan heroism, anti-Semitism, and later the horrors, suffering and slaughter of war.

However not everyone was disoriented, jobless, hopeless and rejected by society in the 1930s. Many Germans simply did not want to see any of the barbarities committed by the Nazis. Many only saw the rebirth of the Fatherland, without looking too closely at the price being paid for it. There was no place for criticism, objections and democracy within the Nazi Party. Hitler held that democracy was the mastery of the herd over the intelligentsia, the mastery of the true energy through the dead weight of massed numbers. The Nazi organisation was built on discipline, the *Führer* commanded and every member had to accept, obey, and do what Hitler and his henchmen ordered.

Nazi ideology drew heavily upon a historic nationalism, which it greatly exaggerated. It derived in part from the organic theory of society, which held that the nation was a kind of living organism within which the individual person was nothing more than a single cell. The individual had no independent existence, he received life itself and all his ideas from the culture of the nation into which he was born and by which he was nurtured. The individual person was meaningless outside the collective body. Hitler claimed to represent the absolute sovereignty of the German people. The propaganda presented him as a kind of modern messiah and made him the subject of extravagant popular worship. The new order was thought of as absolutely solid, like one huge monolith in which no particle had any separate structure. Given such a theory, it made no sense to speak of individual freedom, to allow individuals to have their own opinion or to count up individual opinions and votes to obtain a merely numerical majority.

The ordinary party members were told that grand policy was much too complex for common people to judge and understand. They were ordered to be content with a few propaganda slogans and to blindly rely upon the *Führer* and the Party who were always right and always had solutions. Arguments from authority were used to sooth consciences, and false excuses were avidly snatched, resulting in acceptance of the unacceptable. Consequently, one felt one was being represented, never called upon to take personal responsibility or develop one's own ideas. The whole Nazi system was aimed at preventing criticism and conflicts of conscience. It repressed and suppressed any forms of troublesome doubts, and everyone kept to his own sub-group. Members were immured in closed-off areas of life, developing a society of totally isolated individuals with uniform opinions, sterile conversations and standardised discussions between like-minded persons. The structure of the system was often used for a convenient excuse after the war. One would then argue: *'Wir haben's nicht gewußt!'* ('We didn't know') – referring to the crimes committed by the Nazi regime.

Hitler and the Nazis were adept in oratory, and as early as 1928 they established the *Rednerschule der NSDAP* (Party School for Orators). In this institute, created by the *Gauleiter* of Upper Bavaria, Fritz Reinhardt, Nazi leaders were trained in the art of speaking in public, they memorised speeches, arguments, and answers to possible and frequently-asked questions. In 1939, there was also a project by the chief ideologue of the Nazi Party, Alfred Rosenberg, to create an elite Nazi university, a kind of academy for party officials. A monumental central university was to be built on the shores of Lake Chiemsee in Bavaria. This institute, called the *Hohe Schule der NSDAP* (literally 'High School of the NSDAP'), was never founded owing to the outbreak of the Second World War. Other educational centres were also planned for the forming of NSDAP officials: e.g. the Institute for Indo-Germanic Intellectual History (planned at Munich), Institute of Biology and Race Studies (located at Stuttgart), Institute of Religious Studies (at Hall), Institute of Germanic Studies (Kiel), Institute of Ideological Colonial Studies (Hamburg), Institute of German Folklore (Münster and Graz), Institute for Research on the East (Prague), Institute of Celtic Studies (Römhild) and Institute for the Study of Germanism and Gallicanism (Strasbourg).

Since 1921, the Nazi Party had *Parteigerichte* (party courts). These tribunals of the NSDAP – headed by Party chief of justice Walther Buch – developed into powerful bureaucratic mechanisms for controlling and punishing Party members. Set up at *Gau* (provincal) level, the courts turned a blind eye to dishonesty, crime and immorality, except in so far as these affected the reputation, efficiency and unity of the Party. Indeed their real purpose was preserving Party discipline and the authority of Hitler, and settling disputes so as to keep them quiet, rather than to achieve substantive justice between the parties involved or to enforce any moral code. The courts had authority to keep party members in line by subjecting them to fines, loss of employment, social banishment, prison terms and detention in concentration camps.

SALUTE AND OATH

Since 1925, members of the NSDAP greeted each other with the *Deutscher Gruß* (German salute) designed to replace the familiar *Guten Tag* (good day). The Hitler salute was probably introduced by Austrian pan-Germanists, but obviously it was an adaptation of the Ancient Roman salute and similar to that used by Mussolini's Italian Fascists. Standing to attention, the left hand was placed on the belt buckle, the right arm was raised a little higher than the shoulder in a quick upward thrust and one said enthusiastically *Heil Hitler!* while clicking heels. The salute with the rigidly-upflung arm was a reverential gesture to aggression rather than to peace. The German adjective *heil* means whole, not broken, intact, salvation but also healthy. So the salute can be translated as something like the archaic greeting 'hail' or 'long live' expressing both the ideas of a respectful and virile salute, and wishing health and long life to Hitler. For the happy few who might meet Hitler personally, the salute was the same but one said *Heil, mein Führer!* (Hail my Leader!)

It seems that the *Hitler Gruß* was introduced in December 1924 when Hitler was released from prison. It became common practice after 1925, and after the establishment of Nazi power in 1933, the greeting became compulsory at all parades, meetings, official and public events, and strongly advised in daily life including at schools, offices, working places and so on. Germany became a vast camp of Hitler saluters. Failure to use the greeting, or reducing it to an infinitesimal movement of the right arm accompanied by an inarticulate mumble, was regarded as an offence. After the attempt on the *Führer*'s life in July 1944, the *Hitler Gruß* was imposed on the Army in place of the traditional military salute. Within the formations and units of the Nazi Party, the customary way to address was *Kamerad* (comrade) like the Communists.

At the end of a meeting, a gathering, a toast, a ceremony or a speech, the president or the speaker shouted *Sieg!* (victory) and the crowd, the guests or the participants answered *Heil!* while making the Hitler salute. This popular rallying cry was not only the greeting and farewell of the Nazi followers but also a chant screamed in unison again and again in strongly-accented tones to express the German collective joyful triumph on all public occasions.

All official letters and mail were concluded by the formula *mit deutschen Grußen, Heil Hitler* (with German greetings, hail Hitler). As for Hitler himself, when making a speech on the radio or before a live crowd, he addressed the public with *Volksgenossen und Volksgenossinen*, which means male and female compatriots or fellow citizens.

All NSDAP members had to swear an individual *Eid* (oath) going like this: *Ich gelobe meinem Führer Adolf Hitler Treue. Ich verspreche, ihm und der Führern, die er mir bestimmt, jederzeit Achtung und Gehorsam entgegenzubringen.* ('I swear loyalty to my leader Adolf Hitler. I promise to him and to the leaders he will give me, to

Right: The Hitler salute.

serve always in respect and obedience'). Hitler and the Nazis regarded any deviation from this pledge as treason. The slogan 'the *Führer* proposes and disposes' was not an empty one.

COMMEMORATIVE DAYS

The Nazi Party had numerous commemorative days. As one can see in Leni Riefenstahl's 1935 propaganda film *Triumph of the Will* these were grandiose masterpieces of theatrical art with the hypnotic effect of thousands of men marching in perfect order, with music of massed bands, the forest of standards and flags, the vast perspectives of the formations, smoking torches at night, giving a sense of irresistible power, force and unity. Rallies and meetings necessitated a huge organisation and strict discipline for the marshalling, equipping, feeding and then dispersal of – in the case of the annual Nuremberg rallies – hundreds of thousands of men, women and children. They were astounding spectacles intended to impress both participants and spectators. Sanctifying the new regime, they were expected to serve as substitutes for traditional religious high holy days.

January 24 was the day of the celebration of the murder of the Nazi 'hero' of the Hitler Youth movement, Herbert Norkus, with a slow nighttime torchlight parade with solemn songs.

January 30 was the anniversary of the *Machtergreifung* of 1933. On that day each year the German Nation was presented with a lengthy account of what Hitler had taken over and what he had done with the power entrusted to him. The day ended with a public ceremony, broadcast by radio from every street corner in the land, and by torchlight processions. Eighteen-year-old members of the Hitler Youth who had proved their worth were sworn in as full members of the NSDAP on this day.

February 24 was the 'annunciation day' on which the NSDAP had been founded and its 25-point programme published in 1920. Year after year until 1943, Hitler liked to look back on the beginning of his career. The *Führer* presented himself as the 'truest executor of the NSDAP's sacred heritage', he recalled the movement's modest start, the great opposition it had overcome, and emphasised its achievements and successes which guaranteed Germany's victorious future.

March 16 was the National Day of Mourning, or Heroes' Remembrance Day for the victims of the First World War and Nazi martyrs; this was celebrated in the Kroll Opera House with a performance of the second movement of Beethoven's Third Symphony 'Eroica', a solemn cultural occasion attended by the Nazi elite and all foreign diplomats –at least before the Second World War.

April 20 was Hitler's birthday (1889), celebrated with extravagant rituals. On that day delegations from all over the country brought presents, gifts and works of art. These were passed on to the museum in Linz, which Hitler hoped to turn into the greatest art gallery in Europe after the war. Representatives of the youth organisations solemnly pledged their allegiance to the *Führer*. April 20 was an important moment in the ritual of Hitler's worship. The day culminated in a parade of the *Wehrmacht* (armed forces) through the Brandenburger Tor at Berlin before Hitler in his capacity of army supreme commander.

May 1 was National Labour Day –taken over from the socialist and labour tradition – with popular festivals emphasising the Nazi Party's solidarity with the workers (its 'socialist' component) and Hitler's role in the creation of the welfare state.

The second Sunday in May was Mothers' Day (originally invented by the flower trade to boost turnover), during which prolific mothers were rewarded with medals, and young girls reminded of their duty towards the regime: to bear children.

Strenuous efforts were made to introduce a romantic pagan feast on 21 June (the Summer Solstice) dedicated to NSDAP martyrs and war heroes with stirring speeches, night parades, public demonstrations and blazing bonfires.

The *pièce de résistance* of the annual Nazi cycle was during the first week of September: the grandiose Party Rally was held in Nuremberg from 1927 to 1938 in a climate of mystic ecstasy, sacred delirium and nationalist exaltation. For a full week the regime displayed its immense talent in jubilation, colours, lights, music and festivities for its own honour in the presence of thousands of participants. Homilies, slogans and speeches were addressed to the faithful, providing occasions for displays of Hitler's rhetoric. Mass performances, mass settings and mass demonstrations, included parades of soldiers with fixed bayonets in rows of twelve with overhead a *Luftwaffe* display, as well as SS and SA men with colourful eagle standards, and old Nazi fighters who represented the glorious past of the movement. The whole population was mobilised. Women, farmers and workers' organisations, RAD

(Labour Service) uniformed battalions presenting gleaming shovels, disciplined boys and girls of the Hitler Youth, dancing young women from the 'Faith and Beauty' association. Many other overtly or related Nazi agencies, fronts, and services paraded in an expression of the ideal of the national 'racially-pure' community, and the self-dramatisation of Hitler's messianic mission. Each year had a different theme. For instance in 1933 it was the Rally of Victory, in 1934 Rally for Unity and Strength, 1935 was the Rally of Freedom, 1936 Rally for Honour and Freedom, 1937 the Rally in Honour of Work, and 1938 the Rally of Greater Germany. The Party week of September 1939 would have been devoted to Peace, but it was cancelled, and the hundreds of trains prepared for it were used for the mobilisation of the army for the invasion of Poland.

In Autumn, the Harvest Thanksgiving Day on October 1st was a tribute paid to the German farmers emphasising the racist myth of *Blut und Boden* with impressive mass demonstrations, romantic ceremonies, and parades in ancient folk costumes.

November 4 was the *Totengedenktag*, the Day of Homage to the Dead. On November 9 sombre pageantry lent mythical status to the 'blood baptism', the commemoration of the holy anniversary of the abortive 1923 Beer Hall Putsch in Munich. The march to the Feldherrnhalle was repeated in the precise order of 1923, along a route flanked by burning torches, with funeral music, tolling bells, and the slow recital of the names of the sixteen martyrs of the party who were honoured for their self-sacrifice for the Nazi cause. This had a symbolic significance too: commemoration of the past with an eye on the future. The solemn and kitsch commemoration was broadcasted over the whole country.

December 21 (Yule, the Winter Solstice) was a celebration designed to replace the Christian festivals, but in spite of the Nazis' efforts, it did not supplant the traditional Christmas (with fir tree and offering of presents) and Sylvester Eve (New Year). As Christian usage was too deeply ingrained, summer and winter solstices were treated with little reverence, being artificial, too showy and hollow.

The Nazis also revived the *Althing*, an old Germanic institution as a support for their ideology. The Viking *Althing* was originally a tribal assembly of free men, both a kind of parliament and a court of justice. Under the Nazis the custom was emptied of its institutional character, and replaced with a powerful mixture of pagan romanticism, militarism and naïve patriotism to build up recruits for Hitler's war machine. The

Althing became merely a theatrical show held in rudimentary natural theatres incorporating hilly slopes and ancient ruins. The show included music and songs, commemoration of martyrs, military tattoos, pagan oratorios, exhibition of sport and horsemanship, circus acts and reconstructed battle scenes. Even the mystically-oriented SS treated these ridiculous and showy occasions with irreverence.

During the war the prestigious national days were no longer commemorated, or they were celebrated with much less pomp. The mood had shifted from rejoicing to active combat, as many men were drafted. In the last years of the war, feelings were even gloomy as the Allies bombed Germany intensively from the air, and many towns were in ruins.

Chapter 5

Organisation of the NSDAP

UNITS

By 1928 the NSDAP was divided into two main branches. The first one, headed by Gregor Strasser, was devoted to attacking the existing Weimar regime. It had three sections concerned with foreign affairs (headed by Nieland); contact with the press (Otto Dietrich); and infiltration of trade unions and economic structures as well as recruiting for the party (directed by Schumann). The second branch directed by Konstantin Hierl was concerned with building up in advance the structures and the cadres of the future Nazi state; it consisted of Walter Darré (agriculture), Otto Wagener (economics), Hanno Konopath (race and culture), Nicolai (home affairs), Hans Frank (legal affairs), Gottfried Feder (technical and financial affairs), and Baldur von Schirach (youth organisation, created in 1922, soon to become the *Hitler Jugend* for girls and boys) and Schulz (labour service, later to become the DAF). The *Propagandastaffel* (propaganda) was a separate department headed directly by Hitler and Gregor Strasser, later becoming an independent ministry directed by Joseph Göbbels.

After the seizure of power in January 1933, the Party was re-organised to form a pyramidal hierarchy with vertical subdivisions. One of the organisation's leaders was the *Alte Kämpfer* Reinhold Muchow (1905–33).

The lowest ranks of the Nazi organisation were the previously-described NSDAP members. The lowest official was the *Blockleiter* (a *Leiter* was a leader/director/administrator) who was in charge of a Block regrouping a various number of homes with an average of 160 or 240 members. Four to eight blocks formed a cell at village level, or a neighbourhood in a town, called a *Zelle* (headed by a *Zellenleiter*). Three to five *Zellen* composed an *Ortsgruppe* (headed by an *Ortsgruppenleiter*), a group of villages or a town; the *Ortsgruppenleiter* often doubled as the town mayor. A varying number of *Ortsgruppen* constituted a 'circle' or *Kreis* (headed by a *Kreisleiter* who was the lowest salaried official of the NSDAP); the *Kreisleiter* was often the *Landrat* (subprefect), the executive director of a rural county.

Several *Kreisen* formed a region or *Gau* (plural *Gaue*). Roughly corresponding to an English shire, it was headed by a *Gauleiter*. The *Gauleiter* – appointed directly by Hitler and later by Heinrich Himmler – was a very important NSDAP official. He was responsible for all political and economic activities, civil defence and the mobilisation of labour in his *Gau*. He sometimes took on police and security duties. There were originally thirty-seven *Gaue* corresponding more or less to the ancient establishment of Germanic tribes. After the annexation of Austria and the Czechoslovakian Sudetenland, this number was increased to forty-two.

The *Gauleiter* were supervised by a council of *Reichsleiter*. These formed the *Reichsleitung der NSDAP* (main leadership of the NSDAP) with specific portfolios: Propaganda (Göbbels), Foreign policy (Rosenberg), Law (Frank), Finance (Schwartz) and Court of Justice (Buch). The *Reichsleiter* were responsible before the *Stellvertreter des Führers* (vice-president of the Nazi Party) who was initially Rudolf Heß and later Martin Bormann. At the top of the pyramid, Adolf Hitler was naturally the undisputed *Führer* of the NSDAP. All leaders from the *Kreisleiter* down to the *Blockleiter* were appointed by the college of *Reichsleiter*. At the top Hitler aimed at arbitrary power and had no intention of having his hands tied by any constitution. The Nazi Party had no equivalent of the Italian Grand Council of Fascism, which in the end was used to depose Mussolini.

Germany is by tradition a nation with a high intellectual level but the Nazis mistrusted and disliked intellectualism. Hitler hated intellectuals because they introduced criticism, analysis and possible hostile elements, which disturbed his exercise of power. In 1938, of the fifty *Gauleiter* and *Reichsleiter* who formed the 'élite' of the Nazi leadership, only ten had completed an university education, only a few had attended university classes for a while, and the majority had never gone beyond secondary school. Hitler preferred to have people of the same origins as his in his immediate entourage: people with a low standard of education. In the narrow horizon of Hitler's ruling clique, and within his tedious and restricted circle of intimates, docility, capacity of listening, intellectual limitation, petty bourgeois mediocrity and triviality predominated.

RANKS

NSDAP ranks were organised in a military way with the following approximate equivalents:

Mitglied or *Helfer*:	Member or private
Arbeitsleiter:	Private first class
Oberarbeitsleiter:	Corporal
Hauptarbeitsleiter:	Sergeant
Bereitschaftsleiter:	Technical sergeant
Oberbereitschaftsleiter:	Master-Sergeant
Hauptbereitschaftsleiter:	Sergeant-Major
Blockleiter:	Second Lieutenant
Zellenleiter:	First Lieutenant
Ortsgruppenleiter:	Captain
Kreisleiter:	Lieutenant-Colonel
Gauleiter:	Colonel or General
Reichsleiter:	No equivalent (councillor)
Stellvertreter des Führers:	Vice-president (Rudolf Heß, later Martin Bormann)

PARTY AND ASSOCIATED ORGANISATIONS

The NSDAP was made up of two levels of organisations. First the *Gliederungen der Partei* (party organisations) and second the *Angeschlossende Verbände* (associated organisations), which enabled the Nazis to control all administrative and economic functions, police, cultural activities and social life.

After 1934, the *Gliederungen* included the following:

- *Sturmabteilung* (SA).
- *Schutzstaffeln* (SS).
- *Nationalsozialistische Kraftfahrer-Korps* (NSKK, National Socialist Motor Corps).

- *Hitler Jugend* (HJ, Hitler Youth).
- *Nationalsozialistische Deutsch Studenten Bund* (NSDStB, National Socialist German Students' League).
- *Nationalsozialistische Deutsch Doktoren Bund* (NSD-DB, National Socialist German Professors' League);
- *Nationalsozialistische-Frauenschaft* (NSF, National Socialist Women's Organisation).

The *Angeschlossende Verbände* included the following:

- *Dienst Frauenwerk* (Women's Work Service).
- *Deutsche Arbeit Front* (DAF, German Labour Front).
- *Nationalsozialistische Arztebund* (NSAB, National Socialist Doctors' League).
- *Nationalsozialistische Juristenbund* (NSJ, National Socialist Jurists' League).
- *Nationalsozialistische Volkswohlfahrte* (NSV, National Socialist People's Welfare Organisation).
- *Nationalsozialistische Lehrerbund* (NSLB, National Socialist Teachers' League).
- *Nationalsozialistische Kriegsopfer Verzorgung* (NSKV, organisation for veterans and war victims).
- *Beamtenbund* (civil servants' and administrators' league).

Party organisations and associated groups, in their turn, were divided into sub-branches such as the *Kraft durch Freude* (KdF, Work through Joy) organised by the DAF. The *Bund Deutscher Mädel* (BDM, League of German Maidens) was a sub-organisation of the *Hitler Jugend*. The *Waffen-SS* (military SS units) was one of the numerous sub-organisations of the SS.

RIVALRY AT THE TOP

The Nazis were obsessed by order, which was illustrated by parades, processions and meetings but actually, as has already been pointed out, the system was chaotic in order to create energy and rivalry. As already said, Hitler liked to see a good deal of ruthless competition, since he assumed that this way was the only road to outstanding achievement. In the practice the organisations and associations of the NSDAP were separate, and were not supposed to collaborate with each other. The organisation was vertical and each group fulfilled its own specific tasks according to the *Führerprinzip* (orders coming from above). Only a few people, and of course Hitler at the top, had a general view of NSDAP activities. The *Führer* never held cabinet meetings but instead dealt with every branch leader singly by meeting and telling him personally and confidentially (often without written orders) only what he needed to know, when he needed to know it. Under his control, Hitler deliberately allowed the constitution of private empires: economics (Robert Ley), industrial development and air force (Hermann Göring), national building and construction (Fritz Todt), youth movement (Baldur von Schirach), party (Rudolf Heß and later Martin Bormann), security, order and repression (Heinrich Himmler), propaganda (Josef Göbbels) and regional dictators (the *Gauleiter*). These rivalries kept his subordinates weak and greatly increased Hitler's own power as supreme arbiter. Furthermore Hitler exploited the poorly-defined legal competence of various state and party organs. There was considerable ambiguity in the relations between state and party, dualities in state and government, overlapping between the national armed forces (*Wehrmacht*) and the *Waffen-SS*, interdependence of industry, government and civil service and rivalries between the various types of state and party police forces. As already said, Hitler's method of government has often been described as 'divide and rule'; he deliberately left the structure of authority under him unclear, so that no individual henchman or group had too much power. He welcomed tensions and rivalries between them, since it was he who had absolute authority, and only he who could afford to play off one group against another. In the resulting chaos, the *Führer* could operate quite effectively and hold unlimited power in his own hands. Until his final years when he completely isolated himself in his concrete headquarters and bomb-proof command posts, Hitler's preferred company consisted of a ruling clique with narrow horizons including fellow veterans and intimates of the *Kampfzeit*, docile and intellectually limited aides and servants, secretaries and immediate subordinates.

Hitler was not interested in religion, economy, administration, or carrying out a programme of reform. He only wanted power and left the details and organisation to appointed and zealous (sometimes talented) subalterns who would be insignificant without his support. So he was able to concentrate his whole energy in the only activities, which interested him: foreign policy and preparation for war before 1939, as well as grand strategy and direction of operations during the Second World War. The NSDAP was the instrument by which Hitler acquired power in Germany, and Nazi Germany was to be the instrument by which he intended to acquire power in Europe and – in the long term – world domination.

USCHLA

The *Gliederungen der Partei* and the *Angeschlossende Verbände* were co-ordinated by the *Untersuchungs-und Schlichtungs-Ausschüsse* (USCHLA, Committee for Investigation and Arbitrage). This commission, headed by Walther Buch (1883–1949), was established in 1926 to deal with internal accusation, dishonourable acts and moral conduct causing offence to the party. The Commission became soon a feared and secret organisation, sometimes referred to as the '*Cheka* in the NSDAP'. The *Cheka* (Emergency Commission) was the first in a succession of Soviet state security organisations. Essentially a disciplinary body, the USCHLA's functions were to keep a watch on unreliable party members, crush and expel dissidents, and arbitrate disputes between party members. It had almost unlimited power of life and death over members and no appeal against its judgement was possible.

A point of interest is what was destined to the mass of members did not apply to the Nazi 'élite leadership'. Hitler did not want to be a spoilsport to any of his lieutenants. If he demanded the utmost of them he had also to permit them to let off steam as they pleased. As long as they were useful to him, he was not interested in their private lives. In apparent contrast to their leader, Hitler's henchmen were at liberty to indulge their personal whims. Hermann Göring – originally No. 2 in the Nazi hierarchy – cultivated ostentation with unparalleled effrontery, he was a scandalous accumulator of property by looting, one of the most brutal and unbridled practitioners of despotism and was addicted to morphine. Reinhard Heydrich, the ruthless head of the powerful *Reichssicherheitshauptamt* (RSHA, SS Central Security Department of the Reich created in 1939) and Josef Göbbels, head of the Propaganda Ministry, were notorious for their many love affairs. Robert Ley, head of the DAF, was a habitual drunk and a source of amusement even to his supreme lord and master. Ley shared with Heinrich Hoffmann (the official Nazi publisher and Hitler's personal photographer) the title of

44

'National Drunkard'. Julius Streicher, editor of the Nazi anti-Semitic newspaper *Der Stürmer*, was a sadist, a pervert and a pornographer. Ernst Röhm, chief of the SA, was a notorious homosexual and beer-hall bawler. Only when it served a political or personal purpose, would Hitler present himself a scrupulous and scandalised puritan. For example he dismissed General von Blomberg in 1938, allegedly because the General's second wife had been a prostitute but in fact to strengthen his own authority over the army. He agreed to the murder of Röhm and the purge of the corrupt SA leadership in 1934 only when they were no longer useful to him.

Chapter 6

NSDAP Regalia and Uniforms

REGALIA

The Nazi Party did not appeal to reason but to passion. It was an inhuman, heroic and tragic opera, which was everywhere evident through the language of regalia. In the strict sense of the word, regalia designates the insignia of royalty – crown, orb, sceptre etc. But like many other words it has come to be used where it fits conveniently. Regalia have been borrowed by church, civic, military, politic and Masonic fraternities to describe the uniforms and ornaments that make them recognisable to outsiders, and within their own fraternities display their degrees of authority and levels of achievement.

Hitler was perfectly aware of the impact of regalia. Indeed, one is really struck by the extraordinary minutiae that presided to the elaboration of Nazi uniforms, emblems, insignia, armbands, daggers, swords, flags, banners and the like. Hitler had a good sense for symbols and knew something of colours having in his early days of scratching for a living in Vienna painted watercolours and posters for shopkeepers. From the start in the early 1920s, Hitler took such matters as the design of regalia, equipment and uniforms very seriously for he believed that the success of his nascent movement depended to a considerable extent on the use of strong symbols immediately comprehensive and impressive to the people.

THE SWASTIKA AND *HOHEITSZEICHEN*

With a team of competent designers, Hitler worked on many versions of Nazi regalia before deciding on the hypnotic Nazi emblem: the swastika.

Introduced in the summer of 1920 as the party symbol, the black swastika mounted in a white circle on a bright red ground had an eye-catching vividness. Hitler said that the red symbolised the blood of the Nazi Party, the white circle the purity of the German race, and the swastika would remind everyone of the struggle for victory of the German Aryan man over the 'evil forces' of Jewry and Marxism. Cold as ice, strong as steel, sharp as a blade, the symbol the most readily associated with the Nazi was the *Hakenkreuz* (swastika or hooked cross). However the Nazis did not invent the swastika. The *Hakenkreuz* was an adapted Greek cross with four arms of equal length extended at right angles. There was originally no particularly sinister significance in it. In ancient times, the cross symbolised the movement of the sun, it was a charm against the evil eye, a talisman on Buddhist graves, and the word swastika seemed to mean good luck in Sanskrit, which was hardly what it came to mean under the Nazi regime. Swastikas have been in existence for centuries, they were (and still are) found in the pictorial records of religions all over the world (for example, in Egypt, Greece, China, Vietnam, Japan, Persia, pre-Columbian South America and North America). In pre-Christian Scandinavian and German mythology the swastika was the symbol associated to Donner also called Thor who was the god of thunder, rain and fertility. Thor was the son of the goddess Jord and Odin (also called Wotan, the god of wisdom, poetry and war). Donner/Thor is still reminded today in North European Germanic languages as a day of the week: Thursday in English, Donnerstag in German, Donderdag in Dutch or Torsdag in Danish and Swedish. The swastika however did not recall a remote but still tangible historical era; as an ancient and prehistoric symbol of salvation, it was supposed to proclaim the future victory of 'Aryan civilisation'. In the 19th century the swastika became the symbol of German nationalism and racial struggle. Hitler carried on its use from an earlier German anti-Semitic, nationalist organisation called Hammer League founded in 1912 at Leipzig by an engineer called Theodor Fritsch. The swastika was also used by several right-wing militias (notably the *Freikorps* Ehrhardt Brigade) after the First World War. So the emblem of Nazism was not a creation of the Nazis but it had a very striking effect. The Nazi swastika was very often represented standing on one point to give the dynamic impression of an advancing movement. The *Hakenkreuz* appeared everywhere in the Third Reich in many shapes and forms on buildings, uniforms, badges, medals, literature and printing works, official seals, stamps, and so on.

Above: Various forms of swastika and (bottom) the *Hoheitszeichen.*

The other Nazi emblem was the *Adler* (eagle), widely used in ancient and medieval heraldry, and symbolising prestige and strength. The eagle –in various forms and positions, with wings either spread or folded – had already been used by the Egyptians, the Romans, the Carolingian empire, the medieval Holy Roman Empire, the United States of America, by the French emperor Napoleon I and many others. To the German people, it referred to the medieval Reich, and to Hitler's followers it meant the recovery of the German national pride and greatness by way of Nazism. Swastika and eagle were combined with wreath of oak leaves and acorn to form the most distinctive Nazi

Right: Swastika decorating a Native North American headdress.

insignia: the *Hoheitszeichen* (national emblem). The *Hoheitszeichen* had various forms, with outspreading or downwards eagle wings, in metal or in cloth for wear on uniform, headgear, badge and medal, in rubber stamp form for official papers.

Everyone in Nazi Germany in any kind of position, civil or military, was recognisable through the symbolic language of regalia. The theatrical Nazi protocol was distinguished by its insignia in an infinite variety: uniforms, flags, banners, seals, gorgets, cuff titles, symbols and badges indicating function in society and rank. There were medals for varying degrees of valour and achievement, and medallions to commemorate games and rallies. Medals were an obligatory purchase by everyone attending a rally, and the money of course went to support the NSDAP. They also had the effect of making the event seem important and bonding the participants into a united front.

In November 1935 a new *Reichskriegflag* (national war flag) was officially introduced. Combining Nazi regalia and German tradition, it was composed of a red ground, a superimposed white cross at the junction of which was a small white circle containing a black swastika; in the upper left corner of the flag was a small black Teutonic 'iron' cross with white edges.

DAGGERS

Nazi regalia also included weapons such as swords and daggers with subtle distinction of rank and function in the decoration of haft or blade, tabs and lanyards. Introduced in December 1933, a sixteenth-century 'Holbein' Swiss-styled *Dolch* (dagger) was suspended by a chain from the waist belts of high NSDAP functionaries and SA and SS senior officers. Other Nazi organisations were quick to follow, and before long, most branches of the uniform-conscious civil service were also clamouring for daggers of their own. Hitler, keenly interested in regalia

Left: SS Dagger 1933.

Left: *Hitler Jugend* dagger with leather scabbard. The bladecarried the motto *Blut und Ehre!* ('Blood and Honour!').

Below: *Hitler Jugend* leader's dagger.

and eager to support the world-renowned German blademakers' cartel in Solingen, approved many of the designs himself. They were created by students and masters at the state trade schools. Once a pattern had been selected, it was submitted to the *Reichszeugmeisterei* (RZM, National Quartermaster's Department – see below) for final approval.

Only then could members of the organisation purchase and display their new swords, knives, and daggers.

There was a profusion of gleaming blades in Nazi Germany. The late medieval-styled SS dagger had a black wood grip, bearing various decorations such as SS runes, the standard eagle and swastika and motto ('My honour is Loyalty') etched into the blade. The RAD's sidearm was a whittling knife carrying the slogan *Arbeit Adelt* (work ennobles) on its broad blade. That of the Hitler Youth was a knife displaying the motto of the organisation: *Blut und Ehre!* (blood and honour!). The SA had a dagger with inscribed on the blade *Alles für Deutschland* (all for Germany). SA-men who had joined before 31 December 1931 received from Ernst Röhm personally daggers inscribed '*In herzlicher Freundschaft*' ('In heart-felt Friendship); after Röhm's death in 1934, these daggers were either withdrawn or had their inscription erased. Daggers were awarded to qualified members who were members for years, to those who had achieved a set of minimum standards, and passed tests of knowledge of Nazi arcana. The dagger was offered or granted, but although it had to be purchased by the holder, it was not considered a personal property. So when a holder was expelled or had to leave for any reason, the dagger had to be handed back.

THE *REICHSZEUGMEISTEREI*

After Hitler's accession to power, the *Reichszeugmeisterei* (RZM, National Quartermaster's Department) was established in July 1934, with offices in Munich at Tegernseer Landstraße 210. This organisation had exclusive legal authority to design and control quality and costs of uniforms, badges, medals and other regalia, thus ending the flow of improvised, unofficial, and semi-official items. The RZM contracted private firms and state companies to produce all items, which were authenticated by official and legal RZM seals, marks and labels. The RZM was a branch of the Treasury Department of the Nazi Party and made sure that the production of all that they procured was carried out in 'Aryan' manufacturing plants, and with materials of German origin whenever possible. Producers authorised by the RZM could not employ 'non-Aryan' workers, and had to give preference to Party members when promoting workers. Hitler was from the first incapable of delegating authority, in small details as well as in great matters. The

Left: Two examples of RZM control labels on SS items.

design of the smallest part of the most insignificant Nazi regalia had to be submitted to him for approval. Hitler was also a cunning money-maker who lost no opportunity to convert the enthusiasm he whipped up into a flow of cash. In the Nazi Party there was a price tag on everything – admission fees to meetings, membership dues, pamphlets, books and newspapers, as well as the RZM's flags, uniforms, regalia, medals and insignia. The RZM became a flourishing business, selling clothing, equipment and even insurance to thousands of members.

Before the seizure of power in 1933, the necessity of financing their own party meant a real sacrifice for many poor members, but Hitler believed that the true test of his followers' convictions was their willingness to pay their own way. Whatever money Hitler may have received from big businessmen and industrial tycoons, none of it reached the base of the Nazi movement. Funds and donations from the upper classes were managed from 1925 by the Party Treasurer Franz Xaver Schwartz (1875–1947), and used almost exclusively for the support of the NSDAP leadership and headquarters, for the maintenance of certain elite SA groups, and to help pay the enormous cost of election campaigns. The local groups and the lower ranks of the Nazi organisation were financed principally by dues, contributions and collections at meetings. Occasionally a local leader was lucky enough to have one or more generous benefactors or sponsors in his area, but in the early days and even when the Party was officially established, passing the hat was often the only and main source of income for local Nazi groups. Considering that the NSDAP local units did most of the propaganda work, it is not surprising that they were constantly short of money.

The RZM system applied to Nazi Party uniforms, equipment and insignia only. The control did not extend to non-Party organisations, like the Army, Navy and Air Force. Like all other Nazi bodies, the RZM was organised along hierarchical military lines ranging from the *Vorstände der Zeugmeisterien* (Directors of the Quartermaster's Department), to the *Angestellte der RZM* (employees). As early as 1929 the SA set up a Quartermaster's Department to produce, regulate, and provide uniforms and equipment as economically as possible. It should be noted that many SA men were so poor that they could not afford to pay for their own uniforms and equipment.

UNIFORMS

Aside from the programmes to purify the German 'race' by expelling and exterminating Jews and other 'enemies', a key impulse in the social operations of the Nazi regime was the urge to total uniformity of mind and of appearance. The great uniform historian Brian L. Davis once wrote: 'Nazi Germany was a nation besotted with the wearing of >>>

Above: '*Alte Kampfer*' chevron. This was worn on the upper right sleeve by NSDAP members, SA and SS men who had joined before 30 January 1933.

Right: NSDAP *Hauptbereichsleiter's* collar patch. The eagle, swastika and oak leaves were gold on a red background.

Left: NSDAP *Bereichsleiter's* overcoat. **Right:** NSDAP *Gemeinschaftsleiter.*

Left: NSDAP *Oberdienstleiter.* **Right:** NSDAP *Oberbereichsleiter.*

military and paramilitary uniforms of all kinds'. Indeed the wearing of uniforms for everyone was designed to break down social classes, and professional barriers. The uniform provided visible evidence of group cohesion and was intended to stimulate citizens' impulses to join in. Asocials, outcasts, doubters, sceptics, ironists, wits, loners and dissenters would either be absorbed or transformed – or vanish into prisons and concentration camps. Nazi society, both civilian and military, was madly theatrical. At work and in everyday life people went in civilian suits, in unformal and casual dress, in dungarees or protective clothing suitable for everyday wear, but every trade or labour community (including mine workers, postmen, zookeepers, administrative and hospital personnel, bus and tram conductors, train drivers, and many others) had a ceremonial walking-out dress with official insignia and emblems resembling military uniforms worn for formal occasions.

Nazi Party members thus had uniforms, which were worn at parades, rallies, parties, meetings, gathering and whenever they were in official function. The uniform's quality and design varied following the ranks in the party. Basically it was composed of a peaked cap decorated with an eagle holding a swastika in its claws, a white shirt and a (often) black tie, over which a four front pockets tunic was worn. The tunic had collar patches indicating ranks, and displayed various medals and badges. On the left arm members wore the *Hakenkreuzbinde*, a red armband with a black swastika upon a white disc. Each level of leadership was denoted by coloured piping round the cap, collar patched, and around the edge of the armband. Often for senior officers the uniform included riding or straight trousers and riding black leather boots or black shoes. Breeches and high riding boots were intended to associate with such former aristocratic activities as horse-riding, hunting and steeplechasing.

In winter a long duty overcoat or a cloak was worn. The NSDAP dress was usually brown, field-grey or dark blue but senior ranks' summer uniforms were often white. *Alte Kämpfer* wore a special golden chevron on the upper right arm. High-ranking party officials and diplomats had resplendent walking-out dresses, attractive parade uniforms, sumptuous dinner-jackets, tuxedos and frock coats, some of which were created by the famous opera designer Benno von Arent. Often white or fine brown leather gloves added a touch of elegance. The service uniform was completed by the issued of a Sam Browne waist leather belt and shoulder strap with various buckles, rings and clips.

Some members were allowed to carry a sidearm, generally a sword or a dagger and even a small Walther PPK pistol, which was held in a holster on the service belt. When in civilian clothes, members wore the emblem of the NSDAP on a round lapel pin.

Hitler was the only party member to wear a gold 'badge of sovereignty' – an eagle holding a *Hakenkreuz* in its talons – but his everyday tunic did not differ from the ordinary NSDAP member's jacket. Hitler loved theatrical pomp but his own dress was always modest as a matter of careful strategy: among shining, magnificent and beautiful uniforms, his personal simplicity made a modest but striking effect.

NSDAP ANTHEM

From 1930, the official NSDAP anthem was *Die Fahne hoch* ('Up with the Flag') also called the *Horst Wessel Lied*. When Adolf Hitler became chancellor three years later, the *Horst Wessel Lied* was recognised as the German national anthem by a law of 19 May 1933. The lyrics of the song was composed by Horst Wessel, a young Nazi SA man killed in February 1930, and the music was a popular tune in the German Imperial Navy in the First World War. In 1936, a German music critic, Alfred Weidemann, published an article in which he identified the melody to a song composed in 1865 by a certain Peter Cornelius on the melody of a Viennese folk tune.

The following is an English translation of the *Horst Wessel Lied*'s lyrics:

> The flag on high! The ranks tightly closed!
> The SA is marching with quiet, steady step.
> Comrades shot by the Red Front and reactionaries
> March in spirit within our ranks.
> Comrades shot by the Red Front and reactionaries
> March in spirit within our ranks.
>
> Clear the streets for the brown battalions,
> Clear the streets for the storm division!
> Millions are looking upon the swastika full of hope,
> The day of freedom and of bread dawns!
> Millions are looking upon the swastika full of hope,
> The day of freedom and of bread dawns!

For the last time, the call to arms is sounded!
For the fight, we all stand prepared!
Already Hitler's banners fly over all streets.
The time of bondage will last but a little while now!
Soon Hitler's banners will fly over all streets.
The time of bondage will last but a little while now.

The flag on high! The ranks tightly closed!
The SA is marching with quiet, steady step.
Comrades shot by the Red Front and reactionaries,
March in spirit within our ranks.
Comrades shot by the Red Front and reactionaries,
March in spirit within our ranks.

Part 2

Origins and Growth of the Sturmabteilung

Chapter 7

The *Freikorps*

After the collapse of the Second Reich in 1918, a national assembly was elected in January 1919 and met in Weimar the following month to draw up a new constitution, resulting in the creation of a democratic regime called the Weimar Republic. The black red and gold colours of 1848 were adopted for the new regime. By that time Germany was in the grip of social turmoil and near civil war, with Communists and Socialist parties clashing with various nationalist and conservative movements and militias.

The *Freikorps* (Free Corps) were an important feature of German political life in the immediate aftermath of the war. Their history is little known but formed a major episode in the development of the nascent Nazi Party. The term *Freikorps* itself came from the 'free corps', irregular regiments of volunteer skirmishers created in Prussia during the Seven Years War (1756–63). They became famous for the part they took in the Battle of Freiberg against Austria in 1762. The *Freikorps von Kleist* was so successful that it was incorporated into the Prussian Army and consisted of *jäger* (light infantry), dragoons and hussars. The term was later re-used to designate the voluntary paramilitary formations organised by Major Lützow in 1813 as the kernel of an army to liberate Prussia from Napoléon. Continuing the tradition, the post-First World War *Freikorps* were right-wing paramilitary units recruited from 'reliable' officers and soldiers from the demobilised Imperial Army. The German troops returning home after the Armistice found their country torn apart by internal unrest and its eastern borders threatened by the Poles. Right-wing, nationalist and revanchist, the *Freikorps* became the available 'force in being' for the defence of the newly-created Weimar Republic. Though reluctant to support the new Republic, the *Freikorps* fought furiously against Communists at home and against Polish forces on the eastern frontier.

Members of the *Freikorps* were volunteers, very often ex-servicemen, former officers, adventurers and the unemployed, students and youngsters eager to prove their valour. Some of them were fanatical nationalists, and many were men who liked to wear a uniform and felt at home in barracks, indeed men who never settled down into the monotonous routine of civilian life. Besides, unemployment was rife, and many professional soldiers did not wish to exchange the prestige of the uniform, the comradeship and the comparative security enjoyed in a *Freikorps* unit, for the misery and shame of civilian unemployment. The officers, of course, would find such a fall even worse. The image of the First World War as a period of almost unrelieved horror which later developed in Europe, was not shared by all the soldiers themselves when they returned to the post-war civilian world. For many of them this was disappointing and drab, and for some a real deprivation. In many countries the terrible experiences of the war did produce a deep and widespread reaction against militarism, but pacifism was by no means universal. At post-war regimental reunions, veterans maintained their strong wartime comradeship and were able to persuade themselves that the war with its warm fellowship and its dangerous adventures, its inhuman sufferings and petty pleasures, its challenges and triumphs, its economic security and freedom from domestic responsibilities, had really been the happiest time of their lives. This nostalgia for a lost world of security, status and purpose was a significant element in the confused political movements, which gave birth to various forms of populism and fascism in the 1920s and 1930s.

In Germany many ex-soldiers felt they had been betrayed and looked for scapegoats. Many of them indeed believed in the so-called *Dolchstoßtheorie* (the 'stab-in-the-back theory'). This was a political lie, asserting that the German army had not been defeated at the front, but 'stabbed in the back' by traitors, Social Democrats and Jewish profiteers at home, whom Hitler called the 'November criminals' (those who had 'caused defeat' and signed the shameful armistice of 11 November 1918). Many Germans – both civilian and military – were quite willing to blame pacifists, internationalists, anti-militarists, socialists, profiteers and Jews for the defeat. This convenient legend, later brilliantly >>>

Left: German Stormtrooper 1918. This soldier of the Stoßtruppen (special assault unit) wears the 1915 pattern steel helmet, a grey-green tunic without pockets, leather-reinforced breeches, puttees and ankle boots. Equipment includes an entrenching tool, and a gasmask in a canvas pouch. Armament ranged from a Mauser carbine, bayonet, Bergmann sub-machine gun, and grenades. Detachments of Stoßtruppen were of battalion strength and attached to infantry divisions. The fast-moving and hard-hitting stormtroopers were deployed, not in long lines of riflemen as had been habitual, but as small groups of assault infantry, searching and jumping for cover and firing while advancing, by-passing centres of resistance and penetrating wherever they found weakness. They operated with speed, aggression, independence and flexibility. Many of these special elite assault troops were later part of the post-war Freikorps.

exploited by the Nazis, contributed to a belief in the injustice of the Treaty of Versailles of 1919. Some of the ex-servicemen saw in the use of violence the path to power both in domestic and international politics. Militarists and ultra-nationalists saw in war an activity in which mankind justified itself.

The *Freikorps* were illegally organised, and secretly equipped and paid by the then Captain Kurt von Schleicher (1882–1934). They formed small self-sufficient units rather than larger formations. In February 1926, Schleicher was appointed head of the *Reichswehr* (German armed forces) and began the clandestine development of the German army. From 1929 to 1933 Schleicher, an ambitious and unscrupulous schemer, played a deciding role in the political affairs of the declining Weimar Republic. In December 1932 he became Chancellor and attempted to contain the Nazis, hoping to take advantage of Hitler's growing popularity to strengthen his own position. After Hitler's seizure of power he retired to private life, but fell victim to Hitler's vengeance: he was assassinated during the purge of the SA in June 1934.

It is impossible to determine exactly how many men served in the *Freikorps* but the usually accepted estimate is between 150,000 and 350,000. The men of the *Freikorps* wore Imperial Army uniforms and used the old Army's equipment.

They maintained the best of wartime comradeship, and owed allegiance to their commanding officers and not to any government or constitution. Many *Freikorps* were named after their leaders: Ehrhardt, Loewenfeld, Roßbach, for example. They had inherited the tactics and structure of the *Stoßtruppen* (shock/assault troops), self-sufficient elite groups of combatants specially trained for aggressive assault and raiding warfare, which the German Army had developed at the end of the First World War. They were not always really interested in politics, and were less determined political militants than tough front-line soldiers, thirsting for action, action at any price, be that against Bolsheviks, Poles, war profiteers, Jews or the Weimar Republic which had called them into being.

They were dangerous, as they had a wide range of fighting skills and weapons, and were ready to take the law into their own hands. Attempts were made to indoctrinate them politically, but on the whole the *Freikorps* longed for something new, without any clear idea what they were aiming at. They were marching but they were not sure in which direction.

The *Freikorps*' Role in Post-war Germany

The *Freikorps* were covertly supported by the *Reichswehr* as a means of evading the demilitarisation imposed by the Treaty of Versailles. They were charged with maintain order in the streets, breaking up riots and strikes, and repressing left-wing conspirators. It should be noted that by leaving national defence to overtly right-wing units, which seemed to make the protection of the Germany a right-wing monopoly, the leaders of the Weimar Republic committed a major blunder, and this ultimately contributed to their downfall. The *Freikorps* were an anti-revolutionary police force to repress any left-wing take-over, and prevent Germany from becoming a Bolshevik state.

It is almost impossible to find words to describe the disarray of Germany was in at this time, deserted by its rulers and its chief military commander, Ludendorff. By then Germany was a nation marked by defeat, disorder, the accusation of war guilt and the loss of its overseas colonies. To defeat, hunger and unemployment was added the horror of civil war. Germany was in grave danger of falling to Communism (Bolshevism, a sit was commonly known then). In the chaotic post-war period, the Communist threat must not be underestimated. Soviet Russia, based on the doctrines of Karl Marx modified by Lenin, considered itself in a state of perpetual war with the bourgeois capitalist world. Bolshevism, victorious after a civil war that lasted until the early 1920s, instituted a dictatorial regime in Russia which, for all its egalitarian rhetoric, subordinated every aspect of public life, and much of private life as well, commanding from the top, reinforced by arbitrary discipline and a pervasive system of internal espionage. Bolshevism was a serious threat a nightmare which obsessed the middle class and above all the capitalist upper classes of Europe after 1917. The Communists in Germany were a determined and well-organised party which commanded considerable popularity among the lower classes, and enjoyed Moscow's support. They had strong-arm squads, and their propaganda was powerful and convincing, based on the teachings of Marx and Lenin. But to many Germans it seemed to mean bloody revolution, the end of private property, the ruining of the middle class and the elimination of the intelligentsia. Many Germans lived in fear of a Bolshevik takeover. In some places the Communists actually gained power and set up the first 'soviets' (revolutionary councils of soldiers, workers or peasants forming the core of a Marxist society). The danger of the establishment of a Communist dictatorship in Germany provoked a reaction among many people including military men – officers and men alike – who were still strongly inspired by nationalist feelings.

In this confused context, the *Freikorps* went into action. Having rapidly learnt the methods of urban guerrilla warfare and riot control, they put down a revolt led by the Communist Spartacists in Berlin in January 1919 and killed their leaders Karl Liebknecht and Rosa Luxemburg. With equal brutality they smashed an attempt to establish an independent Socialist state in Bavaria in May 1919, and, in June, a similar revolt in the Rhineland. The combination of Army and ultra right-wing factions such as the *Freikorps* made any Bolshevik successes short-lived but the threat from and the fear of Communism did not diminish.

Freikorps units also fought – with reluctant Allied approval – against the Russian Bolsheviks in Lithuania and Latvia in 1919. They were also intended to protect the newly-instituted Weimar Republic from being invaded from the east, notably in Upper Silesia. In this province, claimed by both Germany and Poland in complex rivalries combining Polish patriotism and German economic need, the Allies were unable to prevent fighting between Poles and Germans in 1921. The frontiers had not yet been exactly defined, and the Germans wanted to keep as much as possible of what they considered their own lands, whereas the Poles intended to make as many conquests as possible prior to any treaty. It was impossible to adequately defend the eastern provinces with the limited *Reichswehr*, and it was therefore necessary to supplement it with secret formations. Disguised as non-military *Arbeitskommandos* ('labour battalions' also known as the 'Black *Reichswehr*'), numerous *Freikorps* were attached to the small German regular army, and were at the forefront of this undeclared war.

A THREATENING FORCE

At first, the Weimar Republic supported the formation of the *Freikorps*, but the undisciplined behaviour of some of these units eventually made them obnoxious to the traditional military command and an embarrassment to the civilian authorities. Their victories had pacified Germany and saved it from the Communist threat but they soon became troublesome victors and difficult allies. Some *Freikorps* leaders thought that the regular army had failed, and had to be replaced by a

new model, a fanatical army of volunteer soldiers ready to fight under any circumstances. In some of their leaders' minds was the strong desire to crush Communism, but also the hope of overthrowing the unpopular Weimar Republic, to reverse the Treaty of Versailles, to restore Germany to her rightful position as the greatest power in continental Europe and to put the Army back in its rightful position within Germany.

The *Freikorps* with their personal devotion to individual leaders and their mercenary *Landsknecht* indiscipline, their indifference to law and order and their general political ignorance and arrogance, were manifestly an embarrassment both to the Army and to the Government. Called into being in a moment of chaos and emergency, they were symptomatic of a revolutionary period which both Army and Government were anxious to forget. They had served their turn with brutal efficiency but their

Left: Trooper of *Freikorps Maercker* 1919.
This volunteer wears standard German army uniform with M1916 steel helmet, bayonet, ammunition pouches and M1917 grenades on the service belt, and a Mauser carbine.

Left: Volunteer of *Freikorps Oberland* in Upper Silesia 1921. This Bavarian volunteer wears civilian clothing, the M1916 steel helmet, and a *Patronentragegurte* (bandolier) holding ammunition clips for his Mauser rifle.

Above: M1916 steel helmets.
The man on the left belonged to *Freikorps Hacketau* under the command of *Oberstleutnant* Menz and Major von Falkenstein, which fought against the Communists in spring 1919. The *Totenkopf* (Death's Head), roughly hand-painted on the steel helmet was adopted by several *Freikorps* and later became the emblem of the SS and that of the German Army armoured troops.
The *Freikorps* soldier on the right, belonging *to Kompanie Schlageter* within the *Selbschutz Sturmabteilung* (Self Defence Assault Detachment) *Heinz* in 1921, wears a white swastika on the front of his steel helmet. The swastika was also worn by the men of Brigade Ehrhardt. It was adopted by Adolf Hitler's Nazi Party in 1920.

continued existence was a cause of anxiety to the victorious Allies who persistently demanded that they be disbanded. The Army, therefore, supported the Government in their enactment of a law requiring all individuals and formations to give up illegally-held weapons. The duty of destroying equipment in conformity with the orders of the Allied Control Commission was entrusted to a special Reich Commissioner.

On 10 January 1920, the terms of the Treaty of Versailles came into force; the new *Reichswehr* had to be reduced from 450,000 men

Left: Badge of honour of the *Stahlhelm*. The *Stahlhelm* (Steel Helmet) was a militant right-wing nationalist ex-servicemen's association created in the chaos of the German collapse of 1918. It was founded by the veterans Franz Seldte and Theodor Düsterberg. The president of the association was the soldiers' idol, the legendary First World War commander Field Marshal von Hindenburg. In the 1920s the *Stahlhelm* was a large and powerful organisation playing an increasing prominent part in the Weimar Republic. The association was linked with the Nazi Party and was absorbed by the SA in June 1933. By February 1934 its name had changed to the Nationalist League of Ex-Servicemen.

(including the *Freikorps*) to 100,000 professional soldiers. The newly appointed chief of the *Reichswehr*, General Hans von Seeckt (1886–1936), was determined to rebuild the German forces for future revenge. Seeckt was one of the greatest military planners of all time, and he set to work to turn the tiny German army into an elite corps into which a conscript army could rapidly be drafted when the time came. Knowing that he would never achieve this goal with the unruly *Freikorps*, but only with highly-qualified military professionals, he ordered their disbandment. Several units refused to simply disappear and plots flourished.

On 13 March 1920 some *Freikorps* officers leading the Ehrhardt Brigade, protesting against the government's acceptance of the Treaty of Versailles and their own disbandment, attempted to overthrow the government in Berlin and make the right-wing journalist and activist Wolfgang Kapp (1868–1922) Chancellor. The putsch was not opposed by Seeckt, who did not want to see German soldiers fighting each other. The insurgents seized several ministries in Berlin and issued a proclamation declaring the Weimar Republic abolished. The government was obliged to leave the capital in a hurry and move to Stuttgart. But this initial success turned into dismal failure when Seeckt refused to support the putschists. In the meantime the trade unions had organised a successful general strike, which proved how little popular support the insurgents enjoyed. The ill-prepared takeover failed, Kapp fled to Sweden, his supporters and conspirators were arrested or fled, and on 18 March, the legitimate government returned to Berlin. The failed putsch had clearly shown how fragile the new democratic regime was, and how dangerous armed militias were.

In 1921, all citizens' militias were disbanded. Many ex-*Freikorps* men returned to civilian life, while the best and most reliable units were absorbed into the *Reichswehr* and the *Schutzpolizei* (Security Police, *Schupo* for short). However, some unruly and still-armed gangs of determined, diehard activists took refuge in Bavaria. By then Bavaria had become a hotbed of revolt, reaction and ultra-nationalism against Prussian hegemony. Here these men, who had lived through the horrors of war and had in their disillusionment become disdainful of all civil law and order, re-formed themselves into secret societies and paramilitary organisations dedicated to undermining and ultimately overthrowing the Weimar Republic. For example, after its dissolution the Ehrhardt Brigade continued in the form of a secret underground formation named *Organisation Consul* (OC). Enjoying a strong following among the students of Munich, the OC engaged in acts of violence. In August 1921, its members murdered the former minister Erzberger, and in June 1922 the German foreign minister Rathenau. An attempt to kill the Socialist leader Scheidemann was unsuccessful. A number of ex-*Freikorps* men were recruited by Hitler's nascent NSDAP, as many *Freikorps* right-wingers shared Nazi hatreds and aims: the 'November Criminals', the combined threat of Judaism and Bolshevism, the Weimar democracy, the betrayal of the German soldiers who had fought for the country, the importance of 'racial purity', the great German traditions, the theft of her empire by inferior nations, and of course the implied promise of strong leadership in a revolt against the 'forces of evil'.

The disbanded *Freikorps* were the training schools for the political violence and terrorism which disfigured German life up to 1921, and again after 1929. They merged with the numerous defence leagues, patriotic unions, and veterans' associations, which sprang up in Bavaria, and which were precursors of later Nazi SA private units. The Nazi Party's survival, development and growth were impossible without the protection and violent action of its own special militia. Indeed the Weimar Republic was characterised by political parties having their own armed paramilitary groups such as the monarchist *Stahlhelm* (Steel Helmet, war veterans trained in secret by *Reichswehr* officers), the Social

Democrat *Reichsbanner* (Imperial Flag, supported by the Prussian *Schutzpolizei*); the Communist *Rotefrontkämpferbund* (Red Front Combatant League, supported by Moscow), and the *Antifa* (Anti-Fascist League), just to name the most important. A few years after the armistice of 1918, in defeated and officially demilitarised Germany, many able-bodied men belonged to private political private militias.

Chapter 8

Origins of the SA

GYMNASTIC ASSOCIATION

Hitler was a man utterly impatient of subtle situations, incapable of appreciating or thinking in nuances, of taking people as something other than accomplices or enemies. From the start Hitler denied the effectiveness of the written word, for the obvious reason that it allows contemplation, consideration, thought and reflection. Instead he relied upon the immediate power of the spoken word before a live audience formulated in stark black-and-white statements. Familiar slogans and repeated clichés attempted to reduce complex problems to simple issues. In their speeches the Nazis made great use of hysterical invectives, accusations, verbal attacks against enemies, recitals of injustices, passionate expressions of threats, and real and imaginary fears. The meetings with public addresses (that is political speeches not followed by discussion) were shows of strength expressing a conspiratorial solidarity. They were the key means of propagating Nazi ideology, and the first step to weaken, obstruct and, if possible, get rid of the German democratic government. Now that it is easy to see what Hitler intended, the credulity of his audiences seems difficult to explain, but Hitler seemed to have possessed a strange fascination, appealing to primitive mass emotions in a country where national arrogance had been followed by the humiliation of 1918 and the bewilderment of the early 1920s. Hitler was soon regarded by many as the providential saviour of the country from decadence.

Verbal violence was accompanied by physical violence. This was not an accidental accompaniment to Nazism, it was central to it. National Socialism was presented by Hitler himself as an unceasing struggle, an eternal combat against Germany's enemies both internal and external, real or imaginary. National Socialism was essentially organised hatred. It drew its power and inspiration from the desire to destroy. Hitler was a man at war, a man of hate. His language was the language of conflict, and everything was refracted through the prism of his hateful, warlike and racist mind.

Facing strong opposition, it was of course necessary to protect the nascent party and Hitler the orator in particular. From the outset Hitler was determined not to allow any interruptions while holding a meeting. The first recorded Nazi strong-arm squad was formed on 24 February 1920 at the Hofbräuhaus in Munich when Hitler and other orators spoke in a meeting before an audience of about 2,000. The improvised squad numbered some ten tough and hard-hitting ex-soldiers. Uproar began while Hitler was speaking, the meeting soon being interrupted by Communists and Socialists with chants and catcalls, but the Nazi squad and other sympathisers were strategically placed throughout the hall. Violent clashes occurred, and within a few minutes order was restored. By the time Hitler concluded his speech, most of the audience was on his side, and this was a historic moment of victory. As many other meetings soon followed, the number of improvised protection squads was increased. The organisation and co-ordination of these small units was in the hands of ex-*Freikorps* leader Johann Ulrich Klintsch. They had experienced ex-*Freikorps* men in their ranks, and their structure was copied from the Communist squads. Admission to the protection squads was voluntary. Candidates had to be of irreproachable character with no previous convictions; they had to show idealism and selflessness, they must identify themselves to the ideas of Hitler; they had to be physically suited to the party's demands including fighting, marching and training, and able to react quickly and firmly in an emergency. From the start it was attempted to give them a disciplined military appearance. They were divided into squads, provided with red flags with a black swastika in a red disk (designed by Hitler himself), and issued more or less uniform dress. They chanted slogans, and marched in step. In the streets and at unruly meetings, they obviously did not shun physical violence. Called *Ordnertruppen* (monitor troops), the Nazi squads were also known by the euphemism *Turnvereine* (Gymnastic Association), in order to avoid suppression by the police and to avoid being disbanded by the Allied Control Commission. The *Ordnertruppe* formed Hitler's earliest retinue, including the ex-convict and watchmaker Emil Maurice, a tough young butcher named Ulrich Graf, Hermann Esser, Christian Weber, the ex-Lieutenant Berchtold, Julius Schaub, a young student named Rudolf Heß, and several others. The purpose of the 'Gymnastic Association', as declared in the Party Proclamation of 3 August 1921, was far from sporting, however. It was in fact 'to serve as a means for bringing our youthful members together in a powerful organisation for the purpose of utilising their strength as an offensive force at the disposal of the movement'. In practice, the Nazi strong-arm squads were intended to serve three main purposes: first to keep order and protect the Nazi meetings; second to create an atmosphere of menace that made it risky for anyone to challenge the Nazis openly; and third to attract public attention by provocations, disturbances and riots. Rapidly the Nazi squads gained a reputation as troublemakers, breaking up meetings of opposing political factions, and beating up opponents as part of a deliberate campaign of intimidation. The long-term aim was to undermine the power, the appeal and the public standing of their political opponents. A major goal of the Nazis was the discrediting and annihilation of opponents, the negation of any alternative ideology, communist, socialist, but also conservative, and thus the destruction of democratic political life in any traditional form. At a meeting in Munich on 4 January 1921, Hitler bawled: 'The National-Socialism Movement in Munich will in the future ruthlessly prevent – if necessary by force – all meetings and lectures that are likely to distract the minds of our fellow countrymen.' The statement was blatant enough and the voice correspondingly harsh. There was, however, considerable subtlety in the action that was proposed. The display or threat of physical force is not necessarily repellent to all people. To some people violence had (and still has) a strongly attractive psychological appeal: it certainly had to frustrated Germans nursing their hatreds in the post-war period. To them also, the feeling of being associated with a movement that was surging forward with irresistible power was like an injection of the same power into their veins. But besides both regrettably appealing qualities there was also the propaganda value of terrorism. In pursuing its aims it was bound to attract attention, whether favourable or not. Gradually, the Nazi protection squads were increased in number, notably by the addition of numerous ex-*Freikorps* men when the Weimar authorities decided to disband all armed civilian and paramilitary formations in mid-1921.

THE *STURMABTEILUNG*

The very term *Sturmabteilung* seemed to have been coined by Hitler himself in a speech after a serious *Saalschlacht* (free fight) at the Hofbräuhaus (a famous beer hall in Munich) on 5 October 1921 when he had the opportunity to appreciate not only the protective worth of his squads but also their offensive value: indeed eighty Nazi 'gymnasts' had fought 800 Communist opponents and succeeded in driving them out of the hall. Henceforth the Nazi squads were officially given the name *Sturmabteilung* (SA, Assault Battalion). This title obviously appealed to ex-soldiers and ex-*Freikorps* men because it was associated with the élite *Stoßtruppen* (assault troops) of the First World War. After 1925 the name *Braunhemden* (Brownshirts) was also used because of the light-brown colour of their new uniforms when the Nazi Party was able to purchase cheaply a surplus lot of shirts which had been destined for the colonial troops in Africa.

Before 1925, outwardly the structure of the early SA was based on the military tradition of the *Freikorps*, but they were little more than gangs who regarded themselves as ordinary members of the Nazi Party. Except for a few small details the appearance of the SA was quite similar to regular Army troops. Their uniform consisted of a grey tunic, military breeches, Bavarian or Austrian-style ski-caps, leggings and marching boots, and a swastika armband. Of course, equipping a paramilitary unit like the SA cost a great deal of money. By the end of December 1922, the SA numbered less than 100 men and about forty regular soldiers had secretly pledged their loyalty. Even though the squads were thus on a very small scale, early SA men were often unemployed and had to be provided with food and shelter. Besides, hiring meeting halls and headquarters cost a lot of money too. There were transportation expenses whenever the SA squads travelled as a group. The Nazi Party itself could not supply such funds for it needed every available penny for its own upkeep and propaganda costs. Fortunately, Hitler found a prosperous supporter, Kurt Lüdecke (1890–1960), who agreed to subsidise the first units of Stormtroopers. Being fortunate enough in those hard times to have a reasonable private income, he was able to offer free meals –a great inducement – and equipment to volunteers. The naïve and irrepressible Lüdecke had joined the Nazi Party in August 1922, and soon felt there was a need to instil into SA men a pride in their special function as the party's

defenders. Hitler agreed to his plan and Lüdecke continued recruiting, accepting only the toughest and most able-bodied men who took an oath of allegiance on the swastika flag and pledged loyalty to Hitler. A band with four drummers and four fifers was formed, drills were held regularly, and every Wednesday night the entire company would assemble in a room Lüdecke had rented above a café where the men were lectured on the political aims of the NSDAP. Every Saturday and Sunday mornings the unit would gather on the outskirts of Munich and drill outdoors. When bad weather prevented this, Lüdecke's connections with far-right *Reichswehr* officers allowed them to use the drill-hall of the 2nd Bavarian Regiment. Soon weapons and military equipment were acquired and stored by Lüdecke. Germany was flooded with the leftovers of the First World War. Uniforms, equipment and even weapons were comparatively easily available for whoever had the money and the right connections.

Lüdecke was also send by Hitler to Italy in 1922 to make contact with Mussolini and get as much support as possible from the new Fascist dictator. In 1924 he also visited the US industrialist Henry Ford in Michigan, to see if the notoriously anti-Semitic founder of the Ford Motor Company would contribute funds to the struggling Nazi Party. Lüdecke also served as the NSDAP fundraiser in Germany. But Hitler's representative in high society achieved little. Important industrialists and wealthy personalities in those early days of Nazism regarded Hitler with suspicion, scorn or detached benevolence, and many feared the revolutionary socialist side of the Nazi programme. At this time, only a few rich individuals (the Harvard-educated businessman Ernst 'Putzi' Hanfstaengl or Siegfried Wagner, son of the composer Richard Wagner and his wife Winifred, for example) supported the Nazis financially. One of the principal sources of money and equipment for the SA was the secret army funds originally set up to finance *Freikorps* units and military intelligence work, most of the aid being given to Hitler on the initiative of one influential Army officer, *Hauptmann* (Captain) Ernst Röhm who was chief of staff to the Munich commandant.

HERMANN GÖRING

Hitler did not personally have to soil his hands with the blood drawn by his Stormtroopers, though there is plenty of evidence to suggest he would have been willing enough to do so if necessary. In a meeting in Munich in November 1922, Hitler declared: 'We are convinced that we cannot succeed without a struggle. We have to fight with ideas, but if necessary, also with our fists!' The Nazis regarded peace as nothing more than laziness and mental atrophy, and it was not considered an idea worth fighting for. With so much thuggery in support, the Nazis were easily attracting followers and the SA became opened to all comers. But besides the elements of physical force, all the theatrical trappings of visual melodrama were soon developed: a symbol (the swastika with its colourful striking effect), a gesture (the *Heil Hitler!* salute), a phrase (*Sieg Heil!* To Victory!), uniforms, and a wide range of simple slogans. The term 'togetherness' fairly describes the superficial sentimental urge of the German nation for unity in the early 1920s. The Versailles Treaty had cast them down and dismembered them, and visual manifestations that the crushed body would not lie down were essential.

Hitler had more than enough brutal leaders to direct the dirty work of the SA. Attempts were made to recruit the celebrated *Freikorps* leader Ehrhardt as chief of the SA but he was contemptuous of Hitler and refused. Instead Ehrhardt assigned one of his trusted comrades, Lieutenant Johannes Ulrich Klintsch to take the job. The first official SA leader was therefore an ex-naval officer, a veteran of the famous Ehrhardt Brigade. But Hitler soon sought and found a more prestigious person to lead the SA.

For a while, in 1923, Hermann Göring (1893–1946) was chief of the Stormtroopers. The son of a judge who had been Resident Minister Plenipotentiary in South-West Africa, Göring attended military school from 1905 to 1911. In 1914 he fought as an infantry Lieutenant, before being transferred to the air force as an observer/gunner and later a fighter pilot. He distinguished himself as an air ace, credited with shooting down twenty-two Allied aircraft. He was awarded the prestigious Pour le Mérite and Iron Cross 1st Class. He was the last commander of the famous 'Red Baron' von Richthofen's fighter squadron. After the war the embittered Göring made a living as a stunt pilot and private pilot in Denmark and Sweden, where he met his first wife, Baroness Karin von Fock-Kantzow. For some time Hitler had been looking for an outstanding soldier, preferably a highly-decorated submarine commander or a highly-regarded airman, a prestigious personality with the war record and personal authority to take over the leadership of the SA. Göring was just the right man for this task, a man who brought with him the prestige of a wartime fighter ace, and links with the traditional Army leadership and the aristocracy. Göring had impulsively given himself to Hitler after he had attended a Nazi Party rally in the early 1920s. The former commander of the prestigious Richthofen Squadron was full of admiration for Hitler, the man who had found the words for which he had been groping, and with which he himself would have wished to express his own undefined ideas. Hitler's movement offered the swashbuckling Göring the promise of action, adventure, comradeship and an outlet for his boundless ambition and hunger for power. As for Hitler, he was flattered to receive support from the highly decorated Göring, a front-line soldier like himself. He always looked upon Göring with a tinge of envy, as he had enjoyed the higher education which he craved for himself. His aristocratic standing impressed Hitler in spite of his 'Socialist', simple working man and folksy pretences. An added advantage was that Göring possessed private means owing to his rich wife, so Hitler did not have to worry about his salary. From the start, the relationship between ex-Corporal Hitler and Captain Göring was a case of two people seeking and finding in each other what they lacked in themselves.

In January 1923, Göring took over from Klintsch as commander of the SA. His appointment was intended to give the SA a respectable public image, but also to counteract the influence of ex-*Freikorps* leaders and to gain some degree of control. Hitler sensed instinctively that within the Nazi Party the SA force was growing and looking elsewhere for its orders. What Hitler expected of the SA was clear and in total agreement with Hermann Göring's conception. It should be organised and trained along strictly military lines, but used only for practical political and propaganda purposes. They should not be allowed to develop into a secret society or become conspirators. They should be seen in public in their distinctive uniforms for street propaganda and at meetings for security purposes. Assisted by Major Hühnlein, Lieutenant Alfred Hoffmann and Major Streck, Göring created the organisation of the SA. He set up the *Oberste Sturmabteilung Führung* (OSAF, Upper SA

Command) and established its headquarters at Schellingstraße 39 in Munich. The loose Munich SA units and companies from Ingolstadt and Memmingen were united in a Regiment called *SA Standarte München* headed by Lieutenant Wilhelm Brückner. This first SA regiment consisted of thirteen companies, plus a technical detachment, and a bicycle unit. The ex-artillery Lieutenant Gregor Strasser was appointed chief of all SA units in Upper Bavaria, and Major Buch was appointed head of the SA in Franconia. Contacts were made with other extreme-right militias with the purpose of forming a 'patriotic combat front'. Efforts were made for the adoption of uniforms and the former artist Adolf Hitler designed a special SA insignia. The use of a uniform, insignia and flags was intended – among other purposes – to erase social differences. It was also intended to give a strong and united image of the Nazi movement. Finally, as the SA was by far not the only extreme right-wing paramilitary militia existing in Southern Germany, the uniform and the swastika were means of distinguishing them from other formations. The salute was that of the German army as the typical Nazi *Gruß* (*Heil Hitler!* salute with raised arm) had not yet been introduced.

After Göring had assumed command, the structure of the SA was clearer and better organised, their ranks had swelled, and they drilled in military style. On parades – but *only* on parades the formations were a model of discipline. In the hope that they would exert a moderating influence, Göring introduced a few of his refined aristocratic friends into the SA. The presence of the hero Hermann Göring with his aristocratic and beautiful wife at Nazi rallies and SA parades made a good number of wealthy people re-examine their first impression of Hitler. But in spite of Göring's efforts, the Stormtroopers were not easily tamed. They were involved in street fights almost every day. Practically every political meeting ended in a free fight with broken chairlegs and beer mugs flying around. Göring's youthful idealism was no match for these hard, ruthless and violent men. Göring was also by nature indolent, lazy, self-indulgent, easily bored and tended to quickly lose interest in what he was undertaking. He also had much greater ambitions than commanding the SA. As an arrogant and self-confident representative of the classical Prussian officer type, Göring soon came into conflict with the SA leadership, whom he despised as a 'crowd of rucksack-wearing beer drinkers with narrow minds and provincial horizons'. Imperceptibly, the new commander was lured away from

Hitler's original precepts, and relations between the Nazi Party and the SA rapidly deteriorated. In spite of Göring's efforts, no one could suppress the rowdy instincts of the SA's rank and file. As many of them were former *Freikorps* volunteers – who were accustomed to swear personal loyalty only to their unit commander – it became clear to Hitler that although he was nominally in command of the NSDAP (and by implication of the SA), he could not expect their unconditional loyalty. Here were the first signs of conflict, which was eventually to plague the Nazi movement right up to Röhm's elimination in June 1934. Hitler was quick to sense the danger, so, to free himself from the pressure of unruly SA leadership, he decided to create another 'praetorian guard'. This new protection squad became the germ of the dreaded SS. It is said that a few selected members of the third company of the 1st SA Regiment Munich were chosen to provide Hitler's personal close protection. This detachment, formed in March 1923, became the special *Stabwache*, soon renamed *Stoßtruppe Adolf Hitler,* a small unit of carefully-selected bodyguards headed by Julius Schreck. In November 1925 this small unit became the infamous *Schutzstaffel* (SS, Protection Squad). Hitler's personal SS bodyguards were bound together by a blind devotion to him: they adopted the Death's Head as their distinctive emblem, and swore an oath of loyalty to him personally. As early as 1925, the SS started keeping dossiers on party and SA members as a check on their loyalty; but it was not until 1931 that this intelligence, investigation and political police role began to be done on a large and efficient scale. In the 1920s the SS was still a barely-considered factor in the Nazi Party, though their increasingly self-conscious assertion of their position as the elite of the movement attracted notice. It was ironic that having created the SA to protect party speakers from their enemies, it was now considered necessary to establish a bodyguard unit to protect the NSDAP leadership, and Hitler in particular, from the machinations and unreliability of the SA. This was already an old story, which has been summed up in one of the most famous of Latin tags traditionally attributed to the Roman poet Juvenal (late first and early second century AD) from his poem Satire VI (lines 346–348): '*Quid custodiet ipsos custodes?*' 'Who indeed watches over the watchers?' Göring resigned as SA leader in September 1923.

During the failed Munich putsch attempt in November 1923, Hermann Göring was at Hitler's side, and suffered a near-fatal gunshot wound when the police opened fire on the Nazi conspirators. His wound had been poorly treated and it was necessary to give him increasingly large doses of morphine to ease his pain. Göring escaped with his beloved wife to Italy and Sweden. He returned in Germany in 1927, and after having made contact with Hitler again, renewed his political activism, but the once slim officer of 1918, the dynamic conspirator of 1923, had become overweight with a jowly face and dulled eyes, addicted to drugs, and suffering from epileptic fits. In May 1928 Hermann Göring was elected to the Reichstag. Until the end of the Nazi regime, *Reichsmarshall* Göring's contradictory personality played a fateful part in the history of Nazism. He was a morphine addict, a charming diplomat, an organiser of the economy, and fumbling chief of the *Luftwaffe*, but he was also a rapacious looter of Europe's great museums. He was a Falstaffian figure whose gross appetites for money, power and art found their full satisfaction under the cover of Nazi activities. In his fabulous sprawling hunting lodge and estate (called Carinhall, located north-east of Berlin) wearing extravagant uniforms and jewels, surrounded by the stolen art treasures of Europe, Göring lived in voluptuous ease while Germany starved. He remained – officially at least – the second man in the Third Reich until Hitler stripped him of his position in the last week of his regime in May 1945. At the Nuremberg trial, the arrogant Göring was sentenced to death by hanging. On 15 October 1946 he committed suicide in his cell, taking a capsule of poison that he had succeeded in hiding from his guards.

Ernst Röhm

The SA Chiefs of Staff were Emil Maurice (1920–1), Hans Ulrich Klintsch (1921–22); Hermann Göring (1923), no-one during the interdiction in 1924 following the Beer Hall putsch, Franz Pfeffer (1925–30), Hitler himself (1930–1), Ernst Röhm (1931–4), Viktor Lütze (1934–43) and Wilhelm Schepmann (1943–5). It should be noted that after 1930, it was Hitler himself who was officially *Oberster SA-Führer* (Supreme Leader of the SA), and it was he who appointed the SA *Stabschef* (Chief of Staff) who – officially – acted in his name. But it should also be noted that from the start the true driving force behind the SA, the man most readily associated with it, was *Hauptmann* (Captain) Ernst Röhm.

Originating from a well-connected Bavarian family of railway officials, Röhm was born on 28 November 1887. After a grammar school education, he attended a military academy and was commissioned in

1908. During the First World War he fought with distinction as a company commander in the 10th Infantry Regiment, of which Ludwig III was Colonel-in-Chief. Röhm was badly wounded three times at the terrible battle of Verdun in 1916. He received the Iron Cross First Class for bravery and was transferred as a staff officer to the 12th Bavarian Infantry Regiment where he displayed excellent organisational skills. This apparently conventional background, however, coexisted uneasily with his homosexuality. Despising all women and rejecting civilian society, he found personal and emotional commitment solely within the monarchist Bavarian Army. The armistice of November 1918 and the collapse of the monarchy struck him like a twin hammer-blow. After 1918 the deeply embittered and disillusioned Röhm remained in the Army and at the same time turned to extreme adventurism by joining the *Freikorps von Epp,* in which he participated in crushing the revolutionary government which the Communists had established in Munich in 1919. Röhm suffered no pangs of conscience when he established the Munich home guard, which was aimed at overthrowing the new constitution, and backed the rightist political groups by the clandestine distribution of concealed weapons, by hiding demobilised soldiers and by associating with political assassins. Indeed, Röhm was far from a figure of gentlemanly military elegance. The tough, professional front-line soldier had a frank aversion to the old generals and to bourgeois prudery. He exemplified a younger generation of soldiers who paraded around exuding a provocative pride. The most innocuous words in his mouth became harsh and violent, almost shocking, an effect perhaps of his ugliness. He was a formidable figure, a bulky powerfully-built man whose hair was cut short, always well-combed and shaved on the sides. His fat coarse face was marked by a wide scar down the side of his nose and chin. Resulting from a serious wound that he had suffered in June 1916 at the battle of Verdun, the scar accentuated his brutal expression. His face, with a low forehead and a pair of small alert eyes and with its double chin and dewlaps, was flushed and blood-flecked, covered with a network of fine violet veins. The end of his nose, the product of plastic surgery, was a caricature, red and round, giving him the look of a grotesque and clownish baby. Röhm was an obese man with a bulging stomach his service belt seemed scarcely able to contain. The banquets at which he gorged himself for hours could not be made up for by the riding exercise he took daily. In his blunt, aggressive manner there was also a hint of brutality. Röhm

had coarse and straightforward manners. He was a fanatical, simple-minded swashbuckler with a weakness for young men. He described himself as immature and wicked. His views were simple and uncompromising, all black and white. He simply divided people into soldiers and civilians, into friends and enemies. From the start he was a soldier before everything else. Although he was deeply monarchist, he had nothing but contempt for the titled and monocled officers of the old order. Instead he wanted a huge, strictly-disciplined people's army, where ability, efficiency and personal merit would be fairly rewarded. He hated capitalists and certainly believed in the so-called 'Socialist' side of Nazism, but had only vague notions of what this would actually involve. Without subtlety he believed and proclaimed that the professional soldiers who had risked their lives for the defence of Germany – and only they – had the right to rule Germany. He once declared to a foreign diplomat, with the air of a sixteenth-century *condottiere*, that he would 'rather come to terms with an enemy soldier than a German civilian, because the latter is a swine and I do not speak his language!' The

Left: Early SA man 1921.

84

French diplomat André François-Poncet, the most elegant and witty of the ambassadors to Berlin, felt that there was 'something repulsive' about Röhm. He was the prototype of the lost generation that sought to perpetuate the values of the trenches, the camaraderie of the front-line soldiers of the First World War, with restlessness, adventurism and latent criminality masquerading as nationalism.

In July 1919 Röhm was transferred to the Bavarian 7th Division and was entrusted with concealing clandestine stocks of weapons from the Allied Control Commission. In this function he showed himself to be a brilliant organiser, and a man who had the front-line soldier's contempt for red tape, influence and all other obstacles in the way of efficiency and good management. On behalf of the defeated German Army he secretly established weapons and ammunition dumps for monarchist and nationalist groups. In Munich alone he amassed 169 light and eleven heavy guns, 760 machine guns, 21,351 rifles, carbines and revolvers, 300,000 hand-grenades and 8,000,000 rounds of ammunition. Röhm also founded and organised a special clandestine political intelligence unit, known as the *Eiserne Faust* (Iron Fist), which provided liaison between different paramilitary groups and extreme right-wing parties. It was through this activity that he infiltrated Drexler's DAP. He attended a DAP meeting, and met another veteran and army intelligence agent, a pale and puny man fired by nationalist passion and visionary ambition: Adolf Hitler. Attracted by Hitler's furious oratory, captivated by his nationalist passion, and hypnotised by the look of exaltation in his eyes, Ernst Röhm quickly joined Hitler's party. He was just the kind of man Hitler needed to help him get his small party from pedantic back-room discussions into open combat in the streets and beer halls. Hitler and Röhm made a formidable combination. Hitler had an exceptional gift of oratory, a faculty for inspiring blind devotion in his followers, and a fund of visionary social panaceas, which he found suitable for Germany. Röhm, on the other hand, was a ruthless practical man of action and a talented organiser. Hitler provided the will, the direction and the 'concepts', while Röhm provided the men – the raw material that would take up Hitler's will and see it enforced. Röhm recognised the importance of political education in the army, but from the start always insisted on the primacy of the soldiers over the politicians. But military effort could be combined with political activity, hence Röhm's interest in the small party founded by Drexler and now ruled by Hitler. He saw in Hitler the demagogue he needed to mobilise mass support for his secret ambitions. Although he regarded membership of Hitler's party as one commitment among many, Röhm's importance for the NSDAP became soon unmistakable. When he joined the SA, he did not come empty-handed. Officially in charge of press and propaganda for the Bavarian *Reichswehr*, Röhm's influence was much greater than his rank of *Hauptmann* (Captain) indicated. Unofficially, the generals took his advice on all political matters, he organised new *Freikorps* units, and he directed the movement of arms to secret hiding-places out of the reach of the Allied Control Commission. Röhm's activities and connections made him a key figure in the so-called Black *Reichswehr*, the clandestine reserve of the reduced German army. When he joined the Nazi Party, he brought with him men from the 19th Trench Mortar Company, and managed to rally a part of General Maercker's *Jägerskorps* (mountain units), men from Captain Löwenfeld's 2nd Naval Brigade and activists from the Ehrhardt Brigade. These experienced veterans, both soldiers and conspirators, had been scattered to the four winds after the failure of the Kapp Putsch in March 1920, and some of these escapees had taken refuge in Munich, calling themselves the 'Consul Organisation' as already mentioned. Ehrhardt, a crusty sea captain and an eccentric character totally unsuited to conspiratorial ways, initially refused to have anything to do with Hitler, but he eventually lent Röhm some of his best men, led by ruthless officers like Lieutenants Ulrich Klintsch, Hoffmann and Manfred Freiherr von Killinger. These men were a welcome reinforcement to Hitler's tiny mobile protection squad, in fact the embryo of the SA. They supplied the strength and muscle Hitler needed to defend his young party against the Communists in the streets. Röhm also channelled Army funds into Hitler's penniless movement, and also persuaded his commanding officer, Major Ritter von Epp and a nationalist poet, Dietrich Eckart, to raise a fund of 60,000 Marks to purchase a weekly newspaper, the *Völkischer Beobachter* ('The Racial Observer') for the NSDAP. Röhm's connections with the Bavarian army and government also allowed Hitler in securing secret protection, significant influence and important patronage to exercise his political activities which included vehemence, verbal aggression, passion, fanaticism, and lies but also, illegal incitement, intimidation and physical violence. Dietrich Eckhart introduced Hitler into bourgeois society and Ernst Röhm arranged links for him with right-wing radicals and important political contacts in the army, far above the reach of a mere ex-*Gefreiter*. The celebrated Röhm, who played a decisive role in helping Hitler to climb the first steps of his political career, soon became one of his closest friends, and one of the few to address Hitler as 'Adolf' and using the familiar form '*du*' (thou). The fact that the influential Captain Röhm supported the activist Corporal Hitler gave the latter a certain status among Bavarian officers, but Röhm was and would remain the only man in Hitler's early career capable of opposing or negotiating with him on equal terms. He always spoke harshly to the point, not troubling to disguise the fact that at times he was making threats in order to have his way. His coarse, direct nature disdained social graces and his interests were confined to military matters alone. Röhm, the tough, hard soldier of fortune, certainly had a profound contempt for professional politicians, a fierce hatred of titled officers and the old Prussian order in general. Unlike Hitler, he never modified this attitude. His homosexual 'depravity' was all too notorious, and effectively barred him from mingling on social terms with his fellow officers. He held in contempt the bigoted attitudes of the times, and this made him a pariah to most of the officer class who looked on him with undisguised contempt and disgust. A strong facet of his character was that Ernst Röhm was far from being as blind a devotee of the demagogue *Führer* as many other Nazi Party leaders were. He used to express his dissatisfaction with Hitler's ideas and acts freely, and on several occasions employed pressure and persuasion.

It also seems that Röhm had been a member of the *Thule Gesellschaft* (Thule Society), a *völkisch* society in Munich during the early post-war period. An offshoot of the German Order, it was named after the legendary kingdom of Nordic mythology, which was supposed to be the homeland of the ancient German race. Outwardly an innocent association composed of intellectuals who wanted to study and promote old Germanic literature, the club was actually a secret society with an organisation akin in its system of branches and secrecy to Masonic lodges. It was devoted to extreme nationalism, race mysticism, racial superiority, occultism and anti-Semitism. The swastika was among the Society's mystic symbols. Thule agents supported the Pan-Germanic dream of a new, powerful German Reich, infiltrated the Communist formations in Munich, stored caches of weapons and ammunitions for violent actions, and approached Anton Drexler's DAP to serve as a liaison to the working class. Many Thulists soon joined the Nazi Party, e.g. Dietrich Eckhart, Rudolf Heß, Alfred Rosenberg and probably Ernst Röhm as well.

In the period 1920–3, Röhm continued to play the ambivalent role of liaison officer between the army and the Nazis. From the start, Röhm had a position of influence on the staff of the infant SA. As he still was officially employed by the Army he could not take direct command but he always kept a protective and watchful eye on the Nazi security units. In fact, the 25-year-old Klintsch was little more than a puppet. More than Göring, Ernst Röhm was the true organiser of the SA, which he would finally build into an effective private Nazi paramilitary formation. Röhm, the monarchist army officer, became a political adventurer, a professional freebooter and swashbuckler with boundless contempt for the pharisaism and hypocrisy of normal civilian life in September 1923, when he resigned from the Army and placed himself full-time at the disposal of Hitler's Nazi paramilitary militia, of which he took unofficial but direct and effective command.

Chapter 9

Development of the SA

GROWTH OF THE SA

Many extreme-right paramilitary associations existed in Bavaria in the early 1920s. There was Hitler's SA but also the former *Freikorps Oberland*, the *Reichsflagge*, and the *Bayern und Reich* league to name but a few. These groups were commanded by former First World War officers, ex-*Freikorps* leaders and by serving officers of the *Reichswehr*. The latter secretly supplied them with funds and weapons. The paramilitary groups were preparing for the day when they would be summoned to save Germany, be that from its foreign foes, the French or the Poles, or from the internal ones: the Marxists, the Weimar government or the Jewish 'profiteers'.

All the melodramatic trappings deployed by the Nazis resulted in a rapidly snowballing in numbers, but the influence of the NSDAP was originally confined to Munich. The SA became a national movement owing to Ernst Röhm's untiring energy, his acquaintances in the underworld of conspirators, and his numerous connections in the Army.

In the early 1920s the *Reichswehr* welcomed the creation of the SA as one more example of the ability of the Nazi movement to attract recruits to the cause of nationalism, and a possible reserve of manpower. Along with other illegal paramilitary organisations, the SA men were allowed to carry out military exercises with the regular Army, and to receive instruction in tactics and the use of weapons. They were provided with sidearms and on occasion were secretly permitted the loan of rifles from government arsenals for training purposes. The SA assumed more and more the character of a private volunteer paramilitary formation, known as *Wehrverbände* (defence units, non-officially tolerated armed group) to combat the Communists. The SA was sometimes regarded as the banned *Freikorps* under a new name. Many senior officers of the *Reichswehr* saw the SA as a chance to build a secret reserve force for the tiny 100,000-man army allowed by the Treaty of Versailles. They admitted that Röhm's force could become a part of the border defences of Pomerania, Silesia and East Prussia where the Polish forces remained a threat. In this early time of Nazism, SA men felt themselves close to the German Army in which most of them had served. The Stormtroopers were gradually no longer limited to staging and protecting meetings and rallies. They acquired an importance of their own as a demonstration of will, power and energy. Although constituting a part of the NSDAP and having to 'render willing obedience to Hitler', it was soon made clear to him that he was an outsider to the SA, and the men who gave the orders were Röhm and his staff officers. In fact the SA was becoming a genuine military force, and figured as a regular formation in the *Reichswehr*'s secret mobilisation plan. Pioneer Battalion No. 7 and Infantry Regiment No. 9 of the Bavarian *Reichswehr* were responsible for the military training of the SA. The Munich SA Regiment, numbering 1,150 in 1923, included an artillery company and cavalry platoons and used Army ranks. Indeed Göring and Röhm had drilled them in military style until the units were able to parade as efficiently as guard formations, but they were always liable to break out, and even Röhm had difficulty suppressing their rowdy instincts. From 1919 to 1923 Röhm was in no sense a subordinate of Hitler but the creator of the SA and the quartermaster of National Socialism. But Hitler wanted the SA to remain a Nazi Party militia whose job was to rule the streets and, with parades, intimidation and violence, wage a political war against political opponents. Before 1923, the SA organisation probably counted less than 2,000 members. When the first national rally of the NSDAP was held in January 1923, the unit had grown to some 6,000 troopers who paraded before Hitler. In that year new units were created and Hitler presented standards to five newly-formed SA regiments. To the existing Regiment Munich I, were added Regiment Munich II, Regiment Nuremberg, as well as Regiment Landshut and Regiment Zwickau –the first two SA units to be created outside Bavaria. In September 1923 Hitler, Röhm and Göring succeeded in creating an alliance, called the *Kampfbund* (Combat League), totalling a force of about 70,000 uniformed activists. This included their own SA men, and most of the extreme right-wing activists of Southern Germany: the *Bund*

Oberland (an ex-*Freikorps* headed by a Munich veterinarian, Dr Frederick Weber), the *Kampfverband Niederbayern* (Lower Bavarian Combat League, headed by Lieutenant Hofmann), the *Vaterländische Vereine München* (Munich Patriotic Association, headed by Zeller), and the *Reichs-Kriegsflagge* (Reich War Flag, another paramilitary militia headed by Captain Heiß). A joint committee was set up with the greatest difficulty in face of the intrigues and rivalry with which the ultra-nationalist formations were riddled. With the support of the venerable and prestigious General Ludendorff as one of the joint leaders, the *Kampfbund*'s partners agreed on two major aims: first, to overthrow the Republic of Weimar; second, to tear up the hated Treaty of Versailles. In the distorted Nazi view the democratic government was branded as the agent of the Allies in despoiling and humiliating Germany. The rebirth of the Fatherland required the destruction of the Republic.

The growth of the SA, however, resulted in a fragmentation of the corps. This became increasingly heterogenous. For example, the ex-*Freikorps* men, who came from a disciplined military and 'patriotic' background, were often rather contemptuous of the 'political' newcomers, some of whom even appeared to have left-wing tendencies.

When the French occupied the Ruhr in 1923, Röhm flung himself into the task of training the SA and the *Kampfbund*, and suggested that its battalions should march on the Ruhr and fight the French. Hitler of course rejected this ridiculous plan for a hopeless battle. The occupation of the Ruhr seemed to Hitler the opportune moment for a general uprising, not in resistance to the French invaders but against the 'November Criminals' and the Weimar Republic. The Ruhr affair and how the SA formations should be used was the first clash between the two men.

The growth of the SA also resulted in an increased need for money. Such generous supporters and contributors like Kurt Lüdecke could no longer provide the funds that now were needed. Fortunately Röhm thought of a cunning way to get Army funds. Two privately-owned corporations were created, one dependant on the other. The basic corporation, the existence of which was secret, was the *Feldzeugmeisterei* directed by Röhm himself. The other, the dependant corporation, was the Faber Motor Vehicle Rental Service, which was operated openly as a business by Major Wilhelm Faber who was under Röhm's command. All this had the secret approval of some officers and army authorities as an ideal cover for concealing weapons and vehicles forbidden by the Treaty of Versailles. Röhm's corporations also served the purpose of making this illegal equipment available to the clandestine reserve Army. Hitler's SA, as one of the many right-wing formations, was entitled to occasional use of this equipment but, as time went on, Röhm quite naturally began to channel more and more material and money to the Nazis. It was not until 1923 that Army authorities discovered the extent of Röhm's illegal practices. The reason the Army did not simply arrest him for stealing government property was that Röhm had many influential friends. Indeed, it was impossible to get rid of him without a public scandal and a full-scale investigation, which would have revealed that the German Army itself was violating the Versailles Treaty.

THE *FRONTBANN*

For the putsch of November 1923, Röhm provided Hitler with secret ammunition dumps, co-ordinated armed bands of right-wing revolutionaries in the form of a contingent of determined *Kampfbund* men who took an active role. The Munich SA Regiment received orders to surround the Bürgerbräu hall; units from inside and outside Munich – not only SA, but also from *Bund Oberland* and other paramilitary organisations – were to reinforce them and to occupy public buildings. All had received weapons from Röhm's hidden arm depots. While an excited Hitler at the head of his faithful followers pushed his way through the hall, fired a shot into the ceiling and proclaimed an insurrection and the national revolution, armed SA men occupied the hall and placed a machine gun in the entrance. As already discussed in Part 1, the next day, 9 November, Göring, Röhm and a group of Party members marched at Hitler's side during the shooting at the Odeonsplatz, which brought the Beer Hall putsch to a bloody end. Several Nazis and SA men were killed, wounded or arrested. Röhm, too, was arrested, put on trial, and found guilty of treason. Protected by his Army masters and influential connections, however, he received only a severe reprimand and was confined for five months in Stadelheim prison.

After the abortive putsch, the NSDAP was outlawed, and briefly renamed the National Socialist Freedom Party. The SA was forbidden too. Röhm was released on 1 April 1924 and received permission from the still-imprisoned Hitler to re-launch and lead the SA. The failure of the putsch, Hitler's trial, and the ban on the SA, far from destroying the Nazi Party, contributed to its spread to other German provinces. >>>

Right: *Frontbann* member. The standard SA uniform was maintained but without insignia, collar patches and badges. Note the neutral white armband.

Right: *Frontbann* Badge.
The *Frontbann* Badge
(*Frontbannabzeichen*) was
instituted in 1932 by the *SA-
Gruppe-Berlin-Brandenburg.*
Intended to commemorate the
Frontbann, it was awarded to
those who had joined it prior to
31 December 1927. The badge
was silver in colour, had a pin
back and measured 20mm in
diameter. It displayed a swastika
with a First World War German
steel helmet in the middle; the

sentence '*wir wollen frei werden*' (We want to be free) was inscribed in
capitals on the arms of the swastika.

As a man accustomed to conspiracies, secrecy and illegal practices,
Röhm established the so-called *Frontbann* (sport leagues, singing and
hunting associations, rifle clubs, and so on) – in fact substitute SA troops
in disguise who performed exactly the same functions. The *Frontbann*
uniform was similar to that of the outlawed SA. A slight change was
the removal of all insignia, badges and collar patches, and the placement
of a black steel helmet at the centre of the Nazi red armband instead of
the swastika. A totally neutral white brassard was also worn. Röhm
built up the force to a strength of 30,000. The formation of the *Frontbann*
brought Röhm his first significant recruits from outside Bavaria. Until
the November 1923 putsch, the Nazi movement had hardly reached
beyond the Munich city limits and Bavarian borders, but now Röhm
was joined by a series of ruthless desperadoes, and nationalist
extremists who eventually made thuggery the hallmark of the SA. This
included, for instance, such men as Captain von Heydebreck, Graf
Helldorff, and Lieutenant Edmund Heines, a roughneck highly
qualified in all sorts of vice. Clearly the failed 'civilian' putsch of
November 1923 had reinforced Röhm's ingrained suspicion of all
politicians. He was responsible for the organisation and leadership of
the SA/*Frontbann*, and although he still believed more than ever in the
primacy of the soldier, he accepted Hitler's political guidance. By then
Röhm was willing to recognise him as a 'reliable comrade', but reserved

the right to oppose him whenever he disagreed with him. When Hitler was released from prison in December 1924, the NSDAP was re-activated. In February 1925 the ban on the SA was lifted and Ernst Röhm was charged with it reconstitution. The temporary *Frontbann* was officially disbanded and the SA started anew.

CONFLICT BETWEEN HITLER AND RÖHM

The SA became – at least officially – a private militia organised and financed by the Nazi Party. More than ever Hitler was determined never to have an independent SA on the lines of the Ehrhardt Brigade *Freikorps*. Röhm, however, insisted that the NSDAP bosses had no business giving orders to his soldiers. In fact Röhm's affirmation of the 'primacy of the soldier' was an idea that was anathema to Hitler. Besides Röhm employed the *Frontbann*/SA units not exclusively for the protection of the NSDAP, but also for rival extreme-right parties, and this of course infuriated Hitler.

Before Hitler and Röhm openly clashed, the latter flung himself into the task of expanding the SA, but he demanded more independence than ever before. The sudden growth of the SA gave Röhm a new importance. His success made Hitler uneasy as the SA threatened to overshadow the power of his own political party. Henceforth deciding to employ only legal methods to win power, Hitler categorically forbade the SA to carry weapons. He repeated his intention of making of the SA a party organisation with its function limited to political, propaganda and security purposes. In his book *Mein Kampf*, written in prison, Hitler had clearly defined the role of the SA: '. . . the training of the SA must not be organised from the military standpoint, but from the standpoint of what is most practical for the party purposes'. The SA was to be an instrument of intimidation, denying enemies the use of the streets and meeting halls. It had to be a body for propaganda subordinate to the NSDAP, not a private army or an auxiliary of the *Reichswehr*. Hitler's aim was the overthrow of the existing system and his method was patience. Unlike most of history's successful dictators, Hitler did not come to power at the head of an army whose loyalty to his person had been won in battle. Ernst Röhm's SA men, however efficient in political street fighting, were not capable of opposing the German police and the *Reichswehr*. Since the early days of the NSDAP struggle, Röhm had sought to convert the Stormtroopers into an armed militia, which in time would absorb and swamp the Army, thus providing Hitler – and himself – with a thoroughly Nazified military instrument. Röhm, who obviously had not drawn the same conclusion as Hitler from the failed November 1923 putsch, still wanted to seize control of Germany by armed revolution. Hitler preferred the tactics of patient legal infiltration. Despise his bluster and violent talk, Hitler was a master at the game of waiting until the forces opposing him had been weakened by their own confusion. He rarely made a frontal attack on a prepared position but promoted rivalry between his enemies. The days of the SA as a *Wehrverbänd* were definitely over. But on the contrary, the happy-go-lucky Röhm envisaged the SA as a citizen's army intended to carry on the political fight by violent means. A violent revolution had to be prepared, and Röhm hoped to achieve his aims by using Hitler's NSDAP. Hitler disagreed and was often disturbed to find that the SA men were not entirely his own. They were often unavailable to his party because of training, manoeuvres, parades or even working for other extreme right-wing parties. When Hitler went to inspect the SA, he was received politely but was not permitted to command Röhm's men. The SA refused to take orders from the NSDAP, and Hitler had no choice but to compromise. Indeed he had to yield, and thus his own most personal creation acquired for him something of the aspect of the moon, which always only turns one side toward the earth.

The relationship between Röhm's militia and Hitler's party continued to be uncertain. The disagreement between both leaders became bitter. The uncompromising fire-eater Röhm became estranged from the Nazi movement and was involved in several controversial homosexual affairs. Unpleasant scandals were widely reported in the national newspapers. Röhm never worried much about his reputation even when his personal leanings were brought to the notice of the party authorities and public opinion. Hitler, until it suited him otherwise, always referred to Röhm's sexual inclination as an 'entirely private matter'. It should be noted that homosexuality had been outlawed in Germany since 1871, but in the liberal climate of Weimar Germany, and especially of Berlin with its café life, bars, cabarets and nightclubs, there had been proposals for decriminalisation. Persecution of homosexuals varied in intensity throughout the Third Reich. After the Reichstag fire of February 1933, decrees were issued against public indecency, homosexual bars were closed, and gay magazines were banned. While many famous members of the performing arts and, of course, Röhm's

SA men and other homosexual Nazis enjoyed an unofficial immunity, castration and imprisonment in a concentration camp were included in the range of punishments applied to the common man. According to the official Nazi ideology homosexual behaviour merited no mercy because of common clichés and traditional prejudices: homosexuals were supposed to be degenerate, mentally diseased, effeminate and cowardly. But behind morality and 'decency', attention was paid to purely arithmetical figures. Male homosexuality was a danger as it appeared to threaten the birth rate of the German community. In terms of population growth homosexuals were zeroes who failed in their duty of racial preservation and growth. In a Nazi Reich hungry for population and obsessed with high birth rates, male homosexuality was an unpardonable crime. What mattered for the Nazis was man, the warrior and begetter of children. Lesbianism, too, was forbidden but it presented no practical reproductive problems. Even a lesbian woman could and *must* bear children at the behest of her spouse.

Under pressure of Ludendorff and other Nazi leaders who complained that Röhm was damaging the NSDAP's reputation, Hitler was more or less obliged to disavow and criticise the scandalous Röhm. Politically isolated and publicly disgraced, Röhm eventually resigned from the NSDAP and from the SA leadership of his own free will on 30 April 1925. A break between the two men resulted which was to last for six years. It was because of Röhm's ambitions regarding the SA – not his sexual orientation – that Hitler broke with Röhm. On Röhm's dismissal, Hitler commented: 'In memory of glorious and difficult days which we have survived together. With heartfelt thanks for your comradeship and in the hope that you will not refuse me your personal friendship in the future.' Hitler had in fact temporary accomplished his aim; he would not have an independent and embarrassing 'military' wing of the NSDAP.

Röhm withdrew entirely from political life. He worked for a while as a travelling salesman and in a machine factory, but failed to establish himself in any civilian career, and had difficult times and personal financial problems. Ernst Röhm's character and sexuality, as well as the accidents of his personal history, made him virtually unemployable in any stable peacetime society. Without a qualified civilian job, without property or a proper home, all he had was his decorations, his military skills and cunning experience as a conspirator. The Bolivian Army was then being reorganised, modernised and trained by an unofficial military mission headed by General Kundl and a group of former officers of the German Imperial Army. Bored, embittered and disgusted, Röhm – owing to his many connections with the *Reichswehr* – accepted with alacrity an offer to serve in the Bolivian Army as a military technical advisor with the rank of Lieutenant-Colonel.

Adolf Hitler could rub his hands. Without much trouble, a burdensome partner, a scandalous rival, and ambitious competitor had been discreetly ousted.

FRANZ-FELIX PFEFFER VON SALOMON

After Röhm's departure Hitler appointed himself *Oberster Sturmabteilung Führer* (Supreme SA Leader). As some sort of protection was necessary for the Nazi Party's work, Hitler encouraged local NSDAP units to organise their own SA squads, which were to be accountable to their provincial *Gauleiter*. The non-Bavarian SA leaders, however, were still suspicious of Hitler, who after all was still only an Austrian-born stranger. The leader of the Nazi Party had to find someone to act as his contact man with the numerous scattered SA groups. On 1 October 1925, Hitler appointed a north German ex-*Freikorps* commander, Franz-Felix Pfeffer von Salomon (1888–1968) as *Chef des SA-Stabes* (Chief of SA Staff). Possibly because Salomon sounded Jewish, the new SA chief preferred to be called Franz Pfeffer or, to sound more aristocratic, Franz 'von' Pfeffer. He had been a prominent *Freikorps* officer leading the *Battalion Münster* and *Westphalia* which had fought on the Baltic and Polish fronts, and in the Ruhr. In 1923 Pfeffer was SA chief in Westphalia and in 1925 *Gauleiter* and SA Commander in the Ruhr. As a Nazi activist he had been condemned to death *in abstentia* by the French during the occupation of the Ruhr, and in Hitler's eyes he was a tough man and a reliable henchman.

Röhm's resignation meant that the SA had to be re-organised according to Hitler's wishes to become firmly subordinate to the political leadership of the NSDAP. In Hitler's mind the tasks of the new SA had not changed a bit: maintenance of order, gathering of intelligence, physical training of the members, disciplined education along pure Nazi lines, and development of devotion to the 'common good'. Hitler had to give Pfeffer considerable power in order to strengthen the alliance with the northern German Nazis. As a token gesture to the SA, Hitler placed his SS bodyguards under the command of the SA hierarchy, but he issued strict directives. The new SA was deliberately isolated from the Army and other military organisations. The men were forbidden to bear arms, but were trained in boxing, wrestling, jiu-jitsu and other martial arts with a view to fulfilling their prime purpose, that of acting as the fist while the Nazi Party proper acted as the brain. On 3 and 4 July 1926, the Nazi Party held its first national meeting at Weimar with 6,000 SA men, Hitler Youth and *Stahlhelm* veterans.

Between 1925 and 1930, Pfeffer von Salomon and his assistants Captain Otto Wagner and Lieutenant Georg Hallermann made important reforms. They introduced orderliness and traditional army drill to SA formations. The aim was to give parade-ground impressiveness and the glamour of a disciplined military appearance. The SA, with its military formations, a hierarchy of ranks, banners, flags and bands, was designed to satisfy the German craving for uniforms and emblems. Pfeffer gave a revealing description of Nazi methods of mass hypnosis: 'The sight of a large number of men, disciplined and coordinated both mentally and physically, with a patent or potential will to fight to the limit, makes the greatest impression upon the citizens. The language of the message which it carries to their hearts is more convincing and compelling than any writing, speech or logic.' In his eyes, it was essential to give an impression of unstoppable force and emotional power. For this purpose, Pfeffer, an ex-Army officer, appointed ex-Army officers to drill his men. In 1928, he created seven *Oberführer* (Brigade Leaders) who organised SA troops along clearer military lines including *Gruppen* (squads about ten or twelve SA men), *Truppen* (platoons), *Stürme* (companies), *Standarten* (regiments), *Brigaden* (brigades) and *Gaustürme* (divisions which coincided with the German provinces). Pfeffer also introduced the typical light-brown uniform, whence the name of Brownshirts given to the SA came from. Actually, the brown shirt became the SA uniform by accident. A certain SA commander named Rossbach had purchased very cheaply a large consignment of brown shirts in Austria originally intended for German troops in East Africa. Rossbach took them back to Germany and issued them to SA men in 1925. Pfeffer was also particularly careful to keep control of SS recruiting, insisting on being consulted for fear lest the SS siphon off all potential SA commanders and thereby strangle the development of the Stormtroopers. As a matter of principle the SS was forbidden to act on its own, and when SA and SS troops were used together, the latter were always placed under the former's commander.

From 19 to 20 August 1927 the Nazi Party held its second annual national rally at Nuremberg with – among other festivities – a parade of 20,000 SA men. By 1928 the SA had become a national organisation with the following regional high commands: Eastern Region with its HQ in Berlin commanded by Captain Walther Stennes; Northern Region with its HQ in Hannover, headed by Major Dincklage; Western Region with it HQ in Cassel under Lieutenant-Colonel von Ulrich; Centre Region with its HQ in Dresden commanded by Lieutenant-Colonel von Killinger; Southern Region with its HQ in Munich, headed by Major Schneidhuber; and Ruhr Region with its HQ in Elberfeld under the command of Lieutenant-Colonel Lütze. In addition there was a SA 'foreign' department headed by Captain Reschny in neighbouring Austria. In 1928 the *Hilfskasse* (Solidarity Fund) was created; it was a pension fund, administrated by Martin Bormann intended to help the families of those killed or disabled in the Party's service. In 1930 the post of General-Inspector was created and entrusted to Lieutenant-Colonel Ulrich whose task was to control the SA corps. Special military units were created, notably a motorised corps (Motor SA) to allow a fast mustering of the force and to increase mobility (see Special Units below). Pfeffer increased the strength of the SA from c. 2,000 in 1925 to over 60,000 by 1930.

At first all seemed well in 1926, but gradually Pfeffer's military instincts began to reassert themselves. Expansion increased the SA's self-confidence and its leadership was increasingly unwilling to accept orders from the political Nazi Party. Surreptitiously the SA organisation was again making itself independent of the NSDAP, and Hitler became suspicious. Apparently the SA was reformed according to Hitler's plan, but the Stormtroopers remained unreliable, disunited and malcontent. Like Röhm before him, Pfeffer began to demand a measure of independence for the SA. Tensions remained and increased again between the SA and the NSDAP, the more so as the new SA chief was a north German, breaking the traditional Bavarian domination of the Nazi movement. Pfeffer and the new SA leaders never abandoned activism and regarded Hitler's growing political success from 1929 onward as little more than the springboard for their own revolutionary armed assault on the Weimar Republic. Pfeffer was unsentimental and Prussian rather than Bavarian in outlook. He was not taken in by the Hitler myth, 'that flabby Austrian' as he called him. He and many high-ranking SA officers had a low opinion of the civilian political branch of the Nazi Party. Elements in the SA continued to challenge Hitler's leadership and demanded a greater say in the running of the NSDAP. In particular they demanded more funds, and insisted on the nomination of SA officers as Party candidates in the Reichstag elections. In fact Pfeffer's concept of the SA differed little from Röhm's. As an ex-officer and *Freikorps* leader the obstinate Pfeffer still thought only in politico-military terms. According to him, the SA was to be a training ground for the Army, but a different army than Weimar's 'neutral' *Reichswehr*. Pfeffer advocated a SA army, both military and political. He announced that the SA was the vehicle for the German army of the future – the very same notion that had cost Röhm his position. The infuriated Hitler could not prevent Pfeffer from having secret meetings with the pro-SA *Reichswehr* officers attempting to involve the tiny Weimar army in the paramilitary training of his Stormtroopers. In the SA Headquarters, in the late 1920s, secret lists were drawn up at SA headquarters of 'annoying' army personalities to be eliminated when the Stormtroopers seized power: Major-General von Schleicher, General Adam, Colonel-General von Hammerstein-Equord and General von der Brussche-Ippenburg, for example. Behind 'revolution' and purges, the height of Pfeffer's ambition was well-paid jobs for himself and his friends in the highest ranks. A series of quarrels remained over matters such as finance, the delineation of responsibilities and the degree of political power to be enjoyed by the SA within the Nazi movement. These important issues were never resolved, and economic distress was producing growing criticism that Hitler's policy was insufficiently revolutionary. In Berlin, Otto Strasser's followers and the SA commanders were drawing closer together. Even Hitler's lapdog Josef Göbbels was beginning to waver. Serious conflicts were latent between leaders of the NSDAP and the local SA. Heated discussions often became purely personal, sometimes blows were exchanged between the rival fractions. SA local leaders often disregarded orders from the *Gauleiter*. In Berlin Göbbels and the NSDAP's work suffered badly from SA rivalry. On the whole, the SA rank-and-file continued to fulfil their propaganda and protection role, if somewhat reluctantly but also followed a more or less independent course, with little interest in Nazi politics, playing at soldiers, going on manoeuvres, marching in uniform, brawling, singing camp songs and drinking themselves into a stupor, while nostalgic veterans tried to recapture the lost comradeship of the trenches.

In August 1927 the SA totalled some 30,000 members, at the end of 1929 about 60,000 and perhaps 75,000 by 1930 as young unemployed men flocked to join the Nazi movement. Pfeffer von Salomon may well have felt that the leader of such a force was entitled to a measure of independence in deciding policy, perhaps even considering taking over the leadership of the Nazi movement itself.

New Generations of SA

The SA provided a haven for adventurous and romantic adolescents but also to undisciplined irregulars and the semi-criminal dregs of the urban slums. During the disastrous economic crisis of 1929–32, the social background of the SA men underwent a significant change. The aging war veterans and ex- *Freikorps* men were gradually replaced with younger people of the declining lower and middle classes. SA men were not recruited from the soft or timid section of society. Many ruined shopkeepers, unemployed white-collar workers, impoverished farmers, jobless *Lumpenproletarians*, poor students, and malcontent déclassés joined the SA. Many were young, attracted by the dynamism of the movement, by its fanaticism and rejection of any compromise, the untold opportunities for 'heroic' deeds, and the constant clashes with political enemies. To these must be added many opportunists, sexual deviants, juvenile delinquents and criminals, the dregs of society, who often rise to the surface in periods of profound dislocation and collapse. Alongside the unemployed, criminal elements indeed infiltrated the SA and, as a result, the perennial underground struggle between the SA and their opponents took on the character of gang warfare reminiscent of Al Capone's Chicago. Fighting raged round the bars and speakeasies, and the nicknames used showed the type of men involved. One SA-*Sturm* in Neukölln, for example, called itself the 'Pimps Brigade', and another in Wedding the 'Robbers'. An SA commander known for his ability to clear streets was nicknamed 'Rubberleg' and his henchmen 'King of the Boozers', 'Revolver Snout', and the 'Bulletmiller'. The grim economic situation exacerbated class antagonism and increased the attraction toward extreme political parties, which proposed radical, populist and demagogic 'quick solutions' and immediate results. During these years, it was not the NSDAP but rather the SA, the Party's strong-arm squads, that was characteristic of the Nazi movement as a whole. The *Sturmabteilung* became a very diverse group of people from various social classes.

The Nazis were seeking the support of the upper and middle classes – especially the conservatives, the big capitalists and the business sector – who feared communism but they also aimed to create a mass movement. Seeking support by appealing to popular desires and prejudices rather than rational arguments, they attracted a part of the working and lower-middle classes. After all, the name of the party, NSDAP, still contained the words Socialism and *Arbeiter* (workers).

It is difficult to make generalisations, of course, but on the whole, the new SA generation were young men, out to prove their virility: over 80 per cent were under thirty, and a large proportion were working-class unemployed. Joining the SA was not often the result of profound thought, nor necessarily indicative of full commitment to Nazi ideology. Many joined on a whim, for fun, to show off, to be 'somebody', having been dragged along by a friend, or simply to have a daily hot meal. In an atmosphere of violence, uncertainty and economic scarcity, people could easily change sides. In the early 1930s, when it became clear that Hitler was the coming man and that his party had a good chance of achieving power, many jobless people – including turncoat Communists – thought he was the man of the future. The winter of 1931–2 was the coldest in Germany for a century. Freezing temperatures and heavy snow struck the land in the depths of the Depression when only a few people could afford warm clothes and coal for their fires. It must never be forgotten that without the Wall Street Crash of October 1929 and the following ten-year Great Depression that affected all Western industrialised countries, the Nazis would probably never have been able to take power in Germany. In February 1932 there were a total of 17,500,000 Germans living on the dole, almost one-third of the population. The lower working class provided more than half of the SA squads, as reflected in the following figures regarding the social origins of SA men (according to the historian Stephen J. Lee in *Hitler and Nazi Germany*). Between 1929 and 1934, 56.5 per cent of SA volunteers came from the urban working class. Only 2.9 per cent were agricultural workers. But 15.4 per cent were unskilled workers, 35.4 per cent were skilled workers, 0.9 per cent from the public sector, 1.5 per cent were apprentices, and 0.4 per cent were servants. The occupational groups of the lower and middle classes represented 32.9 per cent with: 1.3 per cent master artisans, 3.3 per cent non-graduate professions, 8.8 per cent salaried staff, 2.7 per cent civil servants, 10.4 per cent salesmen, 4.3 per cent farmers and 2.1 per cent domestic servants: notably, none were soldiers or NCOs from the *Reichswehr*. The upper middle and upper classes represented only 5.8 per cent of the SA with: 0.2 per cent senior salaried staff, 0.1 per cent senior civil servants, 4.1 per cent university students, 1.2 per cent graduate professions and 0.2 per cent entrepreneurs but, notably again, no senior military officers.

Next to the beefy beer-hall brawlers, the SA also counted a few genuine wealthy aristocrats, such as Count von Helldorf, and Prince Friedrich Christian Fürst zu Schaumburg-Lippe (1906–83), a fervent admirer of Napoléon. Seeing similarities between Hitler and his idol, the Prince joined the Nazi Party and became an *SA-Standartenführer* (Colonel) in 1929. The young Schaumburg-Lippe was a handsome man of medium height and build with fine aristocratic features. He often spoke in public and turned out to be an aggressive orator and able writer. The SA gained considerable prestige from having a genuine prince in their ranks, helping to emphasise that Hitler's movement was representative of people from all social classes and backgrounds.

As one can see the SA was a very mixed body with a few aristocrats and a huge crowd of unemployed members. Those having a job were only part-timers, or 'Sunday' members. The active members, those permanently available for political activities and actual fighting, were (mainly urban) jobless young men who lived and trained in *SA-Heime* (barracks). To jobless and (often disoriented) young men, keen to prove their manliness, the SA re-structured their lives with uniforms and hierarchy. As just said, rank-and-files were young (under thirty), generally poor, often bachelors, always opportunistic, and many of them were aimless and generally without any political background. The cadres of the organisation were usually formed by aging war veterans and ex-*Freikorps* men. In the late 1920s and early 1930s, the aging cadres were gradually replaced with a new generation of young, determined, ruthless and ambitious newcomers who had no hope and nothing to lose.

POLITICAL EDUCATION

Here again it is difficult to generalise but, on the whole, SA-men had a barely-concealed contempt for the Nazi Party, but were fascinated by Hitler, of whom they had great expectations. They had a strong *esprit de corps* for their comrades, and many of them had the feeling of belonging to a select brotherhood, even to an elite force. The penchant for violence that was found in many of them was cynically but cleverly exploited by the Nazis. The kind of war that Hitler glorified – at least in theory – was not fought by masses of hapless conscripts at the behest of generals far behind the lines. It was one that would be conducted by young heroes, 'supermen' who by daring and violence would lead the destiny of Germany to a 'clean and glorious' future. The active and permanent regular SA units were a haven for idealists but also for thugs. For those out of work and aimlessly loafing about on street corners, the SA offered a sense of purpose, what resembled political responsibility as well as a daily hot meal, an uniform, a place to sleep, companionship and something exciting to do. It must be remembered that not all of them were stupid – though many of them were. The SA men were capable of responding to the arguments and appeals that their leaders put to them. Obviously, SA members were exclusively male as Nazi violent political culture praised 'male' virtues of toughness and aggression. They were just as prepared to beat their political rivals as their opponents were to beat them. In Ernst Röhm's own words, 'the SA is not an institution for the moral education of young girls, it is an association of hardened fighting men'.

The SA was a huge, fairly uneducated mass movement, and it was difficult for the Nazi Party and the SA leadership to give this diverse crowd any precise doctrinal formation. Political education included simple slogans, black-and-white concepts, and the so-called 'SA-novels'. These were cheap propaganda books intended to raise the reader's sympathy for the *Sturmabteilung*. Mixing kitsch-style and adventure, political issues and struggle were presented as 'Wild West' stories in Karl May's style with emphasis put on the 'adventurous, courageous and forward-looking' SA men. In these novels, Socialists were depicted as old encrusted bourgeois, and Communists were either criminals or misled brave fighters who in the end understood Nazi ideals and joined the SA. The SA were also issued the so-*SA-Liederbuch* (songbook), a 294-page pocket-sized booklet published in 1932 by Joseph C. Huber Verlag in Munich. The songbook included an introduction by Ernst Röhm, poetry by Dietrich Eckhart, and various lyrics of military, marching, patriotic, and German folk songs. In the back of the book several pages were left blank on which texts and lyrics could be added by would-be poets.

It was, of course, difficult for Hitler and even to the SA leadership to channel the violent behaviour of these young men into domestic politics. Hitler's problem was to keep the spirit of the SA alive without allowing it to go too far into revolutionary action. What Hitler most feared was a head-on collision with the police, above all a conflict with the German Army. The combination of mass unemployment, the breakdown of traditional political allegiances and a culture which embraced violent aggressive values raised the Nazi movement to become the most successful practitioner of violent street politics that Germany had ever seen.

THE RETURN OF RÖHM

Before the election of September 1930, the Berlin SA mutinied and wrecked the headquarters of the NSDAP. Their main grievance was their pay but deep discontent against the party also came to the surface. Berlin *Gauleiter* Josef Göbbels and SA Chief of Staff Pfeffer von Salomon proved unable to handle the crisis. Hitler had to intervene personally to control the rebels, led by the Berlin SA Chief Walther Stennes. Stennes was a small, elegant man about thirty-five years old with blond hair and blue eyes who always wore a neatly-pressed uniform. The typical son of a rich Junker family, he had won many citations for bravery during the First World War. In 1919, he joined the *Freikorps Pfeffer* and became second in command. When Pfeffer later became chief of the SA, he appointed his friend Stennes to a high position in the SA organisation.

Hitler went round one beer hall after another promising the SA rebels better pay, telling the mutineers that the party was on the eve of victory and assuring them that bad leaders would not be in the future allowed to come between him and the faithful rank-and-file. After an exhausting night Hitler had restored his authority. He levied a special tax to increase the SA's pay, and promptly took the opportunity to dismiss Pfeffer von Salomon. Pfeffer was invited to resign (he later became *Gauleiter* of Westphalia), and Hitler himself re-assumed the position of *Oberster SA-Führer*. In the electoral success that followed, the incident was soon forgotten – but not by Hitler. Ignoring the warning by Dr Leonardo Conti (senior medical officer at Stennes's headquarter, later *SS-Obergruppenführer* and the head of the Reich Health Service), he let Stennes remain as Berlin SA Chief. Conti was right and he was soon to start another rebellion.

Hitler of course did not have the time to be both head of the Nazi Party and chief of the SA, and soon was looking for a new commander for the SA. He needed a capable men who could keep the local units under control and yet was bound to him by strong ties of loyalty. It was a job that Göring had once held and now wanted again. Indeed Göring realised that it was one of the most powerful posts in the Nazi Party. But instead of appointing Göring, Hitler made a very curious move. He wrote a letter to Bolivia in which he reminded his dear Ernst Röhm of past loyalties. Remembering his old friend's parting words ('You have only to give the word – Be at the Siegertor at 6 AM on such and such a day with your men – and I shall be there'), he persuaded Röhm to leave La Paz and to come back to Germany in order to reorganise the SA, which had now fallen into disarray. Given the obvious political differences between the two men about the role of the SA, Hitler's decision might seem rather odd. Varied explanations have been provided. Both men had always been personal friends, and before Röhm had left for Bolivia, he had become reconciled to Hitler despite the latter's ungrateful treatment of him. Hitler was self-confident and believed that in the long term he held the stronger hand. He had good reasons to think that the infamous and despised Röhm would be nothing without his backing. In him, he hoped to find the man to handle the crisis, to pull the Stormtroopers together and keep them in hand. No-one could deny Röhm's abilities, and his loyalty had stood up to tests few others would have submitted to. Röhm had made a brilliant career in Bolivia, and was pleased with his work as a military advisor in South America but apparently was tormented by the sexual deprivation he suffered there where his favourite form of activity seemed to be unknown. An unexpected 'comeback' into German political life, rehabilitation, and an official recognition of his talents were attractive and flattering prospects. Moreover, Ernst Röhm probably believed that Hitler's problems in 1930 would enable him to gain concessions for the SA that were unobtainable in 1925. As for his rival Göring, he had no choice but to swallow his dissatisfaction and accept Ernst Röhm's appointment. But the new SA chief had now made another powerful enemy.

RÖHM'S CLIQUE

Ernst Röhm was officially appointed SA Chief of Staff on 5 January 1931. Armed with Hitler's blank cheque, Röhm rebuilt his personal life and gathered around him his old clique composed of a dissolute crew of adventurers, men with a reputation for corruption, debauched perversion and violent criminality. Sadists, drinkers, old friends and opportunistic young *Lustknaben* (male prostitutes), and common thugs were granted official responsibilities in the SA senior leadership. Röhm made no efforts to hide his proclivities. 'I do not consider myself a good man' he once said, 'I have no such pretentions'. From a sort of dissolute bravado, Röhm surrounded himself with youths whom he chose for their physical beauty and their overt homosexuality. Ignoring all remonstrations, he flaunted himself in company with young sons of the aristocracy forming his retinue, a brilliant staff with the faces of perverse angels: *Standartenführer* Hans-Joachim Count von Spreti-Weilbach (head of the Munich SA), Baron von Falkenhausen and the Prince of Waldeck, for example. Röhm's personal aides-de-camp and friends were handsome, fair-haired, blue-eyed young 'Aryan' men such as *Gruppenführer* Bergmann, *Gruppenführer* Edmund Schmidt, *Gruppenführer* Hans Hayn, *Gruppenführer* von Krausser (Adjutant on the SA General Staff), *Gruppenführer* Georg von Detten (head of the SA political branch), *Obergruppenführer* August Schneidhuber (appointed Munich prefect of police) and his private secretary Rolf Reiner. The handsome Karl Ernst (a former hotel doorman and a bouncer in a café frequented by intellectuals) attracted Röhm's attention. In April 1931 Ernst was promoted to the rank of *Obergruppenführer*, placed in command of the Berlin SA, appointed Reichstag deputy and attached to the supreme leadership of the SA. A personal friend of Prince August Wilhelm von Hohenzollern, Ernst spent the money from public collections on dissolute orgies. Another of Röhm's friends was Edmund Heines. Born in July 1897, he had served as a junior officer in the First World War, and had been a member of the freebooting *Roßbach Freikorps* after the war. He joined the SA and the Nazi Party and became a member of Röhm's intimate circle. He was expelled from the SA May in 1927 by Hitler himself allegedly for corruption, and debauchery – in fact he had called the *Führer* a 'dishrag'. In 1929 Heines was sentenced to five years' imprisonment for murder but soon released in a general amnesty. On Röhm's energetic insistence Heines was reinstated and appointed *SA-Obergruppenführer*, given command over SA men in Silesia, and placed as chief of police at Breslau where he directed a network of procurers of young boys. One, Peter Granninger, also drew a large monthly salary of 200 marks for the job of finding handsome boyfriends and organising the festivals of debauchery which Ernst Röhm and his staff enjoyed. Granninger had been one of Röhm's partners since 1928, and was now given cover in the SA Intelligence Service to keep Röhm and his friends supplied with fresh young men. His main hunting ground was Gisela

High School in Munich whence he recruited no fewer than eleven boys whom he first tried out himself before passing them on to Röhm and his highly dubious clique. Other men placed in high positions by Röhm were old pals from the early days such as *Obergruppenführer* Hans-Peter Heydebreck, a thin bony man who had lost an arm in the First World War and was one of the moving spirits in the *Freikorps*. Heydebreck had fought in Silesia in 1919 against the Poles, in defiance of the terms of Versailles, with the brutality of the brigands who ravaged Germany during the Thirty Years' War. He had been a Nazi Party member since 1922 and, in June 1934, Hitler had honoured the soldier-adventurer by naming a village on the Polish frontier after him.

With his immediate circle, Röhm spent happy days and nights in his beloved Berlin, sampling the delights of the Kleist-Kasino, the Silhouette nightclub, and the Turkish baths. He also held boisterous banquets and orgies at his headquarters. Röhm's men were exempt from punishment. Theft, corruption, misappropriation of funds, sex with youths under age, even rape and murder, all were 'political'. Hitler was fully aware of most if not all of the loose morality in the Nazi leadership, from Röhm's homosexuality to Ley and Göbbels's extra-marital escapades. He did not openly encourage it, but did little or nothing to stop it. Hitler was part panderer, part avuncular father-confessor. In his more mellow, less lonely moments, he regarded his 'Old Fighters' who were his personal retainers, as part of his family. He seldom fired anyone, security from gossip being one of the pragmatic motives for this.

However, fierce indignation was voiced from within the Party. Many Nazi leaders complained that Röhm and his scandalous gang were damaging the reputation of the NSDAP. However in the period 1931–3, Hitler strove frantically to seize power. As he badly needed his able SA commander's organisational skills and unquenchable drive to achieve his goal, and because he could not afford to imperil the efficiency of his private force because of morale scruples, Hitler turned a deaf ear to complaints about Röhm's wild drinking orgies, debauchery and corruption and the low behaviour of his immediate circle.

RÖHM'S REFORMS

Although a debauched pervert, Ernst Röhm was unswervingly loyal to Hitler personally, even though their opinions differed on matters of policy. He was also a talented organiser. He possessed an astonishing capacity for hard work, organisation and efficiency, and had the ability to instil these qualities into his subordinates. Röhm embarked on a fundamental restructuring of the *Sturmabteilung*. The SA headquarters at the notorious Brown House at 45, Briennerstraße, Munich, became the focal point of Nazi activity in Germany. The Brown House was a solid-looking three-storied building in the most aristocratic avenue in the capital of Bavaria. Soon Röhm's huge energy turned plans for reform into action.

He created special bodyguard units, known as *SA-Stabwachen*, to protect himself and other key SA leaders. Members of these units were selected from the most reliable SA men. They wore the standard SA uniform including the brown-painted helmet. Other reforms quickly followed. The former *Gruppen* were renamed *Scharen* (squads); the ten or twelve men of the *Schar* were encouraged to look upon themselves as a band of comrades bound together by common ties of friendship as well as by loyalty to the *Führer*. Anyone who, from his own initiative, succeeded in raising a *Schar* from among his friends or workmates, was entitled to have the unit named after him. So squads came to existence more or less spontaneously, for example, from men who had been at school or university together, or from desperate unemployed workmen fired from their factory by the effects of the economic crisis. *Truppen* (platoons), *Stürme* (companies) and *Standarten* (regiments often recruited from a particular area) were retained, but new units were created: the *Sturmbann* (battalion) and the *Untergruppe* (division, replacing the former *Gausturm*). Most important was the creation of the so-called *Gruppen* (the agglomerate of several divisions), which constituted powerful bodies. The *Gruppenführer* who headed these large formations were officially answerable to Hitler, but in practice were under Röhm's authority. In July 1932 Röhm established a yet larger SA unit – the *Obergruppe* (roughly equivalent to an army corps) headed by a *Obergruppenführer*. With vigour and determination Röhm increasingly stamped his authority on the SA and succeeded in curbing his troops' excesses. Another SA mutiny in Berlin helped him dispel the doubts expressed by several NSDAP leaders about his abilities.

The reforms and the reorganisations made by Hitler and Röhm, however did not bring to an end the rebellious tendencies within the Berlin SA. Dr Conti's prediction came true and Walther Stennes prepared to strike once more. Stennes's second revolt was another unsuccessful SA rebellion fomented by the *Gruppenführer* of the regional SA in Berlin. The pretext for the second Berlin SA mutiny came in February 1931 when Hitler, determined to win power legally, ordered the SA to refrain from street fighting and again forbade them to carry weapons. Stennes regarded the order as a betrayal of basic revolutionary principles and a treacherous departure from the strong proletarian and 'socialist' element in Nazism. He was also bitterly dissatisfied with Hitler who, he assumed, was making too many compromises with wealthy conservatives in industry, the landowners and the regular Army. Stennes and his men wanted the rejection of legal means and instead subversive violent action now. Stennes's SA men were also overburdened with work from the strenuous election campaigns, but there were also serious internal friction between the Nazi Party and the Berlin SA. As always, the exasperated Stennes demanded more funds, and greater SA participation in policy-making. Furthermore, many members of the Berlin SA were former Communists who did not want to see the Nazi Party abandon the fight against the reactionary capitalists. When Stennes's demands were rejected, he and a few desperate followers decided to form a breakaway movement. They occupied the Berlin *Gauleiter*'s headquarters and the offices of the Nazi newspapers *Der Angriff* (edited by Göbbels) on the night of 31 March 1931. Now the rebels rejected Hitler's legal path: they announced their plan to remove Göbbels, and to form their own dissident SA corps in Berlin. This time the threat of secession was serious because Stennes had allied with Otto Strasser's 'anti-Hitler' Black Front. This dissident radical wing of the Nazi Party represented the 'socialist' tendency, demanding the nationalisation and state control of business and industry. Strasser's faction alienated potential supporters of Hitler who demanded that the Nazis renounce this policy.

Stennes and his followers gained control of the meeting places of the SA men still loyal to Hitler after a barroom battle, with several men being injured on both sides. The secessionists planned a major demonstration in the naïve hope that Hitler might turn NSDAP policy to their views. Realising that the SA might be on the verge of exploding, Hitler, with Röhm and several loyal SA units, came to Berlin in a hurry. For four days, Hitler and Röhm went from beer hall to beer hall begging, cajoling and promising better pay, and assuring them that no reprisals would be taken against those who returned to the ranks. The appeal was successful since it was the case that the secessionist movement was small, isolated and deprived of significant support. By the exercise of their brilliant personalities, Hitler and Röhm managed to convince most of the SA rank-and-file to return to their duties. The isolated rebel leaders were expelled from the Nazi movement, and thus cut off their source of funding. When the rebels' funds ran out their last supporters melted away and only a few rank-and-file stormtroopers followed the rebellion. Röhm was thus able to isolate Stennes and quell the revolt, with the help of the Berlin police force and Himmler's SS – a fact worthy of mention. The disillusioned Walther Stennes was expelled from the SA for insubordination and his life hung by a thread. Fortunately he was the nephew of a cardinal and had influential friends (one of whom was none other than Hermann Göring) who discreetly helped him leave Germany before the vengeful loyal SA and SS could kill him. He later went to China where he served as commander of Chiang Kai-shek's personal bodyguard. As for Otto Strasser he left Germany in 1933, moving to Canada. After the war he returned to Germany still hoping to play a political role, but his anti-Semitic and Nazi past made him highly unpopular in denazified post-war Germany. He died in 1974.

Stennes's second unsuccessful revolt was followed by a purge, allowing Röhm to dismiss several SA senior officers from Pfeffer's time, and to replace them with his own henchmen, accomplices, clients and friends. The repression of the revolt also increased the image of Hitler as a man respectful of legality, and the *Reichswehr* now accepted recruits who belonged to the Nazi Party, and soldiers and officers were allowed to attend Nazi meetings. Hitler then also gained the support of the Agrarian League and the German Nationalist Party. Such support was of great value to him. The quelling of Stennes's rebellion also demonstrated the importance taken by the puritanical SS as a loyal security force. Having fought their way through the tangled web of competing authorities, they would henceforth act rapidly and silently on Hitler's orders. In late January 1932, the SS were officially charged to carry out police duties within the Nazi movement.

In early January 1933, Röhm successfully repressed another SA mutiny. This time it was launched in Ansbach, Franconia, by the dissatisfied provincial SA commander Stegmann against the *Gauleiter* Julius Streicher. After these firm actions, which reinforced Nazi unity and the apparent respect of legality, Röhm still had an outrageous reputation, but his scandalous private life was brushed aside for he proved a brutal, excellent and tenacious commander with an overt and valuable loyalty to Hitler. He concentrated on recruiting from within the young working class, the unemployed workers, white-collar jobless and the impoverished farming population. The re-organised Brownshirts – closely modelled on the organisation of the Army – became an effective instrument of mass proselytization and terror.

In the winter of 1929–30, Hitler began his conspiracy to gain power. In order to achieve his goals he needed three things: men, money and votes. The men were the members of his Party, sympathisers and SA troops who used violent pressure and intimidation against political opponents. Money, apart from the minor dues paid by the members, was provided by industrial magnates and tycoons who now regarded the Nazis as a useful shield against Communism and whom they thought to utilise for their own ends. The votes came from the use of Göbbels's clever propaganda, which exploited the fear, discontent and profound uncertainty among the German people, the possessors and the dispossessed alike. Göbbels staged monster meetings with rousing military tunes played, banners and standards carried into the hall, until the Speaker himself appeared amid shouts of *Heil*. Searchlights illuminated the platform and Hitler's voice was often drowned out by thunderous applause. This atmosphere gradually affected those who had come out of curiosity or vague sympathy. They were drawn into the vortex of excitement and frenzy, of chiliastic hope and deep hatred, which pervaded the meetings. Hundreds of thousands of Germans fervently hoped that Hitler and his Nazi movement would free them from their misery and suffering, and would establish a strong, glorious and respected State, from which the Communist threat would be forever eliminated.

Chapter 10

The Role of the SA Before 1933

Propaganda and Hooliganism

The SA played a significant (but not decisive) role in providing Hitler with the keys to power. During the *Kampfzeit* (the 'Time of Struggle', the stormy years before 1933 before Hitler came to power), beer halls and beer cellars played an important role. Practically every brewery, particularly in Munich, had large drinking halls and smaller rooms, used not only by individual customers but also hired as meeting places by groups, clubs, associations or political parties of every colour. The Sterneckerbräu was the place where Hitler attended his first meeting of Drexler's DAP on 12 September 1919. The famous Bürgerbräukeller was where Hitler had made his ill-fated putsch in November 1923. The Torbräukeller near the Isar Gate was the centre for SA recruitment. Other beer halls used by the Nazis for meetings were the Hofbräuhaus, the Eberlbräuhaus and the Löwenbräuhaus.

Göbbels and Hitler recognised that speaking, not writing, was the essence of effective propaganda. Journalism was degraded to a populist tricks, and propaganda raised to a deceiving art. Anything that would help to attract attention, to create an impression of energy, determination and success was pressed into use: slogans painted on walls, posters, demonstrations, rallies and mass meetings, all with crude and unrestrained demagogy with insulting language, personal attacks, populist rhetoric and unrealistic proposals and promises. Public meetings, with the dramatic utterances of the live performer, were designed to capture the attention of an audience excited by the contagion of collective enthusiasm and mass hysteria. The street also played a major role. The SA advertised Nazism to the German public.

Kitted out in their brownshirt uniforms, the tough and arrogant SA drove in mobile propaganda units with vans equipped with loudspeakers, they elbowed their way into the crowded beer halls, they propagated Nazi ideology, by spreading pamphlets and placards, chanting slogans, and bawling their cry of *Sieg Heil*! They marched in the streets and turned to their advantage anything that had a mental or physical appeal in the way of military discipline and martial sound-effects, making politics a continuation of combat and war. They paraded in the streets of German towns, marched *en masse* in impressive rallies and meetings, and torchlight processions at night. During organised parades the SA battalions were models of discipline, marching by with mechanical precision, carrying red banners stamped with the swastika, the pounding of their boots in the street in rhythm with the music of the fife-and-drum band. The thunder of hundreds of SA marching boots on cobblestoned streets was not easily forgotten. It gradually acquired a sinister and demoralising significance for those not wearing them. The essential purpose of such events was to display strength and physical force, to create a sense of power and feeling of unity, showing to all that the success of the Nazis was irresistible. The vigour and zeal of the SA was in sharp contrast with the dull routine way in which the established rival and opposition parties went through the motions of electoral campaigns. Being on average much younger than the members or leaders of rival parties, the SA had a physical energy and militancy that the middle-aged bureaucrats of the bourgeois and socialist parties could not match. The sight of apparent discipline and the loud and rhythmic strutting of SA troops marching through the streets in a time of chaos, the impression of energy in an atmosphere of universal hopelessness, seemed to have won many people over.

It was indeed propaganda that Hitler had in mind. The SA men were intended to be the shock troops of a revolution that would never happen. This was the great misunderstanding between the *Führer* and the SA. Raised in the spirit of the *Kampfzeit*, the majority of SA members took Hitler's supposedly 'socialist' programme seriously. The ordinary SA men often openly admitted that Hitler represented something 'new and different'. Many of them were unemployed and inclined to put some of the blame for this on people targeted by the Nazis: their former capitalist employers, Democrats, Socialists, Communists, foreigners and Jews. Recruiting was greatly helped by the economic disaster which Germany was suffering more than any other nation in the early 1930s.

With no money, nowhere to go and no prospects for the future, hopeless SA men devoted their entire time to Nazi activism. They could get their meals from the SA soup kitchen, but the burden of supporting their family (at least for those who were married) fell upon their wives. Those young men who had no jobs, no family and no home could be accommodated in SA *Heime* (homes). These were usually in the back rooms of beer halls or empty buildings whose proprietors were Nazi sympathisers. Often their brown uniform was their only suit of clothes, and even it had been sold to them on credit from the SA Field Ordnance Department. Those desperate men – both ruthless ruffians and sincere idealists – had nothing to lose and no other hope than the Nazi movement's victory. They were sometimes convinced of the need to serve Germany in her hour of need, and many of them were generally ready to sacrifice themselves for the movement, giving up time and personal safety in the expectation that they would someday receive tangible compensation. Therefore most SA men did not fear violence. Since the creation of the movement, they were political agitators but also streetfighters. Political gatherings during the *Kampfzeit* often degenerated into agitation and violence as the Nazis fought their political opponents, tried to break up their meetings and protected their own gatherings from disruption by rivals. Violent incidents followed in rapid succession and the atmosphere of violence and cycle of revenge intensified. The SA kept the German people in a state of permanent >>>

Opposite page: SA Propaganda poster (after Hans Schweitzer). Nazi propaganda made extensive use of posters. One of the most talented designer of Nazi political poster was Hans Schweitzer, better known under his pseudonym of 'Mjölnir'. The poster shown here was made for the election of 1932. Bearing the slogan 'National-Socialism, the organised will of the nation' it is a typical example of Nazi propaganda: simple, emotional and powerful. In vigorous lines, it displays the profiles of three SA men. The one in the background is an older man, obviously a war veteran, the one in the middle is middle-aged, and the one in the foreground is a wounded young man. The different ages show the unity of the Nazi movement. All three of them are idealised caricatures of racially-pure 'Aryans' with fair hair, ice-cold blue eyes and strong jaws. They look in the same direction (victory) and radiate a powerful expression of virility, aggressiveness and determination, which nothing seems to be able to stop.

116

Left: Commemorative badge for the Breslau Rally of 1933.

excitement by incessant activity, marching, sustained efforts of propaganda, and agitation not only during the election campaigns but all the year round.

In the spring of 1928 the liberal Gustav Stresemann (1878–1929) came to Munich to deliver an election speech. He had been Chancellor from August to November 1923, an opponent of the Beer Hall Putsch, and was now Foreign Minister dedicated to reconciliation with France. Five hundred SA men pushed their way into the hall and broke up the meeting by singing the national anthem *Deutschland über alles*. The audience rose to their feet and also began to sing. The Foreign Minister on the speaker's platform obediently joined in, looking ridiculous in the eyes of the world. In the crucial crisis after the Depression of 1929, the Nazis intervened in the problems of the peasants and middle class. When a farmer or a shopkeeper was forced to declare bankruptcy and his home and property was put up for auction, they would turn up in large numbers for the sale. Then they would interrupt the auctioneer with ridiculous questions, or outbid serious buyers only to say later that they could not pay. If all else failed, the SA men would start a fight, interrupting the sale. By such violent actions the Nazis and the SA gained the reputation of being like Robin Hood, the 'good guys', the protectors of impoverished farmers and ruined middle-class shopkeepers from the greed of 'Capitalist Jews'.

In 1931, by calculated hooliganism in the theatres, the SA forced the government to ban the further showing of Lewis Milestone's film *All Quiet on the Western Front*. The film had been adapted from the German novel by Erich Maria Remarque. Made in 1930, the film was bold, interesting and strongly anti-militarist, a key example of a crusading film against war. It was totally committed to showing the pointlessness and evil of war. It gave war its true face, that of degradation and bestiality that applied not only to the First World War, which was portrayed, but to all wars. This was obviously totally in opposition to

Nazi ideology. As a protest Göbbels organised a plot. He distributed to members of the Party, SA and Hitler Youth a number of tickets for the cinemas where the film was being shown in Berlin. The Nazis (in plain clothes) crowded into the cinemas and during the showing created disorder by booing, released mice, setting off stink bombs in the dark and molesting people in the audience. The rowdiness was such that the police were called but when they arrive could find no obvious culprits as everyone present merely stated that they wanted to see the film. The following day, the Nazi press was full of the story of the so-called 'spontaneous' eruption of popular anger against this 'scandalous, unpatriotic and anti-German' film. The local authorities capitulated, and the Board of Film Censors revoked permission for public showing of the movie as like to be the cause of more disturbance to public order. The Nazis were jubilant, as intimidation and terror on the streets could now dictate the government's actions.

However, the activities of the SA were often harmful, radical and violent. The SA carried out anti-Semitic attacks, notably in 1931 on the day of the Jewish New Year when SA troops led by Count Helldorf and *Gruppenführer* Karl Ernst attacked Jews, Jewish-owned property and shops on the Kürfürstendamm in Berlin. Violence was also used against Communists, Liberals and Democrats in numerous meeting disturbances, brawls, night ambushes and riots. Basement taverns, corner cafes and SA Homes served as bases or 'fortified' positions in the combat zone. Whole rows of streets were in the grip of a kind of urban guerrilla warfare that raged through the tenement districts and the grim terrain of the networks of alleys between the tall old buildings. Only massive intervention by the police was able to temporarily quell the fighting in which some were killed and many more injured.

BATTLES AGAINST THE COMMUNISTS

On rare occasions, Communist militias and the Nazi SA would ally to fight together against the Weimar Republic's *Schutzpolizei* (republican state security police). The *Rotefrontkämpferbund* (the Communist Red Front Fighters' League) was, however, the main opponent to the SA. It would be wrong to see the German Communists as the 'good guys' simply because they were anti-Nazi. They were, on the whole, as thuggish and violent as their opponents. Nazism and Communism were totally different doctrines with only one thing in common: the strong desire to overthrow the Weimar Republic by force and the establishment of a dictatorship based on race (and the extermination of the Jews) for the former, and on social class (the destruction of bourgeoisie and capitalism) for the latter. The Red Front had been created in 1924 as the German Communist Party's militia. Trained by Russian officers and financed by Moscow, the Communists called themselves anti-Fascists. At its height the German Communist Party numbered 150,000 militiamen wearing jackboots, a green tunic, cap, breeches and a red armband, and bearing a red flag. Only the Communists could rival the Nazis in methods of social agitation, but they deliberately limited their appeal to the proletariat – the working class regarded collectively. They were also hampered by the rigid creed of Stalinist ideology as orders and strict instructions were issued from Moscow. For example Stalin had forbidden all collaboration and alliances with the Socialists. Unlike the Communists, the Nazis were flexible: they could react more quickly and turn sudden events to their advantage. They could also appeal to the powerful sentiments of nationalism and patriotism, which provided a wide audience, while the Communists were exclusively concerned with the lower working classes, and could easily be denounced as agents of an evil 'Jewish' foreign power. Hitler indeed intended to unite the discontented of all social classes.

The Communist Party had its own strong-arm units, which were usually armed with the same weapons as their opponents: clubs, truncheons, sticks and knives, and occasionally pistols. All the main parties had their organised groups of bullies during the Weimar Republic, and there were continual breaking-up of rival political meetings, beating-up of opponents, raids in 'enemy territory', attacks on enemy taverns and beer halls, and bloody street battles resulting in many activists being wounded and even killed on all sides. As early as November 1921, there was a battle against the Communists at the Hofbräuhaus in Munich in which Emil Maurice (at that time head of Hitler's personal bodyguard) and Rudolf Heß (Hitler's secretary) distinguished themselves and were wounded. Hitler considered the fight at the Hofbräuhaus the baptism of the SA.

On 14 and 15 October 1922 in Coburg, Hitler, personally leading a force of some 800 SA men, defied a police ban on marching through the town with music and flags. The provocation resulted in a pitched battle in the streets with the Socialists and the Communists. The violent incident was reported in the press and served to make Hitler's name

Left: Coburg Medal. This medal was introduced in 1932 on the tenth anniversary of the fighting. The oval medal displayed a small outline of Coburg castle at the top, a sword and a swastika in the middle, and an outer scroll bearing the inscription 'With Hitler in Coburg 1922-1932'.

known to a wider public. A special ten-year anniversary medal was designed in 1932 and awarded to those who had taken part in the Coburg fight.

In February 1927, the Nazis hired the famous Pharus Hall in Berlin, which was especially associated with Communist meetings. This choice for a large Nazi rally was in itself a deliberate act of provocation. This open challenge resulted in a *Saalschlacht* (a free-for-all) between the opposing sides, followed by a scuffle with the police resulting in several casualties on both sides. In June 1931 a gunfight broke out in the streets of Altona (a suburb of Hamburg) when the SA was holding a parade. Activists of the *Rotefrontkämpferbund* opened fire with rifles and pistols. The Communists were only defeated when the *Schutzpolizei* brought troops, machine guns and armoured cars against them.

At Braunschweig (Brunswick) on 17 and 18 October 1931, a large Nazi meeting was organised on the Franzensfeld ground as a show of menacing strength. Some 104,000 Party members, sympathisers, Hitler Youth and SA men were transported by forty special trains and about 5,000 vehicles mustered by the Nazi Motor Corps. Private planes were hired to tow gigantic posters with swastikas, while the participants paraded before Hitler, Röhm and other Nazi bigwigs. Hitler presented newly-created SA and Hitler Youth units with their flags. He declared that this manifestation was the last before he would obtain power. On the night of 18 October, the Communist opposition decided to disrupt Hitler's show of strength. Riots developed into street battles in the town resulting in several SA men and Communists being killed. To commemorate the event a Nazi badge was later issued, known as the *SA Treffen Braunschweig 17-18 Oktober 1931*. The Brunswick meeting had a tremendous effect both in Germany and abroad. The British *Daily Telegraph* remarked that it constituted the preparatory act of a march on Berlin, but Hitler claimed in an article in the *Saturday Review* that he would never act illegally. The deadly clash, and the impressive and provocative display of force shown at Brunswick, alarmed the Weimar authorities. Rumours that the Nazis were planning the seizure of power by force pushed the government to react. In December 1931, the authorities ordered a ban on the wearing of all political uniforms. The Communist units and the Nazi formations (including the SA, SS and Hitler Youth) were forbidden. In April 1932, the police went into action against the Nazis. Throughout Germany, the SA and SS were searched, and some arrested. However, this proscription did not stop street violence and political riots, as Röhm was a master at camouflaging his clandestine organisation. With the ban lifted on 16 June 1932, a state of virtual anarchy prevailed in the streets of Germany. The SA troops were in evidence everywhere again and four private armies confronted each other: the Nazi SA, the Communist Red Front, the Social Democratic *Reichsbanner* and the Nationalist *Stahlhelm*. The scale of political violence continued to mount and the worst and most violent fighting occurred between the Nazis and the Communists. There were 461 political riots in Prussia alone between 1 June and 20 July 1932, in which eighty-two people lost their lives and over 400 were wounded. July 1932 saw a recrudescence of political violence between Nazis and Communists, notably in Königsberg before the national elections. These urban skirmishes, known as the 'Night of the Long Knives' (not to be confused with the other Night of the Long Knives, the campaign of assassination unleashed on 29–30 June 1934 against the SA) resulted in no less than ninety-nine dead and hundreds of wounded. No sooner as the ban on uniformed militias was lifted, that another battle took place again in Altona in July 1932 between Nazis and Communists who were more aggressive and provocative than ever before. The riots (known as >>>

Opposite page left: Red Front Communist.
The *Rotfrontkämpferbund* (Red Front Fighters' League), affiliated to the KPD (German Communist Party) was banned in 1933.

Opposite page right: *SA-Scharführer*, 1933.

Above left: SA Badge *Treffen Braunschweig 17-18 Oktober 1931* (Commemorative Badge for Battle of Brunswick in October 1931).

Above right: SA Medal for Loyal Service.

the 'Altona Bloody Sunday') lasted for two days and only ended when the police brought in armoured vehicles. Eighteen men lost their lives and some 265 were wounded.

Another incident was typical of the violent political climate and of the atmosphere of menace created by the SA in the early 1930s. At Potempa in East Prussia five members of the local SA murdered a Communist leader named Pietrzuch. The assassins were arrested, and condemned to death according to a special emergency law promulgated to repress political murders. *Gruppenführer* Heines, his staff and a significant force of SA men disturbed the verdict (in August 1932) by threatening the tribunal and the Weimar Republic with a major uprising leading to a terrible civil war. This obliged the tribunal to back down and let the murderers go free. This was an immense loss of prestige for the government and a huge victory for Hitler's movement.

In 1931, the Nazi Party claimed more than 4,000 wounded all over Germany. For the year 1932, in Berlin alone, the SA reported eighty-two dead and about 400 severely wounded. Reports of such brawls in the newspapers and on the radio brought publicity to the Nazis and helped develop the image of SA men as both heroes and martyrs. All through the *Kampfzeit*, funerals of Nazi 'heroes' killed in street-fights or ambushes were staged as emotional ceremonies, dramatising violence, exploiting the political situation and turning it to the advantage of the movement.

Exceptionally again, companies of Stormtroopers were allowed to assist the police in keeping law and order. This occurred notably during some of the Nuremberg Party celebrations held before 1933. This was cunningly arranged between the pro-Nazi mayor of Nuremberg and Julius Streicher (*Gauleiter* for Franconia, and editor of the Jew-baiting weekly newspaper *Der Sturmer*) who was in charge of the organisation of the rally. On such occasions the SA had the temporary official status of auxiliary police for the maintenance of public order. This temporary legality was useful in quelling, with the approved strong-arm methods, any opposition that cropped up. Hecklers interrupting the rally were seized and beaten up with truncheons by the official police and semi-official Stormtroopers. Before 1933, it was still possible to protest. Attacks on Nazi members were qualified by the Nazi press as 'ill-organised incidents fomented by Jewish and Marxist elements, which were no more than typical of the unrest that permeates the whole nation, and will continue to do so until power has been gained by a strong man leading a strong party that will vanquish the system of majority rule, rebuild the nation economy on the ruins of international capitalism, and insist that every citizen has an obligation to the Fatherland!'

THE BOXHEIMER PAPERS

For the leadership and most SA men, who conducted politics in an atmosphere of violence and semi-legality, the idea of a violent putsch was never ruled out. What was the purpose of this formidable force of fighting men if not to seize power? The Stormtroopers were the uprooted and disinherited who had absolutely nothing to lose and everything to gain by a civil war. Into this situation came a mysterious affair.

In November 1931 the police of the State of Hesse had seized incriminating documents at the house of a certain Dr Wagner, at Boxheimer Hof – after which they became known as the Boxheimer Papers. The documents drawn up consisted of a secret internal party working draft, a proclamation to be issued by the SA in the event of a Communist rising, and suggestions for emergency decrees to be issued by a provisional Nazi government after the Communists had been crushed. The documents stated, amongst other things, that those who resisted the Nazis, who refused to co-operate, and who were found in possession of weapons were to be judged by court martials presided over by Nazis and executed. Another emergency measure proposed was the abolition of the right to private property. The SA was to be granted the right to administer the property of the State and of all private citizens. Work was to be made compulsory without reward, and people were to be fed by a system of public kitchens. The Boxheimer documents clearly indicated the Nazi Party's totalitarian ambitions, and were also an indication of the mood of frustration and restlessness for power which consumed some Nazis and some SA leaders, and which Hitler was as yet powerless to fulfil. As can be imagined, the discovery of the Boxheimer Papers caused a huge sensation, and Hitler was seriously embarrassed. He declared, probably truthfully, that he had known nothing about them, and had he known, he would have disavowed them. When Hitler firmly re-expressed his adherence to the policy of legality, and underlined his insistence on democratic methods, the German authorities declined to take action against the Nazis, and the whole affair was soon forgotten.

THE NATURE OF SA VIOLENCE BEFORE 1933

In an atmosphere of violence, punching heads and bawling slogans was – for many SA men – as much for fun as an ideological action. The SA directed their violence against opponents by breaking up meetings merely by making a lot of noise or by throwing chairs and hurling beer mugs around, according to local custom. They raided 'enemy' territory, sacked offices, attacked individuals and made life uncomfortable for newspaper vendors and billstickers. The SA were meant and trained to conquer, dominate and rule the streets. The public space was their trench, as it were, and thus the ideology of First World War trench warfare was transferred to the battles of the SA. Youngsters who had been schoolboys during the war could now show their mettle together with the genuine veterans and older soldiers. During electoral campaigns the SA marched and rode in swastika-draped trucks through the streets, chanting slogans, pasting posters everywhere and distributing pamphlets. They did not beg for votes, they demanded the backing of the German public with conviction, devotion and passion using simple slogans, but always with insolence and arrogance, often with energetic words, and sometimes with intimidation and threats. Their appearance in public was always determined by a paramilitary style: uniforms, disciplined parades, martial bands and waving flags. But the SA also always deliberately provoked trouble. They did everything they could to dramatise the violence they themselves incited, but their strategy was less one of terrorism or civil war than a tactic of violent pressure and hooliganism. Some SA men were probably mere hooligans, and (perhaps) only a minority were real convinced Nazis and politically involved revolutionaries. The SA thrived in an atmosphere of violence and attracted many of the young toughs and brawlers who loved a good fight for its own sake. It is, however, important not to exaggerate the violent nature of the SA and the importance of political violence before the Nazi seizure of power. In the first place, as has already been pointed out, Hitler came to power via official and legal ways. He was not given the keys to the Chancellery by the SA and a violent revolution in the street, but by backstairs intrigues with conservative forces and support from the influential capitalist and conservative factions at the highest level. Hitler had experienced the folly of a violent and illegal putsch in November 1923. Nazi violence in the period 1925–33 was rife and harmful, but it had fairly clear limits. Nazi and SA activists were ruthless, brutal and fanatical, and responsible for much of the political violence which occurred in Germany, but they were never so foolish as to stage frontal armed assaults on the Weimar Republic. Attacks by the SA on police stations or Army barracks – targets where serious resistance could be expected and where real issues of political power were at stake – were never launched. Events such as those of Coburg, Altona and Brunswick were exceptional. On the whole, the violence in which the Nazi movement was engaged before January 1933 was, if one may say so, rather 'limited'.

It must be noted that there was no real breakdown of public authority in Germany as had occurred in Italy before Mussolini's March on Rome. Until July 1932, the Weimar Republic was able to defend itself. It had sufficient means to intervene against rioters, and possessed enough strength to crush any uprising whether from the nationalist extreme right or the Communist extreme left. The *Schutzpolizei* had been created

right after the First World War by the Ministry of the Interior with a double mission: to fight against internal subversive armed groups (of the left or right), and to constitute an additional military force to help the reduced *Reichswehr* to oppose any aggression or invasion from abroad. Therefore the *Schupo* were uniformed, lived in barracks and received a professional military training. They were armed with pistols, rifles and machine-guns and equipped machine-guns, armoured troop carriers, armoured cars and trucks. The police remained firmly under Social Democratic leadership and acted as efficiently against the extreme Right as against the extreme Left. The leadership of the *Reichswehr*, too, was faithful, and nowhere fraternised with the SA. On the contrary, many professional officers and soldiers equally disliked their proletarian character and their military incompetence. This dislike of the SA in higher army circles was reinforced by the fact that many

Left: Early SA man with Nazi flag (c. 1921).

of the SA leaders came from the *Freikorps* and were, in their eyes of very conservative generals, dangerous revolutionaries and adventurers who could not be trusted. The officers of the tiny German *Reichswehr*, although reduced to 100,000 men by the Treaty of Versailles, was one of the most important groups of the German ruling class. The Army was non-political only in the sense that it usually did not interfere in the disputes within the establishment. Officially the Army represented the national interest, and officers and men were requested to refrain from politics and serve the state aloof from political strife. However, should the establishment be threatened by force, such as by the Communists or Nazis the Army probably would have become political. It had, of course, close connections with the industrialists and armaments manufacturers, and naturally the senior officers were nationalistic and adamantly opposed to the Treaty of Versailles. On this point they agreed with Hitler, and in 1930, when Hitler started to be taken seriously, NSDAP propaganda was making headway in the *Reichswehr*, especially among young officers who were attracted by the Nazi promises to restore the size and glory of Germany's fighting forces. It should also be added that from 1930 to 1933, the Weimar Republic was no longer ruled in a parliamentary way but by a government which relied on the confidence of the old president, Field-Marshal Paul von Beneckendorff und von Hindenburg (1847–1934) who was easily influenced by his entourage particularly by the all-powerful General von Schleicher, the grey eminence of the Army. The government ruled by issuing emergency decrees, which were later submitted to the Reichstag for approval.

The SA was only one of the tools by which Hitler achieved his aims. But these were paradoxical, as National Socialism mobilised violence and hooliganism but did so in the defence of the social order. Nazism simultaneously used both roughness and respectability, and promised both radical change and the upholding of traditional values. The Nazi propaganda machine pictured the SA as defenders of decent national values and their enemies as decadent thugs whom only force could contain and defeat. The cunning Hitler always posed as the defender of order and morality, and presented himself as the man who acted violently for the good of Germany against evil foreign powers, the Democrats, Jews and Marxists. A great part of Hitler's popularity came through his capacity to reassure, and the false image of a respectable, moderate politician created by his propaganda. The rest was due to his ability to deliver spectacular but short-lived results. This paradox partly explains his success both in attracting support and in being able to establish a dictatorship once he had taken power.

SA Martyrs

Hitler's propaganda was based on complete opportunism. It sharpened itself against the whetstone of both its successes and its setbacks. In Göbbels's own words, it had to be strict in principle but elastic in application. He saw to it that every funeral of an SA man, Hitler Youth or any other Hitlerite who had been killed in street fighting or ambush was turned to advantage.

As already said in Part 1, the name Horst Wessel is strongly associated with a song, the infamous *Horst Wessel Lied*, and the man who wrote that song, Horst Wessel, entered Nazi mythology by way of 'martyrdom'. Wessel was born on 9 October 1907 from a good middle-class Berlin family. In 1926 he joined the SA, and in 1929 was appointed leader of SA-Troop 34, based in the Friedrichshain district, where he lived. In October 1929 he dropped out of university to devote himself full-time to the Nazi movement. Wessel had written a poem, a simple marching song (titled *die Fahne Hoch*, 'Up with the Flag') extolling the glories of National Socialism, which had been published in *Der Angriff* in September 1929. The poem was set to a traditional tune and became the anthem of the NSDAP after his death. Wessel corresponded to the idealised Nazi representation of the Nordic German: tall, blue-eyed, blond and handsome. On 23 February 1930 this 'ideal Germanic' young man was shot by a certain Albrecht 'Ali' Höhler (who was an active member of the local Communist Party). The murderer was later killed without trial in retaliation by Wessel's Nazi friends. Göbbels, with a vast outlay of propaganda, managed to turn Wessel into the idol of the movement and a shining example to German youth. Göbbels cleverly manipulated Wessel's death and chose to make him a symbol of Nazi idealism, a venerated martyr, and a national hero. Wessel's funeral was taken over by the Party and Göbbels himself gave the customary oration. The *Horst Wessel Lied* was sung for the first time in public, and Wessel himself was sanctified as the warrior crowned in death. His martyrdom became the theme of the movement and lasted as long as the regime itself. Photographs, propaganda posters, films, epics, commemorative cantatas and even idealised sculptures of Horst Wessel

Above left: Commemorative badge for Leo Schlageter Day.

Above right: Emblem of ZG 26 'Horst Wessel'.
Zerstörergeschwader 26 (ZG 26) 'Horst Wessel' was a *Luftwaffe*
'destroyer' (heavy fighter and ground attack) wing equipped with
twin-engined Messerschmitt Bf 110s.

were made and displayed everywhere. Street and squares in Berlin and
everywhere in Germany, as well as an SA regiment were named after
him. A training ship of the *Kriegsmarine* was christened *Horst Wessel* for
the purpose of training the members of the Marine-HJ (the navy branch
of the Hitler Youth). Several *Luftwaffe* squadrons bore his name. In 1944
the hero's name was given to a *Waffen-SS* unit, the XVIIIth *Freiwillige
Panzergrenadier Division Horst Wessel*. A film, *Hans Westmar*, a retelling of
the Horst Wessel legend, was made in 1933. The movie – originally
entitled *Horst Wessel* – was an idealised film biography in which all
unsavoury details of his life were suppressed. As Wessel's actual life
was rather dull and laughable, the film was retitled *Hans Westmar*, and
was re-cut after a private showing to boost its propaganda value.
Directed by Franz Wenzler, it had Paul Wegener playing the Communist
leader, and Emil Lohkamp playing Wessel / Westmar, trying to recruit
the East Berlin masses to National Socialism before being shot by the
Communists. The film imitated Soviet techniques of documentary
realism, particularly in the final funeral sequence. It ended with a vision

of the Nazis seizing power, the usual hagiography in front of swastika flags and marching masses with martial music thundering out. Another attempt at making an idealised portrait of the SA was the film *SA-Mann Brand*, which was produced in June 1933. Directed by Franz Seitz, it was a glorification of the SA by using a primitive Manicheism. It presented violent but 'just' combats against the 'evil' Communists, and warned against the danger of Bolshevism. Another movie, *The Rights of Man* made in 1934, glorified the *Freikorps* defending Germany against the Bolsheviks at the end of the First World War.

In all these movies, the message was clear: '*Wir sind opferbereit*' ('We are ready for sacrifice'). Death was a small price to pay for the love of Hitler. One had at all times to be ready to sacrifice everything, including parents, relatives, friends and oneself, for the Nazi movement. The SA films – kitsch, vibrant, passionate, emotional and lyrical – were, however, box-office disasters. They were so unsuccessful that Göbbels changed his propaganda tactics. As he put it: 'The SA's place is in the streets not on the screen.' Nevertheless there were many attempts at making an idealised portrait of Nazi youth and the SA. Between 1933 and 1939 about forty propaganda movies, especially targeting a young audience, were produced.

Another important martyr in the Nazi mythology was Albert Leo Schlageter (1894–1923). Schlageter was a war veteran, a former *Freikorps* activist, and a member of the NSDAP and SA. During the French occupation of the Ruhr in 1923 he was active in opposing the French authorities, and headed a clandestine sabotage network. He was denounced, arrested by the French military police, tried for espionage and sabotage, and executed on 26 May 1923. His death was quickly avenged by the Nazis. A few days later, a squad murdered the man – a schoolmaster Walther Kadow – who had allegedly betrayed him to the French. It is believed that the assassins included Martin Bormann (later to become Hitler's assistant and secretary) and Rudolf Franz Höss (later commander of the Auschwitz extermination camp). Schlageter was elevated to the level of a national hero, a patriotic martyr who had given his life for Germany. A monument was erected in his honour in 1931, a selection of his letters was published, his life and death formed the subjects of numerous plays, movies and books, notably the basis for a drama written by Hanns Johst. His name was also given to many Nazi units, SA regiments, RAD battalions, Hitler Youth groups, and also to a *Kriegsmarine* sail training ship.

Part 3

The Organisation of the SA

Chapter 11

A Military Organisation

THE NUMBER OF SA MEN

The exact number of SA personnel is difficult to determine, as different historians give different figures. In the early 1930s the figures quoted vary according to whether veteran's associations such as the *Stahlhelm*, auxiliary units, youth organisations and other extreme-right wing formations are included, and also whether the great increase in the first year of Nazi rule is allowed for. The approximate number of genuine SA men was probably 2,000 in 1923, 30,000 in 1924, 60,000 in 1930, 220,000 in 1932, and between 2 and 4.5 million in 1933–4? In June 1933, Ernst Röhm himself estimated the figure at nearly 2,000,000.

According to the historian Brian L. Davis in his book *Flags of the Third Reich (3): Party & Police Units* (Osprey Publishing), the SA totalled 4.5 million men in 1933, and its composition was as follows:

- 300,000 uniformed men of the original SA, known as 'Tradition SA', including Hitler's Protection Squads (the SS);
- 1,000,000 war veterans of the *Stahlhelm*;
- 1,500,000 war veterans of the *Kyffhauserbund*;
- 200,000 members of the *SA Reiter* (cavalry), recruited from riding clubs and rural areas;
- 50,000 sailors of the *SA Marine* (navy) recruited from boating and watersports clubs;
- 100,000 soldiers of the Border Defence Auxiliaries Units;
- 50,000 specialists from the Engineering Branch of the *Technische Nothilfe* (TeNo, Technical Emergency Service);

- 60,000 medical personnel from the German Red Cross and Samaritan League;
- 100,000 university and technical college students, and 150,000 secondary-school pupils, forming the *Hitler Jugend* (the Hitler Youth);
- 150,000 ex-members of various *Freikorps*;
- 200,000 members of the Oberland Flying Association;
- 200,000 civil servants;
- 20,000 *Ehrenführer* (Honorary SA officers);
- 420,000 men from the uniformed units of various right-wing political parties (e.g. the *Reichsbanner*) incorporated into the SA.

RANKS

The SA was the first paramilitary force formed by the Nazi Party and a system of ranks and insignia was developed for it, which was eventually adopted by other Nazi paramilitary groups, associations and services, for example, the SS, the NSKK, the *Waffen-SS*, the TeNo, the *Volkssturm* etc. As has already been said, Göring and Salomon reorganised the SA along military lines in the mid-1920s, and Röhm carried out a further reorganisation after 1931.

In the period 1920–3, there were only four SA ranks: *Oberste SA-Führer* (Supreme SA Leader), *SA-Oberführer* (SA Senior Leader), *SA-Führer* (SA Leader) and *SA-Mann* (SA Trooper). After its re-establishment in 1925 after being banned following the Beer Hall Putsch, new ranks appeared in addition to those existing before the ban; *Gruppenführer* (Group Leader or Major General), *Standartenführer* (Regimental Leader or Colonel) and *Sturmführer* (Company Leader or Second Lieutenant). In the late 1920s rank was indicated by collar insignia and white bands worn around the *Kampfbinde* ('fighting' or 'combat' arm band). That of a *Gruppenführer* (squad leader) had one band, *Zugführer* (platoon leader) two bands, *Hundertschaftsführer* (company leader) three bands, and *Regimentsführer* (regiment leader) four bands.

After 1928 the SA adopted an expanded system of ranks and began displaying a version of collar insignia consisting of pips and collar bars to denote rank and position. The SA also introduced unit collar insignia, worn opposite the badges of rank, as well as a system of shoulder straps to denote rank. New ranks were created including *Sturmbannführer* (Major), *Sturmhauptführer* (Captain); *Haupttruppführer* (Sergeant-Major), *Truppführer* (Sergeant) and *Scharführer* (Corporal). In 1932, the SA >>>

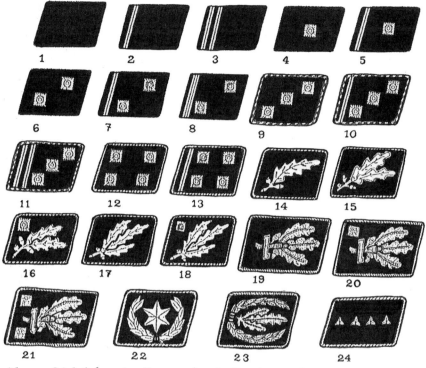

Above: SA left-hand collar patches indicating rank.

1. *SA-Mann* (after 1938 *SA-Sturmmann*).
2. *SA-Sturmmann* (after 1938 *SA-Obersturmmann*).
3. *SA-Rottenführer*.
4. *SA-Scharführer*.
5. *SA-Oberscharführer*.
6. *SA-Truppführer*.
7. *SA-Obertruppführer*.
8. *SA-Trupphauptführer*.
9. *SA-Sturmführer*.
10. *SA-Obersturmführer*.
11. *SA-Sturmhauptführer*.
12. *SA-Sturmbannführer*.
13. *SA-Obersturmbannführer*.
14. *SA-Standartenführer* (above this rank, the insignia was worn on both collar patches).
15. *SA-Oberführer*.
16. *SA-Brigadeführer*.
17. *SA-Gruppenführer*.
18. *SA-Obergruppenführer*.
19. *SA-Brigadeführer* (second design 1944–5).
20. *SA-Gruppenführerführer* (second design 1944–5).
21. *SA-Obergruppenführer* (second design 1944–5).
22. *SA-Stabschef*, Röhm himself.
23. *SA-Stabschef* (new design from 1934 to 1945).
24. *SA-Standartengeldverwalter* (senior officer in the SA Finance Department 1931–3).

adopted the final versions of its ranks and insignia versions, which would remain practically unchanged until the end of the Second World War. This included a system of bars and square stars from the rank of *SA-Mann* (Private) to *Obersturmbannführer* (Lieutenant-Colonel), and a system of oak leaves and stars from the rank of *Standartenführer* (Colonel) and above.

SA Ranks and Army Equivalents (as from 1939)

Non-commissioned ranks

SA-Sturmmann	Private
SA-Obersturmmann	Private 1st class
SA-Rottenführer	Lance Corporal
SA-Scharführer	Corporal
SA-Oberscharführer	Sergeant
SA-Truppführer	Staff Sergeant
SA-Obertruppführer	Sergeant Major
SA-Haupttruppführer	Sergeant Major

Junior officers

SA-Sturmführer	Second Lieutenant
SA-Obersturmführer	First Lieutenant
SA-Sturmhauptführer	Captain

Middle-ranking officers

SA-Sturmbannführer	Major
SA-Obersturmbannführer	Lieutenant Colonel
SA-Standartenführer	Colonel

Senior officers

SA-Oberführer	No equivalent
SA-Brigadeführer	Brigadier General
SA-Gruppenführer	Major General
SA-Obergruppenführer	Lieutenant General
SA-Stabschef	Chief of Staff

UNITS

The early SA units were formed of *Gruppen* (squads), *Truppen* (platoons), *Stürme* (companies), *Standarten* (regiments), *Brigaden*

Left: *SA-Standartenführer* (Colonel).

(brigades) and *Gaustürme* (divisions). The SA *Gausturm* corresponded to the Nazi Party *Gau* (region) and was, in theory at least, subordinate to the party leadership.

After his return from Bolivia, the re-appointed *SA-Stabschef* Ernst Röhm made sure that the military character of the militia was preserved. Due to the SA's expansion, its structure was modified. The smallest unit was a *Schar*, corresponding approximatively to a squad numbering between eight and sixteen *Sturmmannen* (SA men or privates) commanded by *Rottenführer* (Lance Corporal) and *Scharführer* (approximatively corresponding to the rank of Corporal). Three or four *Scharen* formed a *Trupp* (platoon) commanded by a *Truppenführer* (Staff Sergeant). Three or four *Truppen* formed a *Sturm* (like a reinforced company), commanded by a *Sturmführer* (Lieutenant). Three or four companies constituted a *Sturmbann* (battalion) placed under command of a *Sturmbannführer* (Captain). Three to five *Sturmbanne* formed a *Standarte* (regiment) headed by a *Standartenführer* (Major or Colonel). Three to nine *Standarten* formed an *Untergruppe* (sub-group or sub-division) or *Brigade* (brigade) headed by a *Brigadeführer* (Brigadier

General). Several brigades formed a *Gruppe* (a division) under the command of a *Gruppenführer* (Major General). The *Gruppe* replaced the *Gausturm* and the *Gruppenführer* were answerable to Röhm, not the local *Gauleiter*.

In July 1932 Röhm created an even larger SA unit called the *Obergruppe* (an army corps headed by an *Obergruppenführer*, Lieutenant General) composed of several *Gruppen*. After the purge of June 1934, the *Obergruppen* – regarded as too large and too powerful by the NSDAP leadership – were abolished, leaving *Gruppen* as the largest SA formation. By that time there were twenty-two *Gruppen*: Ostland (Eastland), Westfalen (Westphalia), Niederrhein (Lower Rhine), Berlin-Brandenburg, Pommern (Pomerania), Thüringen, Westmark, Niedersachsen (Lower Saxony), Sachsen (Saxony), Nordmark, Mitte (Middle Land), Südwest (South West), Schlesien (Silesia), Franken (Franconia), Hochland (High Land), Bayern-Ostmark (Bavaria), Osterreich (Austria), Nordsee, Hansa, Hessen, Ostmark, and Kurpfalz (Palatinate). Their number increased after 1940 to twenty-nine *Gruppen* including new units called Tannenberg, Oder, Elbe, Neckar, Donau (Danube), Alpenland, Sudeten, Warthe, and Böhmen-Mähren (Bohemia-Moravia).

Ernst Röhm had the title *SA-Stabschef* (Chief of Staff). The SA high command, created by Hermann Göring in 1923, was the *Oberst SA-Führung* (OSAF). The OSAF was a headquarters similar to that of the *Reichswehr* (German Army). It included branches for administration, operations, training and recruitment.

SA Units

SA formation	Military equivalent	Size
Schar	Squad	8–16 men
Trupp	Platoon	3–4 *Scharen*
Sturm	Company	3–4 *Truppen*
Sturmbann	Battalion	3–5 *Sturme*
Standarte	Regiment	3–5 *Sturmbanne*
Untergruppe	Brigade	3–9 *Standarten*
Gruppe	Division	several *Brigaden*
*Obergruppe**	Army Corps	several *Gruppen*
OSAF	High Command	

*Abolished in 1934.

In 1931 there were seven *Obergruppen* (later ten indicated by the Roman numerals I to X), twenty-two *Gruppen* and 121 *Standarten* including specialised SA units. One of the important tasks of the SA was the protection of NSDAP party meetings, speakers and senior leaders. For this purpose regular, salaried *Stabswachten* (staff guards) were created. These were usually recruited from jobless men. They formed guard detachments of guards living in *SA-Heime* (barracks) and they were the only regular element of the force. In fact the bulk of the SA were 'Sunday' soldiers, civilian paramilitaries, veterans and reservists who served only in their free time. As seen above, when Röhm took over in January 1931, the SA numbered roughly 80,000–100,000 men; a year later he could claim between 220,000–300,000.

The weapons used by the Stormtroopers were the usual arsenal of the criminal fraternity. These included *Knüppeln* (rubber truncheons or 'india-rubbers'), iron chains, crowbars and knives. Officially the SA was not allowed to possess firearms – as Hitler had ordered – but they had numerous revolvers ('lighters'), and even grenades, rifles and machine guns.

FINANCES

The Nazi Party was extremely expensive to run. It had thousands of officials on the payroll often without clearly-defined functions. Apart from senior officers, no one in the SA was paid. As mentioned above, a part of the SA consisted of unemployed men who lived in SA messes and barracks. Obviously their upkeep cost a lot, and the SA leadership was greatly concerned with financial matters. Funds were managed by the *SA-Geldverwaltung* – a financial department established in 1931. These were raised from the party itself by membership dues, from street collections by SA men rattling their boxes and asking passers-by to spare a few coins, from the sale of 'essential' Party publications which members were always being pressed to buy, from admission charges and collections at important meetings, from souvenirs such as the rally medals, and from fines for non-attendance at party activities. The Nazis were as ruthless in their financing as in everything else. The Party was never reluctant to squeeze every pfennig from every pocket, and thus made heavy demands on its members. Even the unemployed SA men had to hand over their benefit money in return for their food and shelter.

But these sources of income could not cover all the expenses of Nazi activities, as shown by the freedom with which money was spent. Hitler had more funds behind him than could be easily accounted for. It has never been easy to trace Hitler's finances. After the war, at the trials of the Nazi criminals at Nuremberg, efforts was being made to establish responsibility for the rise and financing of the Nazi Party. Business exists for profits and to a great extend these depend on a country's internal stability. There were therefore undoubtedly significant secret subsidies from supporters of law and order, people anxious to see the defeat of Communism in Germany, for example the Rhineland coal and steel magnates, shipping companies, international corporations, insurance companies and industrial leaders, big businessmen and bankers. Were the Nazis also financed from abroad? Probably. Henry Ford (1863–1947), founder of the Ford Motor Company, was a notorious anti-Semite and admirer of Hitler, whom he certainly supported financially. How much all this produced in hard cash is impossible to say, but it was probably millions of Reichmarks. At the same time, the industrialists who gave money to Hitler as the most likely barrier to social revolution had the agreeable feeling of behaving altruistically. Hitler continued to make use of the socialist concept of the 'common good' because it sounded modern, uplifting and progressive to those searching for social equality, but he was only anti-capitalist when the capitalists were Jews.

In return the rich subscribers influenced the Nazi Party's economic policy. Hitler, anxious to keep these magnates friendly, rapidly repudiated the anti-capitalist elements of the Nazi programme. He promised the capitalists that he would suppress the trade unions and persuaded them that his plans would greatly benefit big business. These promises were kept and this increased the gap between the Nazi Party and Röhm's SA. In fact the Nazi Party and later the Nazi state were organisations marred by corruption, criminality and oppression. The bureaucratic structures and the large budgets provided plenty of opportunities for officials to make money for themselves by putting their hands in the till. Many Nazi leaders (such as Ley and Göring) made scandalous personal fortunes by directing official funds into their own pockets.

Notably, Hitler made frequent use of air travel for election campaigns and travelling to rallies throughout Germany between 1930 and 1933. This was very expensive, but it was not just done for speed and convenience. Hitler's propaganda experts exploited the highly symbolical spectacle of the leader descending from the sky in his modern all-metal shining trimotor Junkers Ju 52. Erhart Milch (later to become state secretary in the Reich Air Ministry and chief of the armaments division of the *Luftwaffe*) was the head of the German civilian airline Lufthansa. He was also a secret member of the Nazi Party, the convenient result being that Hitler and other Nazi leaders never had to pay any air fares. Ironically Lufthansa was heavily subsidised by the Weimar Republic, which thus contributed to the success of its bitterest enemy.

After the seizure of power in 1933 the *Adolf Hitler Spende* (Adolf Hitler Fund) was set up. This foundation was created and run by the Party Treasurer Martin Bormann. Funds were collected by more or less open extortion, mainly from Jewish businessmen. Only German industrialists and businessmen who voluntarily and liberally contributed to the fund could expect to profit from their association with the Nazis. Bormann obtained from Hitler a monopoly over this special fund, and discouraged other party members to establish similar funds for themselves. This therefore gave Bormann a powerful position in the Nazi hierarchy. The fund was used for the benefit of the Nazi Party in the widest sense, including holidays and handouts for senior members, SA and SS men, or for setting up new Nazi offices (e.g. the Ribbentrop Bureau as a rival to the Foreign Ministry).

In an attempt to become self-supporting the SA acquired a tobacco company and sold their own brand of cigarettes, called Sturm. Financing the SA, however, was always a problem for the Nazis. At *Gruppe* level, the SA finance department was managed by a *Gruppengeldverwalter* who wore a silver laurel leaf on a red patch on both collar patches, piped in silver. Under him came the *Untergruppengeldverwalter* who wore a silver or gilt laurel leaf on the left collar patch, and the abbreviation of *Untergruppe* on the right collar patch. At regiment level funds were administrated by a *Standartengeldverwalter* who had four silver three-pointed stars on the left collar patch, and the regimental numeral on the right patch. At battalion level funds were run by a *Sturmbanngeldverwalter* with three silver three-pointed stars on the left collar patch, and the *Sturmbann / Standarte* number on the right patch. At company level a *Sturmgeldverwalter* was in charge with two silver three-pointed stars on the left collar patch, and the *Sturm/Standarte* numerals on the right patch.

Chapter 12

Uniforms and Flags

EARLY UNIFORMS

Nazi uniforms were aimed at encouraging members to conform while at the same displaying evidence of their uniqueness. They were instantly recognisable through their uniforms and regalia. In the early period 1919–22, NSAP members, 'Gymnastic squads', *Sturmabteilung* men and Hitler's other partisans had no standard uniforms. As Hitler's movement was essentially 'southern' and Bavarian in composition, his men wore casual civilian clothes with a preference for southern German folk dress. These included Tyrolean hats with feathers, Austrian ski-caps, mountaineering gear, wind jackets, anoraks, short overcoats, hunting outfits, *Lederhosen* (typical Bavarian leather shorts), thick woollen stockings tucked into mountain trousers and heavy marching shoes or mountain boots, for example, as well as dark blue caps, shirts, greatcoats or casual tunics or mountain-styled jackets, and work trousers. To these civilian clothes were added paramilitary attire such as items of First World War *feldgrau* army uniforms (including puttees, tunics, trousers, and even the 1915 steel helmet), quite similar to those worn by the former *Freikorps*. Obviously war medals and *Freikorps* decorations were proudly worn on the chest to emphasise the 'patriotic' character of the early Nazi squads. The only common item was the *Kampfbinde*, a red brassard or armlet bearing a black swastika inside a white circle, which was always worn around the right upper arm.

THE GREY UNIFORM

By January 1923, when Hermann Göring was SA Chief of Staff, it was decided that a recognisable and martial-looking uniform was essential, and a more or less standard SA uniform was thus issued. Although it was difficult to provide all the SA men with a uniform (and indeed civilian and paramilitary items were still widely worn), the early SA grey uniform bore a strong resemblance to the uniform of the Austrian infantry in the First World War. Simple and functional, it included a double-breasted grey waterproof jacket (worn buttoned to the neck), white shirt, black tie, and field grey or dark green trousers. Footwear included either puttees or thick oiled woollen socks with mountain-shoes or black leather riding boots. Headgear consisted of a grey *Bergmütze* (ski- or mountain-cap) with two buttons in the front below the black/white/red national cockade. The outfit was completed with a leather waist belt and cross strap. The *Kampfbinde* continued to be worn as before.

BROWN SHIRTS

Banned after the failed putsch of November 1923, the SA was re-activated in February 1925. As has already been said, a surplus consignment of German army tropical brown uniforms (intended for General Paul von Lettow-Vorbeck's troops in East Africa) had been discovered in Austria. The whole stock was purchased for a low price by the Munich SA commander, Gerhard Rossbach, and the SA uniform underwent a radical change. The grey tunic and ski-cap were replaced with the more familiar 'brownshirt' uniform. From 1925 onwards the SA uniform included brown uniforms (albeit of various shades) giving the SA their other name *Braunhemden* (Brownshirts). This included a soft brown képi, a brown shirt with two breast pockets (actually a sort of short blouse with a shirt underneath) with a brown tie, dark brown or black breeches and black riding boots. In November 1926, rank bands on the brassard were replaced by stars on the left collar patches. As already said above, as the corps expanded, new ranks were introduced and these were indicated by coloured piping, bars and oak leaves. Various symbols, letters, initials, numerals and figures in different colours and pipings on the right collar patch were used to indicate unit, region and specialisation.

During the economic crisis of 1929–33, the ranks of the SA were swelled by thousands of the unemployed and destitute. Uniforms and equipment were then paid for by the Nazi Party. A system of sponsorship was set up, and a welfare section was established for the

Above: SA *Hoheitszeichen*. The metal *Hoheitszeichen* (National Emblem) – combining the German eagle and the Nazi swastika – was worn on the front of the SA kepi.

Left: Early SA kepi. Tan-coloured mountain-style cap with the national cockade, c.1923.

poorest members. As previously mentioned, funds came from bankers, businessmen, industrials and capitalist who supported the Nazi movement. The uniforms, and in particular the complicated and expensive system of collar insignia, underwent a number of changes.

The 1925 soft kepi had a horizontal peak and a chinstrap, and from 1929 its front was decorated with one button and the Nazi emblem (an aluminium eagle holding a wreathed swastika in). In addition there was a brown forage cap called the *Lagermütze* (camp cap) and the drivers of

Above: SA Headgear.

The most noticeable feature of the SA uniform was the kepi, which was modelled on the ski cap of the elite mountain troops of the Kaiser's Army. It was a curious, almost childish hat, a messy sort of soft French képi with a small peak, and a needless chin strap, very often used. No one surely had the courage to laugh out loud at this ludicrous little cap, but must certainly have felt the urge to giggle, especially when it was worn by the fat Ernst Röhm. Hitler was once photographed wearing the ridiculous SA cap, and was so embarrassed by his appearance that he forbade the publication of the picture.

Left. *Truppführer*'s kepi. Right: *Scharführer*'s kepi of the SA mountain unit *Gruppe Hochland*, 1933.

---

the Motor SA (motorised corps) wore a special crash helmet. The government ban on all political militia from December 1931 to May 1932 had a temporary effect on the SA uniform. The government had said that if the SA adopted a more respectable form of dress then the ban would be lifted. In response a 'less aggressive' khaki uniform was introduced. It included a brown képi, a four-pocketed khaki tunic, a brown shirt and a brown tie, and matching trousers. Instead of the aggressive marching boots, the 'soft' uniform included normal civilian

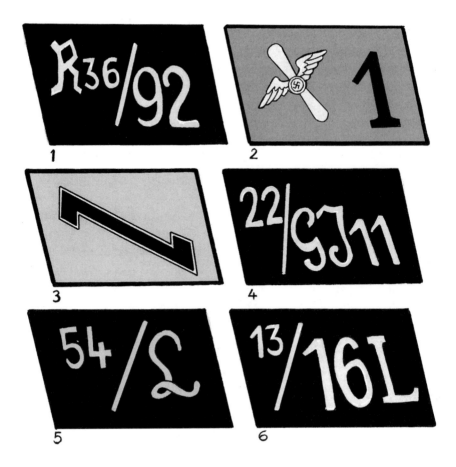

Above: Examples of SA collar patches (right side indicating unit)

1. Reserve 36th *Schar* of *Standarte* 92.
2. *Flieger SA Standarte* 1.
3. Adjutant of the OSAF 1929–32.
4. *Sturm* 22 of *Gebirgsjäger Standarte* 11.
5. *Sturm* 54 of the *Leibstandarte*.
6. *Sturm* 13 of *Standarte* 16 (Regiment List)

shoes. However, the new uniform was not widely issued and the 1925 'brown' uniform remained in general use.

In 1933, coloured side panels were added to the kepi and epaulettes with coloured piping, abbreviations and aiguillettes were introduced to indicate rank. The SA headgear and uniforms were redesigned in 1933 and 1936 but on the whole did not undergo major changes. >>>

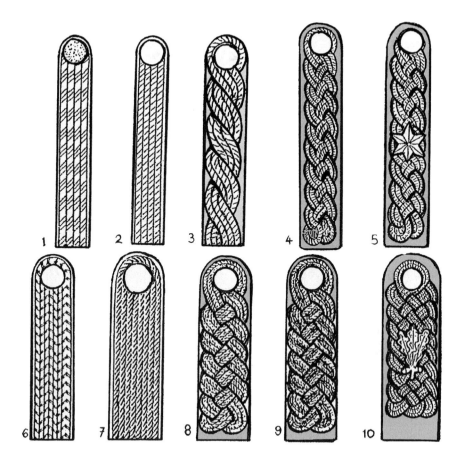

Above: SA shoulder straps.
1932–9.
1. *SA-Mann* to *Obertruppführer.*
2. *Sturmführer* to *Sturmhauptführer.*
3. *Sturmbannführer* to *Standartenführer.*
4. *Oberführer* to *Obergruppenführer.*
5. *Stabschef.*

1939–45
6. *SA-Mann* to *Obertruppführer.*
7. *Sturmführer* to *Sturmhauptführer.*
8. *Sturmbannführer* to *Standartenführer.*
9. *Oberführer* to *Obergruppenführer.*
10. *Stabschef.*

Left: *SA-Sturmbannführer* (Major). **Right:** *SA-Gruppenführer*, 1933.

Left: *SA-Truppführer, 1926.* **Right:** *SA-Standartenführer, 1932.*

Left: *Scharführer Gruppe Hochland,* 1933.
The *Lederhosen* (leather shorts) and *Wadenstutzen* (thick white stockings) were traditional male dress in southern Bavaria and Upper Austria. These items were authorised to be worn with the brown shirt and kepi. The collar colour for *Gruppe Hochland* was light blue and an *Edelweiß* flower (the traditional emblem of German mountain units) was usually worn on the left side of the kepi.

Opposite page left: *SA-Mann,* 1933.

Opposite page right: *SA-Mann* in full marching order, 1934. On certain occasions such as route marches, field exercises, ceremonies or commemorations, SA men carried full marching equipment including backpack, blanket, mess tin, bread bag, water bottle and dagger.

Senior SA leader's belt buckle with the motto 'Our Leader – Our Faith'.

All SA members wore colours on the right collar patch to indicate the formation a member belonged to. The following was the standard colour scheme in 1944:

Red and gold:	SA Chief of Staff
Red and white:	SA Supreme Command
Red:	SA Group Staff
Yellow:	Schleisen Group
Green:	Thuringian Group
Blue:	Hessen Group
Brown:	Westmark Group
Light blue:	Hochland Group
Orange:	South west Group
Pink:	Alpenland Group
Light blue with gold pips:	Sudeten Group
Black:	Berlin-Brandenburg Group

Above: SA belt buckle.

Each SA man was issued with a Sam Browne belt with various types of buckle decorated with the eagle and wreathed swastika, some bearing the motto '*unserer Führer – unser Glaube*' ('our Leader – our Faith'). Some SA units were allowed to wear a black cuff title indicating in Gothic silver lettering the name of their *Standarte* (regiment) or qualifications on the lower left arm. SA men who had enlisted before January 1933 were granted the prestigious *Alte Kämpfer* gold chevron, which was worn on the left upper left arm. High-ranking officers of the OSAF wore the *Achselband* (aiguillette), a looped ornamental cord on the right shoulder. The red *Kampfbinde* remained in general use for all ranks until 1945.

Introduced in December 1933, a sixteenth-century Swiss-styled *Dolch* (dagger) was suspended by a chain from senior officers' belts. On the blade SA daggers carried the motto '*Alles für Deutschland*' ('All for Germany'). SA men who had joined before 31 December 1931 received daggers personally from Ernst Röhm daggers inscribed '*In herzlicher*

Freundschaft' ('In heart-felt Friendship'). After Röhm's elimination in 1934, those daggers were either withdrawn or had the inscription erased. Everything already said about Nazi daggers in the previous section (see Part 1, NSDAP regalia) may be applied to SA daggers.

FLAGS AND BANNERS

The SA units had flags, known as *Sturmfahnen* or *Feldzeichenen*, similar to those of the Nazi Party, composed of a black swastika in a white circle on a red field. Early flags were crude by later standards, mostly hand-made with a variety of designs and shapes of swastika. Soon standardised models were produced with a rectangular patch sewn to the corner in the colour, number, letter and emblem indicating the unit concerned. The flag was often fringed and was attached to the pole by white metal rings. Its staff was coloured brown and polished, and decorated with a nickel-plated metal spearpoint. After January 1923, each SA *Standarte* (regiment) had a banner based on the ancient Roman *vexillum*. The design – which became a distinctive Nazi symbol in its own right – was drawn up by Hitler himself. The first four banners granted to >>>

Left: 1937 pattern SA dagger.

Below: SA emblem.

Opposite page: SA *Standarte* banner.
The *Standarte* banner made its first appearance in January 1923.

156

the first four SA Regiments (Munich I, Munich II, Nuremberg, and Landshut) were manufactured by a goldsmith named Gahr, one of Hitler's oldest and most devoted followers. The SA standard produced by Gahr's workshop had the form of a pole surmounted by an eagle holding a wreathed swastika, below which there was a rectangular frame, a hollow 'name box' displaying the letters NSDAP. From the frame was suspended a red flag with a black *Hakenkreuz* inside a white disc. The double-sided banner had a border of silver braid. It had a red/white/black fringe and carried the motto *Deutschland Erwache* (Germany awakes) on the obverse, and the title *Nat. Soz. Deutsche Arbeiterpartei Sturmabteilung* on reverse. It was held by a polished wooden flagstaff 2.30m long. For ease of transport the cloth was rolled up, and the eagle, pole and name box were unscrewed into sections and carried in a special case. The banner of the motorised and equestrian SA Regiments differed in that it hung from a wooden bar at right-angle to the flagpoles. It had no NSDAP name box, and instead the unit numeral appeared on the cloth in the fly canton – the upper right-hand corner. Smaller SA units had their own flags too. The *Sturmfahne* (company flag), for example, was red with a black swastika, with piping and the unit numeral. There were also rigid pennants carried at large parades and, in smaller triangular versions, flown on staff cars.

Flag and standard bearers wore a metal gorget (a metal plate originating from the full metal armour worn by the medieval knight). This was decorated with two buttons, and a central motif consisting of the traditional German *Gardenstern* (an eight-pointed star out). >>>

Opposite page bottom right: SA *Sturm* flag.
The *Sturmfahne* was composed of a black swastika in a white circle on a red background. The unit number was written in a coloured rectangle in the upper left corner.

Opposite page top right: SA standard-bearer's gorget.

Opposite page left: *Sturmfahne.*
The flag-bearer was distinguished by a metal gorget worn on the breast. Gorgets were widely used in Nazi Germany. They identified men on military special duty and policemen in general. Like the arm- and cuffbands, swords and daggers, they indicated special authority. Gorgets also displayed power by suggesting armoured breastplates.

In the centre of the star there was a circle containing an oak wreath, swastika and eagle – similar to that of the belt-buckle. The traditional *Gardenstern* is still in use today, as symbol of the German and Dutch police forces.

The SA banners (and all Nazi flags in general) played an important role. At once dramatic and menacing, waving in the wind, proudly paraded by standard-bearers in the streets, draped about vehicles, or hanging from buildings, they greatly contributed to the awe-inspiring parades and rallies, and their numbers was often impressive. They were regarded as sacred. It was on their unit's flag that SA men swore their oath of allegiance on their unit's flag, so Hitler solemnly declared that no Jew or Communist would ever be allowed to soil the flags with their touch. Hitler called upon the Stormtroopers to vow that they would defend the banner to the death. When left unattended, flags and banners had to be stood upright, and on no account was the cloth to touch the ground, as this was symbol of defeat. It was also forbidden to lean them against a tree, a building or the like, as this was a sign of neglect. Flags were consecrated by in a ritual ceremony. After the failed putsch of November 1923, the ceremony became theatrical and impressive, and acquired a solemn quasi-religious grandeur. The attempted putsch had been a disaster, but it allowed the Nazi Party to develop its own liturgy with its first sixteen martyrs and its first sacred relic, the holiest of holy flags, the so-called *Blutfahne* ('blood flag'). This was the flag that the Nazi conspirators carried during the failed putsch. The bullet-torn cloth was soaked by an unknown person in a pool of blood on the street right after the firing, and the blood-stained cloth became a sacred Nazi litem. Each regimental SA flag and banner was symbolically rubbed by Hitler against the holy *Blutfahne*, symbolising the transfer of the blood of the martyrs and making thus new units ready for sacrifice. In July 1926, the sacred *Blutfahne* was handed over to the SS by Hitler. This move greatly enhanced the status and reputation of Hitler's tiny bodyguard formation, but was greatly resented by the SA. 'This banner' Hitler said, 'has now achieved the holiness of the Holy Grail. I shall personally see to it that it is used for the holiest of purposes – the consecration of those who link their fortunes, good or ill, with the struggles of the Fatherland!' The *Blutfahne* was always carried by a tall, lean man with a small Hitler-type moustache, named Jakob Grimminger (1892—1969), a privileged and envied position he retained until the collapse of Hitler's Reich in 1945. Grimminger, a WWI veteran, one of the original Nazis and an enlisted *SS-Mann* in 1926 reached the rank of *SS-Standartenführer* in April 1943, and was decorated with the Golden Party Badge, the Blood Order (No. 714) and the Coburg Badge, three of the most important decorations of the NSDAP. Grimminger survived the Second World War, and was put on trial by the Allies in 1946 for being a member of the SS and carrying the *Blutfahne* for nineteen years. He was not sent to prison, but all of his property was confiscated.

The Stormtroopers' badge was also designed by Hitler himself in 1923. It was composed of the styled letter S evoking a sort of lightning and letter A. Both letters were white on a light blue circle. All SA uniforms, equipment, medals, flags, and other items were produced and sold by the *Reichszeugmeisterei* (see Part 1). As early as 1929 the SA set up its own Quartermaster's Department to produce, regulate and provide uniforms and equipment as economically as possible. It should be noted that most of SA men were too poor to buy their own uniforms and equipment.

Chapter 13

Sondereinheiten (Special Units)

Röhm's SA proved an effective and successful fighting force in meeting halls and street battles, and to Hitler that was all that mattered. The *Führer* looked forward to future wars of conquest for which a proper professional army was required, not a street-fighting militia. In spite of Hitler's opposition, Ernst Röhm made no attempt to conceal his opposing view and to express his vast ambitions. In 1931 he had not changed his mind about the role of the SA, and was still determined that it would take over from the German Army in the near future. With this aim in mind, part of the SA's structure was that of an army in miniature. The special units, known as *Sondereinheiten*, were intended to form the nucleus of a future army, and particularly encouraged the development of military skills. Composed of volunteers selected for their particular abilities, they were divided into the normal SA formations including *Schar, Trupp, Sturm, Sturmbann* and *Standarte*. Members of the *Sondereinheiten* wore the normal SA brown uniform, to which were added specialisation badges, collar patches with distinctive badges and piping, and often an *Armelstreifen* (cuff title) worn on the sleeve. Some men of the special units, however, had specific uniforms, headgear and equipment adapted to the requirements of their special duties. As with the SA 'street formations', none of these 'military special units' was officially allowed to be armed. However, until their elimination in June 1934 the SA had secret stockpiles of weapons, either illegally provided or 'loaned' from secret army stocks, purchased on black market or smuggled in from neighbouring countries like Austria. For training purposes small-calibre rifles, hunting weapons, military pistols, rifles, grenades, and machine guns were discreetly used. The future SA army was backed up by various logistics services,

162

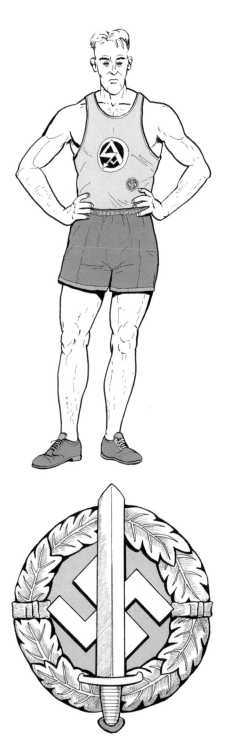

administrative departments, bands, security and police forces. Just like the regular Army, the Special Units had *Waffenfarben* (branch of service colours). For example, that of the *Oberste SA-Führung* was carmine and that of the SA Chief of Staff was scarlet.

The SA also had a cadet school for boys, founded by Ernst Röhm, at Feldafing near Lake Starnberger, south of Munich, which opened in April 1933. It was intended to train future SA leaders. The selected pupils, mostly sons of SA veterans, were known as *SA-Jungmannen*

Top left: SA sports kit.
Sport played an important role in the training of the SA special units, and each man was issued a *Sportanzug* (sports kit). This consisted of a white cotton singlet (bearing the SA emblem and eventually the SA sport badge), brown or black cotton shorts with an elasticated waistband, and low brown/black leather lace-up shoes generally worn without socks. In addition to this, each man was issued a pair of swimming trunks and often a warm two-piece dark blue tracksuit.

Left: SA Sport Badge.
The silver SA Sport Badge was awarded for proficiency in tests generally of a military nature.

Above: MSA crash helmet.   **Above:** Qualified Driver's Badge.

(Young Men of the SA). The main educational aims went without saying: ideological reliability and physical fitness. The standard of education was pitiable, and it proved difficult to find enough pupils. The final examination consisted of essays on optional subjects and an oral test by members of the teaching staff. Graduates could enter the SA corps with the rank of *Truppführer* (Staff Sergeant). This cadet academy was an attempt to compete with the *Nationalpolitische Erziehungsanstalten* (NPEA, National Political Training Institutes) better known as *Napolas*. Created in April 1933, they were special schools for the training of a loyal, fanatical and disciplined Nazi elite.

The main SA *Sondereinheiten* were as follows:
The *Motor Sturmabteilung* (MSA) were motorised units, created in April 1930 in order to provide rapid transport by car for party dignitaries and by truck for the quick mustering of SA troops. Their origin was in the so-called *Kraftfahrstaffeln* (motorised teams), a small and rather disorganised fleet of motorcycles, private cars, vans and trucks which the Nazis acquired as early as 1922. Under the command of Christian Weber, they were employed to transport SA leaders, shock troops and equipment. The MSA units were inspired by Mussolini's *Squadristi* and played a significant role during the *Kampfzeit*. As National Socialism appealed to technicians, engineers, mechanics and drivers, and as the vital role of

trucks and cars had been recognised by many military experts, there was also a semi-civilian auxiliary transport organisation affiliated to the Nazi Party, the *Nationalsozialistische Kraftfahrer Korps* (NSKK, Nazi Motor Corps). The Nazis paid great attention to modern means of transport. Hitler was keen on cars and aircraft and after the seizure of power in January 1933, a wide network of *Autobahn* (motorway) was begun and the *Führer* ordered the engineer Ferdinand Porsche to design a cheap popular car, >>>

Left: MSA *Hauptruppführer*. This MSA sergeant-major wears a black leather crash helmet, a brown shirt with brown tie, black breeches and black leather boots. He belongs to the *Gruppe Franken* (Franconia) indicated by the yellow collar patches. On the left cuff he has the Qualified Driver's Badge, and on the left breast pocket the commemorative badge for the SA rally at Brunswick in 1931.

Below: MSA collar patch.

the future Volkswagen (People's Car). Members of the NSKK did not require any particular knowledge of mechanics and cars: the NSKK accepted members who didn't even have drivers' licenses. It was thought that the training they would receive would make up for any previous lack of experience. Members of the Motor-SA were trained to drive, repair and maintain cars, trucks and motorcycles. They had to log their driving hours like aircraft pilots, pass tests, and also had to spend many hours of theoretical training in workshops. They wore the normal brown SA uniform with an M and a numeral (indicating Regiment or Battalion) on the right collar patch. A driver's badge (introduced in 1931) was worn on the left sleeve. For dirty work they wore overalls and fatigues. On duty motorcyclists wore the *Schutzsmantel* (protective overcoat), and a standard leather crash helmet with goggles.

The *SA-Reiter* (cavalry) was created in 1930. Recruited from riding clubs and rural areas, it provided the personnel who fed, watered, cleaned and exercised horses. Specialist units craftsmen were formed to maintain harness and equipment, as well as horsemen and drivers and trained vets needed to provide the constant care required. It must be remembered that in the 1930s the mobility of most European armies, including the German *Wehrmacht*, depended more on feet, bicycles and horsepower than on motor vehicles. Horses were used in enormous numbers in the German army throughout the Second World War, not only behind the lines but at the front as well. In fact, throughout the war the majority of German field artillery remained horse-drawn.

SA-Reiter wore the normal SA uniform with gold or silver crossed lances on the right collar patch. This was later replaced with a yellow underlay to the shoulder straps. Veterinary surgeons were distinguished by a black badge with a silver snake. The *Waffenfarbe* was golden-yellow.

The *SA-Nachrichten* was a signal corps formed in 1930. Organised at regimental level, this included specialists operating various equipment such as signal lamps, Morse code, wireless radio and telephone. As signals and communication at this time was still largely an affair of bulky devices, clumsy accumulators, complex tuning systems, tinny

---

Opposite page: *SA-Reiter* and (inset) Horse Medal.
The reverse bore the inscription: *'Für Verdienste um die wehrhafte Ertuchtigung der Deutschen Reiter Jugend'* ('For faithful service in the capable training of young German riders').

Above: SA signaller and (below) a SA signaller's collar patch.

loudspeakers, headphones, crystal rectifiers and short ranges, more traditional means were also used such as runners, cyclists, motorcyclists or horsemen as well as pigeons and *Meldehunde* (messenger-dogs). Members of the SA signal units wore the standard brown uniform with the right collar patch bearing 'Na' (short for *Nachrichten*). In 1933 this was replaced with a *Blitz* (lightning flash), and later with lemon-yellow (their *Waffenfarbe*) piping on the shoulder straps.

The *SA-Gebirgsjäger* were mountain troops recruited from huntsmen, foresters, skiing experts and mountaineers principally in southern Germany and Austria. Note that the German term *Jäger* (the same applies to the French *'chasseur'*) means both a huntsman and a light >>>

Above: SA *Gebirgsjäger*.

Inset: *Edelweiß* badge worn on the cap by members of the Alpine SA (*Gebirgsjäger*). The alpine *Edelweiß*, meaning 'white nobless' only grows above an altitude of c. 1,600me (about 5,500ft). It is thus quite a rare flower, often used as symbol for luck, love or honour.

infantryman. This small troop was intended to grown into special mountain fighting units. They were distinguished by a special emblem, an *Edelweiss* flower placed on the left side of their caps, and a right collar patch with the green initials 'GJ'. They had adapted dress including a *Bergmütze* (Austrian-styled peaked cap), various sort of warm jackets, padded anoraks, and *Bergrock* (climbing tunics), gloves and mittens, and heavy climbing shoes with reinforced soles. Special equipment included rucksacks, skis, ropes, icepicks and other mountaineering gear. The SA *Gruppen* Alpenland, Donau, Hochland, and Südmark (not officially mountain troops but connected with the Alps) wore *Tracht* (traditional South German clothing) including Bavarian-styled *Lederhosen* (leather shorts), *Wadenstutzen* (white knee-length socks) and black or brown shoes.

The *SA-Marine* (Navy), created in early 1934, was intended to take over the German navy in what Röhm hoped was the near future. It had two *Reichsseesportschulen* (schools for sea sport) at Prieros in Brandenburg, and at Seemoos near Lake Bodensee. Both schools were created for training in physical exercises, swimming, rowing, navigation, naval >>>

Right: *SA-Marine* unit number (placed in the upper left corner of the flag).

Opposite page right: *SA-Marine Sturmbannführer*, 1934.
This SA Major wears a soft peaked cap, a traditional dark blue double-breasted jacket as worn by naval officers and dark blue trousers from the SA evening dress. On the right cuff of the jacket he has a light blue band with the name of one of the SA navy schools. On the upper left arm is the red swastika armband. On the left upper breast a badge indicates an Officer of the Watch.

Opposite page left: *SA-Marine Rottenführer*
This SA Lance Corporal wears the white working uniform, composed of a white (or light gray) moleskin smock, white (or dark blue) trousers and the navy-blue *Lagermütze* (forage cap). Rank was indicated by a scheme of bars, chevron and stars on the lower left cuff, here the two red bars of a *Rottenführer*.

Right: *SA-Marine* collar patch.

armament, signalling and communications. The *SA- Marine* had their own unique uniform with special nautical insignia, which no other unit of the SA had. Members wore navy-style dress, including dark blue tunics and trousers and white moleskin smocks for working. The normal SA kepi was replaced with sailors' flat bonnets, peakless hats, and blue caps. An anchor in silver or gold was worn on the right collar patch, and qualified specialists were distinguished by trade badges, for example a red cogwheel for technicians, or a red lightning-flash for signallers. Their *Waffenfarbe* was navy-blue.

The *SA-Flieger* (air force), established in 1930, was intended to train pilots who would one day constitute the *Luftwaffe*. A year later the SS, still under SA control, also created a flying branch, resulting in a common *SA-SS-Flieger Korps*. There was also the *NS-Flieger Korps* (NSFK, Nazi Flying Corps) created in 1932, which was a semi-civilian organisation, not regarded as a NSDAP service. According to the stipulations of the Treaty of Versailles, Germany was forbidden to possess an air force but no clause forbad ballooning and gliding. In the late 1920s and early 1930s, gliding was a national sport, which was greatly encouraged by the Nazi Party as a patriotic activity. Model aircraft and gliders were thus very popular among the German youth. Gliding had strong roots in Germany. The engineer Otto Lilienthal (1848–96) had been a pioneer of aircraft design, gliding and aviation technology. He was killed in Berlin when making his 2,000th public gliding flight. The purposes of the *SA-Flieger* was to promote interest and development of air sports, notably gliding and ballooning, to create a means to channel energy, exploit enthusiasm in aeronautics, further air-mindedness among the SA, and to learn the basics of flying which was the first step in training potential pilots for the future *Luftwaffe*. Members built model gliders and planes, and learned the theory of flight. Simple winch-launched gliders gave future pilots their first experience in the air and produced the powerful propaganda image of a modern nation taking to the skies. Members of the SA flying branch wore the standard brown uniform with, on the right collar patch, a winged propeller. Their *Waffenfarbe* was light blue. In September 1933 the *SA Flieger* ceased to exist. Its men were incorporated into the *Deutsche Luftsportverband* (DLV, German Air Sport League). The chairman of this Nazi sub-organisation was Hermann Göring and the vice-chairman was Ernst Röhm until his death in June 1934. In 1937, the DLV was itself absorbed into another Nazi organisation, the *Nationalsozialistisches Fliegerkorps* (NSFK, Nazi Flying Corps).

The *SA-Pioniere* were intended to become the engineer corps of the new army. Each SA *Standarte* was supposed to have one *Pioniersturm* (engineering company). SA *Pioniere* were to become as highly trained specialists, at the forefront of future combats using their skills and special equipment to clear the way for the fighting units. They would breach barbed wire with cutters or explosives, clear mines, subdue enemy strongpoints and bunkers with assault weapons such as flamethrowers and many different forms of demolition charges. For river crossing it was intended that the SA engineering troop would be equipped with and trained in the use of assault boats with outboard motors, and vulnerable but easily transportable inflatable rubber floats. They also would have assault-rafts and barges, some large enough to ferry guns, howitzers and even light tanks. They would repair, destroy or sabotage bridges, and where no adequate bridge existed, they would

Above: RAZ cloth badge.

Left: *SA-Flieger* collar patch.

Below: RAZ cuff title.

Reichsautozug Deutschland

build temporary one from their pontoon trains. In addition they would clear roads through the rubble of bombed towns and villages, construct field fortifications, dig trenches, set up barbed wire and lay minefields. In the early 1930s, however, these warlike activities lay in the future. In fact the few SA engineering units that were actually created were employed in civilian projects (e.g. land reclamation schemes, notably to convert the marshy Emsland on the border with the Netherlands into farmland). SA pioneers wore the standard brown uniform with 'Pi' (*Pionier*) on the right collar patch. In 1933 this was replaced with a crossed pick and shovel. This too was later replaced with black piping on the shoulder straps. Their *Waffenfarbe* was black. Members of the SA Regiment 10 of *Gruppe Nordsee* (North Sea Group), who contributed to land reclamation, were awarded a cuff title reading 'Emsland'.

The *Reichsautozug Deutschland* (RAZ, National Motor Squad Germany) was a special mobile propaganda unit. Created during the election campaign of 1932 and headed by *Sturmführer* Hermann Schäffer, it was equipped with vans and cars fitted with loudspeakers playing music and propaganda slogans and encouragement to vote Nazi. Members of this small but modern unit wore various uniforms, including SA regular dress with kepi and swastika armband or a brown boiler suit when operating. They were distinguished by a cuff band reading '*Reichsautozug Deutschland*' and a right red collar patch bearing the letters 'RAZ'. It was disbanded in 1937.

The *SA-Streifendienst* was a police and patrol service. Placed under the authority of a *Standortführer* (local district leader), SA policemen wore the standard brown uniform with a yellow armband inscribed '*Standortführer Streifendienst*' in black. This was later replaced with a black cuff title bearing the inscription '*Der Standortführer*' and the name of the district.

The *SA-Eisenbahneinheiten* were SA railway units, which briefly existed in Austria. The right collar patch was decorated with a winged railway wheel.

The *SA-Leibstandarte* was a bodyguard unit stationed at Munich. It should not be confused with the *SS Leibstandarte* – Hitler's personal protection unit, which later became a ceremonial regiment known as *Leibstandarte-SS Adolf Hitler* (LSSAH), and a *Waffen-SS* panzer division known as the 1st *Waffen-SS Panzerdivision Leibstandarte SS Adolf Hitler*. The *SA-Leibstandarte* was a formation with a broadly ceremonial function. They guarded the Brown House, the Nazi Party headquarters

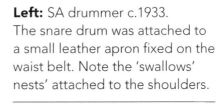

Left: SA drummer c.1933. The snare drum was attached to a small leather apron fixed on the waist belt. Note the 'swallows' nests' attached to the shoulders.

on the Briennerstraße in Munich. It had been a palatial private house until rebuilt by Hitler's favourite architect, Paul Ludwig Troost, in 1931. It was more a display of splendour and might than a place of actual work. The *SA-Leibstandarte* members wore the regular SA uniform with the letter 'L' on the light blue patch of *SA Gruppe Hochland*.

The *SA-Musikeinheiten* were the marching bands. Military music (combined with flags) was an important part of Nazi parades and rallies. Every *Standarte* had a *Musikzug* (a marching band with a various number of musicians) and each *Sturmbann* had a *Spielmannzug* (a fife-and-drum band with about twenty-four members). Music instruments included snare and bass drums, various brass (e.g. horns, trumpets), fife and Glockenspiel (a kind of portable xylophone). Musicians wore the standard SA uniform with the traditional bandsmen's *Schwalbennester* (swallows' nests). These detachable ornementations were

175

Left: SA musician's collar patch.

Below left: SA Doctor.

attached to each tunic shoulder by metal hooks. After 1931 musicians' collar patches were decorated with a stylised Greek lyre.

The *SA-Sanitäts* was the medical corps, which included doctors, nurses, pharmacists and dentists. It was often essential to have these qualified personnel on hand as SA activities were frequently accompanied by violence, at least before the seizure of power in 1933. The first SA medical group had been formed at Munich in 1923 by Dr Walter Schultze. It was further developed by the ultra-Nazi, *Alte Kämpfer* and physician Leonardo Conti (1900–45). Conti also founded the *NS Artzebund* (National Socialist Doctor League), and was appointed *Reichsgesundheitsführer* (Reich Health Leader) in 1939. Promoted to the rank of *SS-Gruppenfüher* in 1941, he was responsible for the murder of a large number of mentally ill Germans in the euthanasia campaign intended to purify the 'Aryan' race. Conti committed suicide in Nuremberg Prison in 1945.

SA medical personnel were often qualified professionals or

students in their final years who volunteered their services for the Nazi cause. They sometimes wore a more-or-less improvised white armband with a red Greek cross until October 1932 when violet collar patches were introduced. Medical orderlies and stretcher carriers continued to wear a white armband with a red Greek cross, while doctors had a collar patch decorated with an Aesculapius staff (a snake around a stick), pharmacists had an A (*Apotheker*) and dentists a Gothic Z (*Zahnartz*). In November 1937 it was decided that the medical symbol should have a more Germanic and Nordic character. Henceforth the *Algiz* or *Leben Rune* (life rune, letter Z in runic alphabet) was used. This rune was placed in an oval badge for doctors, rectangular for dentists, a triangle pointing upwards for pharmacists, and a triangle pointing downwards for veterinary surgeons. Their *Waffenfarbe* was royal blue.

THE HITLER YOUTH

The *Hitler Jugend* (HJ, Hitler Youth) was in fact originally the junior branch of the SA. The first NSDAP-related youth organisation was the *Jugendbundes der NSDAP* (Youth League of the NSDAP), which was announced on 8 March 1922. Gustav Adolf Lenk (born in October 1903 in Munich) was appointed leader of the *Jugendbund* at age 19. In embryo the Hitler Youth was to be disguised much as the SA had been –as a sport and physical fitness club so that the still-prevailing terms of the Versailles Treaty limiting the size of the German Army could be paid lip-service to. The organisation – in fact a breeding-ground for young Nazi activists – was divided into the *Jungmannschaften* (boys aged fourteen to sixteen) and the *Jungsturm Adolf Hitler* (sixteen to eighteen year-olds). It came under the command of the chief of the SA, Lieutenant Johann Ulrich Klintsch, and its 300 members wore uniforms similar to those of the SA. In April 1926, the very descriptive name *Hitler Jugend* (HJ, Hitler Youth) appeared for the first time, revealing the personality cult devoted to Adolf Hitler. On 3–4 July 1926, at the *Reichparteitag* (Party Day) held in Weimar, the Hitler Youth was formally established with Kurt Gruber as *Reichsführer der HJ* (Leader of the Hitler Youth). Gruber was replaced with Baldur von Schirach (1907–74) in October 1931. In May 1932, the Hitler Youth (made up of two main branches for boys and girls) was made totally independent from the SA administration, and became a powerful limb of the NSDAP in its own right, under the dynamic direction of its new leader. After 1933 the >>>

This page: HJ *Rottenführer* (left) and HJ *Stammführer* (right), The *Hitler Jugend* proper was intended for boys aged fourteen to eighteen. Officers were young men aged between twenty-four and thirty.

Left and below: BdM girl. The Hitler Youth had two branches for girls: the *Jungmädelbund* (JM, League of Young Girls, aged ten to fourteen) and the *Bund Deutscher Mädel* (BDM, League of German Girls, aged fourteen to eighteen).

HJ developed into one of the strongest structures of the Nazi regime. It provided a wide range of activities as well as basic military training. The purpose was to take teenagers and turn them into good, fanatical, disciplined Nazis. During the war, the HJ was given a more pronounced military character, notably in the Flak (air defence) role and by the creation of the 12th *Waffen-SS* Armoured Division, which fought in Normandy, France in 1944, in southern Germany, and during the siege of Berlin in the last weeks of the war.

SA RESERVE

SA men over thirty-five, and those precluded from full active service by the nature of their employment, formed the SA Reserve. Men of the

Above: Collar patch of the 11th Reserve *Sturm* of *Standarte* 260 (design worn between 1933 and 1939).

Reserve had to attend three hours service per week and a fortnightly exercise. In November 1933 the SA Reserve was divided into SA Reserve I (SAR I) for men aged between 35 and 45; and SA Reserve II (SAR II) for men aged over 45. Both SAR I and SAR II included older members of the SA but also war veterans of two main *Bünde*: the *Stahlhelm* and the *Kyffhäuser Bund*.

The *Stahlhelm* (Steel Helmet) was a nationalist and monarchist veterans' association, formed at the end of the First World War by Frantz Seldte. The *Kyffhäuser Bund* was another old comrades' association for war veterans. Its name came from the Kyffhausen mountain situated near Frankenhausen, north of Erfurt in the province of Thuringia. Mount Kyffhausen was associated with the legend of the German emperor Frederick I Barbarossa (Rothbart or Red-Beard, born in 1122, reigned 1152–90) who died while leading the Third Crusade. According to several legends, the excommunicated Emperor did not die, but lives forever and remains sleeping under Mount Kyffhausen waiting a final time of awakening. Occasionally the Emperor talks to people who are brought to him by a dwarf, or he appears disguised as a pilgrim. The red-bearded emperor represented the upsurge of German nationalism and imperialism. When Barbarossa finally emerged a thousand-year Golden Age would begin and all wrongs would be redressed, Germany would be restored to her former glory and territorial conquests would be justified. This popular legend was, needless to say, widely used by the Nazis. Both veterans' leagues were absorbed by the SA in 1933. After the purge of June 1934 the SA Reserve was modified. As the corps had been greatly increased by Röhm and as the SA were no longer needed, some of its younger elements were removed to the Reserve. This was then divided into Active Reserve I for men between 18 and 35; Active Reserve II for those aged 35 to 45 and Inactive Reserve for those over 45. SA reservists continued to wear their former uniform, medals and badges, with the addition of an R (for Reserve) and unit number on the right collar patch.

Chapter 14

Other European Fascist Parties and their Militias in the 1930s

In the 1920s, people in Germany and throughout Europe in general had believed that the twentieth century was realising the idea of progress. From 1924 to 1929, there was a period of peace and economic prosperity, international balance and parliamentary democracy. Unfortunately, the Wall Street Crash of 1929 triggered a deep economic depression causing social unrest and the rise of dictatorial regimes, and the end of international security culminating in the Second World War. During that turbulent decade, people began to fear that progress was a phantom. Everywhere the demand was for security. Many nations tried to achieve autarky – that is, economic self-sufficiency – by regulating, controlling, guiding and restoring their own economies. In countries where democratic institutions were strongly established, this trend advanced the principle of the welfare state and social democracy to protect individuals against the evils of unemployment and the free rise and fall of prices in the unpredictable and world market. But in nations where democracy was not so strong, the same economic trend became one aspect of totalitarianism, which spread alarmingly in the 1930s.

The cry was for a leader, a strong man who would act, take responsibility, make radical decisions and get rapid results. This opened the way for true dictators, unscrupulous and ambitious political adventurers whose purposes and solution to all problems, economic, political and social, was war. By 1939, totalitarian or near-totalitarian regimes had been established in Italy, Germany, the Soviet Union, Poland, Spain, Hungary, Greece and Portugal. Only ten out of twenty-seven European states remained democratic: Great Britain, France, Holland, Belgium, Switzerland, Czechoslovakia, and the three Scandinavian countries, Denmark, Sweden and Norway.

In the late 1920s, even within the democratic nations of Europe, there were traditional nationalist and conservative elements but there were also groups and parties which may be categorised as fascist because of their ideology, their authoritarian methods, their propensity for violence, the social background of their members and leaders, and their more or less close relations with Mussolini's Italian Fascism and Hitler's Nazism. European Fascist parties and organisations were extremely varied, but they shared a number of common ideological features: strong nationalism, violent anti-Communism, anti-Liberalism, and anti-democracy. They wanted to eliminate their opponents and replace them by a new authoritarian and corporate state directed by a single strong party. Although they tried to rally the masses, they were often elitist and often (but not always) racist in character. The Fascist parties were conceived as tightly organised semi-military machines by which state and society were to be conquered and later ruled. There was the myth of the magnetic 'leader' who was venerated like a saint by the faithful, who could do no wrong and must not be criticised. Fascism appealed to all groups from the bottom to the top of the social scale, but ardent believers needed enemies with whom they were at war: the profiteers, the parasites, the financial gangsters, the ruling cliques, the rapacious capitalists, the reactionary landowners, the foreigners, (sometimes) the Jews, but even there exceptions were made if it suited the Leader's agenda. It is noticeable that in the 1930s in Europe all extremist political parties –whether left or right – used street violence to intimidate their rivals and impose themselves on society. For this purpose, all Fascist parties had militias like the SA. These private uniformed gangs manhandled, abused and even killed other citizens with varying degrees of impunity as the cult of violence and 'direct action' were also features of Fascism. Indeed the use, acceptance and glorification of violence were was one of the distinguishing characteristics of totalitarian groups. In Fascist ethics, war was a noble thing and the love of peace a sign of decadence. When the Germans occupied their countries after the Blitzkrieg of 1939–40, many members of those parties put themselves at the disposal of the occupiers.

ITALY

The Italian Fascists had their own political paramilitary force, the *Fasci Italiani di Combatto*, or *Squadristi*, better known as *Camicie Nere* (Black

Right: Italian Fascist *Squadrist.* The squads were identified by their black shirts, hence the name Black Shirts, and they became the inspiration for Hitler's SA.

Shirts) after the colour of their uniforms. Created by Benito Mussolini in March 1919, the *Fasci* numbered 17,000 members in early 1920. They were originally composed of *arditi*, disgruntled veterans of the First World War, later joined by many other malcontents and mere opportunists as the Fascist Party gained power. Fascism, as created by Mussolini, was basically an authoritarian form of government, a terrorist dictatorship using totalitarian methods and emphasising chauvinist ultranationalism, militarism and aggressive imperialism, idealisation of 'manly' virtues, conservatism, anti-democracy, xenophobia, contempt for the 'weak', anti-intellectualism, irrationalism and an all-embracing conception of the State which had to control every aspects of life. In fact, the vague Italian Fascism constituted an incoherent and unintelligible justification for any actions undertaken by the *Duce* (Leader) and his henchmen. The Black Shirts were reorganised in 1922 into the *Milizia Volontaria per la Sigurezza Nazionale* (MVSN, Volunteer Militia for National Security), which lasted until the Italian Armistice in 1943. Headed by Mussolini himself, who had the title of Commandant-General, they were important troops for the *Duce* when he seized power after the march on Rome in October 1922. The Black Shirts were a great inspiration for all Fascist and ultra right-wing forces in Europe in the 1930s. The MVSN derived its basic organisation from the structure of the Ancient Roman Army, including *Squadra* (Squad), *Manipolo* (Platoon), *Centuria* (Company), *Coorte* (Battalion), *Legione* (Regiment) and *Zona* (Division). Ranks also closely approximated those of the Roman Army. In 1933 Adolf Hitler was made *Caporale Onorario* (Honorary Corporal). The uniform was the basic Italian army dress, either grey-green wool or khaki drill jacket with a black shirt and tie, black collar patches bearing silver *fascio* (the Roman bundle of sticks wrapped around an axe), a black fez with tassels, riding breeches or baggy 'Turkish' pants, and leather boots or puttees. The MVSN provided security police, which employed violence, intimidation, terror and murder against Mussolini's opponents. Members of the MVSN also formed anti-aircraft units and combat formations, which were used in the Abyssinian Campaign in 1935 and during the Second World War.

GREAT BRITAIN

In 1932 the British politician Sir Oswald Mosley (1896–1980) created the British Union of Fascists (BUF). Mosley's personal charm and charisma and the sweeping, seductive arguments of Fascism combined during the Depression era in England to enlist some 30,000 members, and a small SA-like militia by 1934. The party adopted the Fascist salute, a lightning-bolt in a circle as its emblem, and the black shirt as its uniform. The British Blackshirts, the active members of the movement, regarded themselves as an elite and acted as an escort and bodyguard

Left: Member of the British Union of Fascists.

for the Leader. They became notorious because of the violence they used to silence and remove all hecklers and demonstrators in the best SA style. The national climate and the political structure of Great Britain did not favour the growth of Mosley's BUF, however. The movement was proscribed and broken up in 1940 and its leaders imprisoned. One of them, William Joyce (1906–46) escaped and went to Germany to offer his services to the Third Reich. Nicknamed 'Lord Haw Haw', Joyce worked for Göbbels's propaganda service, broadcasting pro-Nazi radio programmes in English. Arrested in May 1945, he was returned to Britain to stand trial. Condemned to death for high treason, he was hanged in 1946. As for Oswald Mosley he was released from prison in 1943 and moved to France in 1951, where he lived until his death in December 1980.

UNITED STATES OF AMERICA

In the USA there was a Nazi Party called the German American Bund, or German American Federation (German: *Amerikadeutscher Bund*; *Amerikadeutscher Volksbund*, AV). It was established in 1936 in Buffalo, New York, repacing the Friends of New Germany (FONG), the new name being chosen to emphasise the group's American credentials after press criticism that the organisation was unpatriotic. The Bund was led by its German-born *Führer* Fritz Julius Kuhn (1896–1951) and only American citizens of German and 'Aryan' descent were allowed to become members. The Bund's main goal was to promote a favourable view of Nazi Germany and fight American boycotts of German goods. The Bund held rallies and parades with Nazi insignia and rituals such as the Hitler salute. It had a paramilitary branch similar to the SA whose uniformed members attacked their enemies and opponents: Jews, Communists, Socialists, Democrats and 'Moscow-directed' trade unionists. In 1939 Kuhn was arrested and jailed for tax evasion and embezzlement. In 1942 the US authorities denied the Bund and all other pro-Nazi groups the ability to operate freely. Kuhn's US citizenship was cancelled, and after the war he was deported to Germany and died in Munich in December 1951. It should be noted that the First Amendment to the United States' Constitution guarantees freedom of speech, and allows political organisations great latitude in expressing Nazi, racist and anti-Semitic views. Accordingly there are still neo-Nazi groups in the United States today like the National Socialist Movement, the National States' Rights Party, the American Nazi Party, and several others.

FRANCE

In the 1930s France had several extreme-right organisations and fascist parties. The *Action Française* (AF) was a conservative monarchist movement created in 1899 by the writer, journalist and intellectual Charles Maurras (1868–1952), Léon Daudet (son of the novelist Alphonse Daudet) and the historian Jacques Bainville. The AF asserted that the decadence of France was due to the Protestants, the Freemasons and the Jews who formed an evil state within a state. From the start the AF was thus virulently anti-individualist, anti-democratic, xenophobic, anti-Semitic, traditionally Catholic, conservative, nationalist and monarchist. The AF had a newspaper called *Revue de l'Action Française* and a strong-arm force called the *Camelots du Roi* (King's newsvendors). The *Camelots* were not uniformed, but armed with clubs, sticks and canes as they were frequently involved in riots and other acts of violence. The AF was always a movement of a small minority, but its ideology orientated towards the past rather than the present nonetheless had a significant influence on the French Right and extreme Right.

In 1925, one of the AF leaders named Georges Valois sought to emulate Mussolini's movement by founding an openly Fascist party called the *Faisceau*, made up of AF dissidents and discontent ex-servicemen. Financed by the wealthy perfume manufacturer François Coty, Valois soon quarrelled with Maurras, and the *Faisceau* remained a marginal and meaningless groupuscule of extremist fire-eaters. During the Occupation of France (1940–4), the AF enthusiastically supported Marshal Pétain and the Vichy government which put into practice many aspects of Maurras's ideology, notably the harsh measures against the Jewish community. The AF was banned by the French authorities in 1944.

The *Mouvement des Jeunesses Patriotes* (MJP, Movement of Patriotic Youth) was founded in 1924 by a prosperous industrialist named Pierre Taittinger. Actually the youth branch of the older *Ligue des Patriotes* (Patriots League), the MJP was headed by the conservative General De Castelnau. The league had a vague political programme combining anti-communism and anti-parliamentarism. The movement had paramilitary squads called *Phalanges Universitaires*, inspired by the Italian model and headed by Roger de Saivre – later Pétain's Chief of Cabinet. The Patriot movement claimed to have 100,000 members in 1934 – an exaggeration of course. After the dissolution of all such groups by the Léon Blum government in 1936, Taittinger's movement was re-launched as the unsuccessful *Parti Républicain National et Social*.

The *Croix-de-Feu* (Cross of Fire), created in 1927, was originally a non-political club of about 2,000 First World War veterans who had been awarded the Croix de Guerre, France's highest award for bravery. In 1929, the small elitist association was placed under the command of a new leader, Lieutenant-Colonel François de La Rocque Séverac. The social and economic crisis as well as Colonel de La Rocque's prestige and energy gave it a sudden impulse. In 1931 the association numbered 15,000 members, 80,000 in 1932 and probably 150,000 in 1934. The *Croix-de-Feu* constituted a significant electoral lobby, a popular political force and a powerful conservative league. Every Sunday *Croix-de-Feu* members and supporters paraded on the Champs-Elysées in Paris with waving flags and medals proudly worn. The association had defence squads called *Dispos*, organised along military lines in *mains* ('hands', each of five men) who were used to fight communists and other enemies of France. Although de La Rocque has often been presented as a sort of French Mussolini, his political programme was neither fascist, racist nor anti-Semitic. Set out in a book published in December 1934 and called Service Public the Colonel's doctrine was rather vague, influenced by a kind of social Catholicism, traditional nationalism, the unity of the French nation, economical liberalism, protection of the family, and a mystical souvenir of the First World War frontline veterans. After the dissolution of the leagues in 1936, the Croix-de-Feu was reformed as a new party called the *Parti Social Français* (PSF), which counted some 800,000 members in 1938.

After the failure of Valois's *Faisceau*, the veteran officer Jean Renaud created in 1933 a new movement called *Solidarité Française* (French Solidarity) with the financial support of the millionaire perfume industrialist and press tycoon François Coty. With the backing of his newspapers the *Figaro* and *l'Ami du Peuple*, *Solidarité Française* developed the common fascist themes: nationalism, anti-parliamentarism, anti-Semitism and anti-communism. The megalomaniac Renaud and Coty claimed to have 300,000 members but probably had only 4,000–5,000 active members in reality. *Solidarité* included a few uniformed bodyguards pompously called the *Brigade d'Intervention* wearing blue shirts, Alpine berets and black trousers. In the end, Coty's political commitment was fatal to his business. He was ruined and *Solidarité Française*, deprived of funds, was disbanded in 1936.

The overtly Fascist *Parti Socialiste National* (PSN) was created by Gustave Hervé and Marcel Bucard in 1928. Bucard was a First World War veteran who had organised Georges Valois's shock troops in the *Faisceau*. Originally closely related to *Action Française*, Bucard's PSN was a total fiasco. The ultra-revolutionary Bucard created another formation in September 1933 called *Francisme* with fascist Italy financial support. The new party, directly copying from Mussolini's style, had only a few thousands members and a small uniformed militia called the *Main Bleue* (Blue Hand). Banned in June 1936 the unsuccessful *Francisme* survived with difficulty until 1939 under various names, with only a few hundred members.

The *Organisation Secrète d'Action Révolutionnaire Nationale* (OSARN, Secret Organisation of National Revolutionary Action) also known as *Comité Secret d'Action Révolutionnaire* (CSAR, Secret Committee for Revolutionary Action) occupied a very particular place amongst French fascist organisations of the 1930s. The OSARN/CSAR was ironically nicknamed *Cagoule* (cowl or hood) by the Action Française -members being called *Cagoulards* (hooded ones), probably because members of the committee were compared to Ku-Klux-Klan men. Hoods were never worn, of course, except perhaps on a few occasional top-secret meetings, but the name alone, evoking both secrecy and terror, had a striking effect on the public at large. The OSARN/CSAR was created in 1934 by the engineer Eugène Deloncle (1890–1944). Cagoule kept the Orleanist monarchism and strongly anti-republican line of the Action Française, but added the rhetoric of Fascism, and the use of violence with a precise purpose: to take power in France by forces in order to thwart a supposed communist plot and to restore the monarchy or at least establish a military dictatorship. The secret organisation (members were not supposed to know each other) originated from a few radical *Action Française* members who wanted no more talk but immediate violent subversive and terrorist action. Members were generally conservative monarchists or ultra-nationalists, war veterans, and officers and NCOs from the army reserve. Their main enemies were '*la Gueuse*' (the French Republic), the 'Reds' (communists), the '*youpins*' (the Jews) and the '*Boches*' (the Germans). Members were carefully selected, and undertook a symbolic initiation rite influenced by medieval knighthood and had to swear the following oath of loyalty: 'I swear on my honour, fidelity, obedience and discipline to the Organisation. I swear to keep secret and never to try to find out the identity of the chiefs!' The oath was sworn '*Ad majorem Galliae Glorem*' ('For the Greater Glory of France') on a tricolour flag. Sometimes, the rite and oath were reduced to a less noble and cruder warning: 'If you ever reveal our secrets, we'll shoot you!' and these words were not an empty threat; several indiscreet, talkative and imprudent members and traitors were indeed executed. *Cagoule* was an instrument of civil war and was strictly organised in a military way. It was composed of light squads (seven men) and heavy squads (twelve men). Three squads formed a unit of twenty-one men or thirty-six men; three units formed a battalion with an average of seventy men; three battalions formed a regiment numbering about 250 men; three regiments formed a brigade of about 750 men; and three regiments formed a division numbering about 2,000 men. The organisation had several secret headquarters, a special intelligence service, violent action commandos (called groups Z) and secret mobilising centres. There was also a logistic branch including transport units and a medical service. According to Eugène Deloncle some 12,000 men were ready for action in Paris and 40,000 members all over France. These figures were obviously untrue and there were undoubtedly only a few thousand active *Cagoulards*. During their secret meetings, the OSARN/CSAR members did not wear a hood but sometimes a uniform composed of a black beret, a leather jacket, riding breeches, a waist belt and ammunition pouches. However, the committee was a secret organisation and for most of the time the members wore civilian clothes. When in action, they were armed with weapons ranging from clubs and truncheons to pistols and modern submachine guns. Some groups had grenades and machine guns. Arms were purchased from or supplied by Italy, or provided by accomplices in the French army or stolen from the army arsenals where the OSARN/CSAR had many sympathisers notably the prestigious First World War hero Marshal Franchet d'Esperey. *Cagoule* had secret subversive networks lobbying within the French army, called *réseaux Corvignolles*, led by Commandant Georges Loustaunau-Lacau. Arms and explosives were stockpiled in secret depots. *Cagoule* had a secret prison concealed in a house in Rueil-Malmaison near Paris where suspects and kidnapped enemies could be held and interrogated. Obviously *Cagoule*'s organisation needed a lot of money. Funds were provided by robberies and hold-ups, but also provided by Italian Fascists and by several important industrialists and capitalists who feared Communist influence in the *Front Populaire* government in 1936. *Cagoule* had good contacts with Italy and the organisation received Beretta submachine guns to murder opponents of Mussolini who had taken refuge in France (notably the anti-fascist brothers Carlo and Sabatino Rosselli, assassinated in June 1937). The secrete organisation employed indoctrination and psychological means but also subversion and violence. It was responsible for the sabotage of weapons and equipment intended for the Republican Spanish forces (notably blowing up American-made aircraft passing through France).

In the hope of provoking a civil war and a putsch, *Cagoule* perpetrated systematic terrorist attacks with explosives causing significant damage and killing several people. However, in spite of its oath and secrecy, *Cagoule* was an unstable, clumsy and dilettante organisation. The conspiracy was gradually infiltrated by the police. Some members were identified and arrested. Some of them talked, resulting in the arrest of several OSARN/CSAR leaders. In the end, what was intended to be the driving force of a violent revolution and civil war ended up as a ridiculous farce. The secret organisation was entirely broken up in November 1937. After the French defeat of June 1940, radical members and the main leaders of *Cagoule* split into three groups: some of them joined the Resistance or followed General Charles De Gaulle and

Right: *Cagoulard* member of a combat group of the CSAR. Being part of a secret organisation, members of the CSAR did not wear uniform in public, but when violent actions were carried out, members could wear a *Canadienne* (a thick leather tunic), which could presumably offer some degree of protection.

the Free French in London, others stayed in Paris and collaborated with the Germans, and others joined Pétain's Vichy regime.

The *Parti Populaire Français* (PPF, French Popular Party) was created by the ex-communist leader Jacques Doriot (1898–1945). From a modest socialist family, Doriot was a worker who was active in the *Parti Communiste Français* (PCF, French Communist Party). In May 1924 (aged twenty-six) Doriot was a prominent member of the central committee of the Party and mayor of Saint-Denis (a suburb near Paris) in 1931. Doriot seemed to have a bright future within the communist organisation, but his career was disrupted by quarrels with the other rising star of the PCF, Maurice Thorez (1900–64). The opposition and rivalry between the two chiefs led to an explosive situation and Doriot was expelled from the Party in June 1934. From then on, the embittered Doriot felt a strong hatred for his ex-comrades and in revenge decided to launch a rival organisation. The *Parti Populaire Français* was founded in June 1936. It rapidly became a Fascist group recruiting vengeful ex-communists like Doriot, disillusioned unemployed, ultra-nationalists, anti-democrats and various dissatisfied lower-class persons. Funds came from capitalists, bankers, tycoons and from Fascist Italy. Doriot's success was rapid and, according to the PPF newspaper *Emancipation Nationale*, the new party had 100,000 adherents in October 1936, 200,000 a year later and 300,000 at the beginning of 1938. In fact the PPF never counted more than 60,000 paying members. Nevertheless, the PPF was a dynamic formation with an obvious Fascist ideology based on anti-communism, corporatism, nationalism and anti-parliamentarism. It had Fascist rituals with the Roman salute, ceremonies, mass meetings, flags and violent bodyguards. In 1937 Doriot's party adopted a more moderate profile but a more racist and anti-Semitic character in order to be attractive to Catholics, the bourgeois and middle class. These efforts and compromises were, however, in vain, and by 1939 Doriot had failed to meet large popular liabilities. After the defeat of 1940, Doriot became one on the most zealous Nazi collaborators. He was notably one of the co-founders of the *Légion des Volontaires Français contre le Bolchevisme* (LVF, Legion of French Volunteers against Bolshevism) – a military unit that fought on the Eastern Front with the German *Wehrmacht*.

The *Parti Socialiste de France* (PSF) was created by Marcel Déat (1894–1955). Déat, a war hero and teacher of philosophy was an ex-socialist leader who had been expelled from the Socialist Party and who, like Doriot, had created his own rival party in November 1933. Gradually the

Right: LVF Volunteer.
As France was not officially at war with the USSR, the LVF was incorporated into the German army as the 638th Infantry Regiment.

PSF became more and more hostile to socialist values, embracing nationalism, corporatism and fascism, its slogan being: 'Order, Authority and Nation'. During the war Déat was a committed collaborator, and the pro-Nazi leader of the *Rassemblement National Populaire* (RNP, National Popular Union), a new party, which espoused anti-Semitism, totalitarianism and thoroughgoing collaboration with the occupiers.

During the Second World War, particularly after the summer of 1941 when the Germans invaded the Soviet Union, many members of the French Fascist parties collaborated with the Nazis. They joined the anti-Communist armed forces – under German command — resulting in the creation of the LVF (see above), and the *SS Sturmbrigade Frankreich* (the *Waffen-SS* Assault Brigade

France). In late 1944, the remnants of the LVF, the French SS, various other French police formations (notably members of the *Milice Française*) and pro-Nazi paramilitary units were amalgamated into a single formation designated the *33rd Waffen-SS Grenadier Division Charlemagne*.

DENMARK

The Danish pro-Nazi Party DNSAP (Danish National Socialist Workers' Party), founded in 1930 by a cavalry officer, Captain Lembecke, was an exact copy of the German NSDAP. Headed by Fritz Clausen in 1940, the DNSAP had a militia, called *Storm Afdelinger* with brown shirts similar to the German SA. Some of the *Storm Afdelinger*, under the command of the young Danish pro-Nazi leader Christian-Frederik von Schalburg, enlisted in the *Waffen-SS* to form the *Frikorps Danmark* with government blessing and the reluctant permission of the King of Denmark.

NORWAY

The pro-Nazi *Nasjonal Samling* (NS, National Union) and an SA-like militia called the *Hird* (1,500 members) were created in May 1933 by the ex-communist Vidkun Quisling. Ideologically dominated by orthodox Lutheranism, romantic nationalism, authoritarianism and corporatism (anti-Semitism became a dominant factor only after 1940), the NS had good contacts with the Nazis. After the occupation of Norway in April 1940, some men of the *Hird*, under police chief Jonas Lie's command, enlisted in the *Waffen-SS*.

SWEDEN

In neutral Sweden there were a number of Nazi sympathisers active in two small rival parties headed by Birger Furugord and Sven Olov Lindholm. Collaboration, whether willing or coerced, never produced the large number of volunteers the Germans had hoped. Both parties only provided a few pro-Nazi activists, police auxiliaries and *Waffen-SS* recruits.

SWITZERLAND

In the German-speaking areas of neutral Switzerland there were a few tiny far-right nationalist and national-socialist organisations such as the

Left: Member of the Norwegian NS *Hird*.
The uniform was greyish blue. The emblem of the *Hird* was a yellow disc with a sun cross and two swords on a bright red background.

Kampfbund, the *Schweizer Heimatwehr,* the *Eidgenössische Sammlung* or the *Germanische Leitstelle* (a German international recruiting office) directed by Franz Riedweg who had close contacts with his German neighbours. In the 1930s these minor groups were regularly outlawed and disbanded but often reappeared under other names. During the Second World

War, they provided a handful of collaborators, police auxiliaries and volunteers for the *Waffen-SS*.

THE NETHERLANDS

In the Netherlands, the pro-Nazi *Nationaal-Socialistische Bewering* (NSB, National Socialist Movement) was created in 1931 by Anton Mussert who declared after German troops had occupied his country in 1940: 'Hitler is the liberator of Europe!' The NSB was the largest Nazi movement outside Germany claiming 28,000 members in 1940 and 100,000 by 1942. The NSB had an SA-like militia called *Weerafdeling* (defence detachment) and a youth movement (called *Nationale Jeugdstorm*) whose members were encouraged to enlist in the *Waffen-SS* and other Nazi military units. The Germans also pushed ahead with forming the *Allgemeene SS in*

Right: *Untersturmführer Germaansche-SS in Nederland,* c. 1943.
This Second Lieutenant of the Dutch SS wears the typical black SS uniform with the wolf hook emblem of Mussert's NSB party on the cap and left sleeve. Unit identity is displayed on the right collar patch, and rank on the left collar patch.

197

Nederland, which came into being in September 1940 and was re-titled *Germaansche SS* in November 1942. The proposed 'European Ideal', as put forward by the *Waffen-SS*, had considerable appeal to the youth of Holland. The Dutch made the largest contribution to the *Waffen-SS*. In the end of 1944 there were some 12,000 on active service with more in paramilitary, security and police units.

BELGIUM

In Belgium, there were (and still are) two ethnic groups divided by history and language: Dutch-speakers in northern Flanders and French-speakers in southern Wallonia. In Flemish Belgium, there were a few small pro-Nazi organisations. The party *Alles Voor Vlaanderen-Vlaanderen Voor Kristus* (AVV-VVK, All for Flanders, Flanders for Christ) was an extreme right-wing Christian nationalist organisation secretly formed in the Belgian army in 1917. After the First World War, influenced by Charles Mauras's *Action Française* and Mussolini's Fascism, the AVV-VVK was headed by Joris van Severen. The party had a militia founded in 1929, wearing green shirts and armed with clubs. Van Severen was later rejected by his former comrades and created a new organisation called *Verdinaso*.

The *Verdinaso*, short for *Verbond van Dietsche Nationaal Solidaristen* (League of Germanic National Solidarity) was founded in October 1931. One of its aims was the creation a new state including Belgium, Netherlands and Luxemburg. A disciplined and uniformed militia formed the nucleus and the backbone of the movement, the elite of the coming new order, but the *Verdinaso* always remained the league of a small minority.

The pro-Nazi *Vlaamsch Nationaal Verbond* (VNV, Flemish National League), created in October 1933 by Raymond Tollaert and Staf De Clerq, had a paramilitary militia called the *Zwarte Brigade* (Black Brigade) and a motorised corps, the *Dietsche Motor Brigade*. Extolling the virtues of national solidarity, and praising Hitler's regime, the VNV's aim was the union of all Dutch-speaking people in Belgium and Netherlands in a new Europe dominated and ruled by Nazi Germany. The league never developed into a strong party.

The extreme pro-Nazi Party *De Vlag*, meaning the flag but also short for *Vlaamsch-Duitsche Arbeitgemeenschap* (Flemish-German Work Association) was created by Jef van de Wiele in 1935. It was by far the most pro-German party, supporting the annexation of Flanders by the Reich.

One of the men most praised by the Nazis was the French-speaking Walloon Léon Degrelle (1906–94) who was the leader of the ultra-Catholic, anti-Semitic and nationalist *Christus Rex* party. This pro-Nazi Party had Rexist Confederations organised for trade, industry, agriculture, artisans, youth groups and SA-like protection units to ensure order at meetings and demonstrations: the *Garde Wallonne* (party bodyguards), the *Formations de Combat* (combat groups) and the *Brigade Volante* (motorised corps). During the Second World War, Degrelle co-operated with the German occupiers. A Walloon Legion was formed to fight with the Germans in Russia, in which Degrelle served from the bottom upwards until he became a high-ranking officer. By the end of the war Degrelle commanded the *28th Waffen-SS Freiwilligen Grenadierdivision Wallonien* (*Waffen-SS* Volunteer Division Wallonia).

Above: Emblem of the Rexist party.

In the long term, Himmler envisaged the ultimate creation of a new western Germanic state to be called 'Burgondia', bringing together the Netherlands, Belgium and north-eastern France. Burgondia would be policed and governed by the SS and would act as a buffer to protect Germany proper from invasion. For this purpose Himmler established replicas of the *Allgemeine SS* in Flanders (*Allgemeene-SS Vlaanderen* created in September 1940) and the Dutch *Nederlandsche-SS* in November 1940. Members of these organisations retained their own languages and customs, and came under the jurisdiction of their own pro-Nazi governments. In May 1942 the same was done in Norway (*Norges-SS*) and in Denmark in April 1943 (*Germansk Korpset*, later called the *Schalburg Korps*). These four foreign *Allgemeine SS* organisations formed the Germanic SS, which totalled some 9,000 members. Their primary task was to support the local police by rooting out partisans, subversives and other anti-German elements. In December 1940, the northern pro-Nazi parties and organisations, including a few men from Lichtenstein, provided few thousand

Right: *Scharführer (Schaarleiter)*
Germaansche-SS in Flanders
This Flemish SS Staff Sergeant
wears the black SS uniform with a
silver swastika on the peaked
cap, the runic SS badge on the
left sleeve, and a cuff title
reading *SS-Vlaanderen*.

volunteers. These were regrouped into two infantry regiments: *Standarte Nordland* and *Standarte Westland*. With the addition of various service units and the *SS-Artillerie Regiment 5*, they made up the *Waffen-SS* Germania Division. For propaganda reason the name Germania was changed into a highly symbolic designation of *V. SS Panzerdivision Wiking* (5th SS Armoured Division Viking).

HUNGARY

Germany was not the only defeated nation which suffered greatly under the restrictions of the harsh Treaty of Versailles after the First World War. Hungary lost two-thirds of her former territory, many natural resources were taken away, and important industries and markets were handed over to the new nations created after 1919. Not surprisingly democracy was discredited in the eyes of many Hungarians, and fascism, anti-Semitism and anti-Communism

Right: Emblem of the Arrow Cross Party

In heraldry this symbol was called a 'cross barby' or 'cross barbée' also *croix tournée* or *croix cramponnée* (French *crampon* = hook). It shows four barbed fish-hooks or fishing spears, and suggests the biblical phrase: 'Follow me, and I will make you fishers of men.'

appeared in the form of secret societies and political parties. The largest of these movements was the *Ebredo Magyarok Egyesulete* (EME, Association of Awakening Hungarians), and the *Magyar Orszagos Vedero Egyesulet* (MOVE, Association of Hungarian National Defence). The MOVE was headed by the anti-Semitic, anti-Habsburg, and anti-capitalist Julius Gömbös. In 1945 his name was given to the third *Waffen-SS* division formed from Hungarian volunteers, the *XXVI Waffen Grenadier Division der SS Gömbös*. There was also the *Nyilaskeresztes Part* (Arrow Cross Party) created in 1935 and led by Ferenc Szálasi, modelled on the German Nazis, which led a government of national unity at the end of the Second World War. All these movements had paramilitary units similar to the German SA.

Part 4

Zenith and Fall
of the SA

Chapter 15

The SA After the Seizure of Power

AUXILIARY POLICE (*HILFSPOLIZEI*)

The legal appointment of Hitler as Chancellor of Germany on 30 January 1933 was followed by an extraordinary explosion of joy amongst his followers who had been waiting for this moment for years. That night the he SA and the *Stahlhelm* held a vast torchlight parade outside the Chancellery in Berlin. For hours the massed ranks marched in along the Wilhelmstraße and cheered Hitler who stood at the window of the building surrounded by his closest collaborators. The seizure of power had been realised in perfectly constitutional fashion, a fact that deeply angered the top SA leadership. However, by that time Ernst Röhm's hopes and ambitions were high. The radicals in the SA, those who still believed in the early Nazi programme, expected an economic rather than a political revolution. Hitler shook them by such actions as restoring Krupp von Bohlen and Thyssen to the leadership of the Employers' Association, and by dissolving the Combat League of Tradespeople (small shopkeepers hostile to the big department and chain stores). After achieving power, and particularly after the elections of 5 March 1933, the Nazis dealt ruthlessly with all real or imagined opponents. By that time, the SA had grown tremendously, as it was open to all who wanted to join. Membership rose from roughly half a million in early 1933 to probably about two million a year later, while some historians say four-and-a-half million – but, as has already been discussed, the exact number remains unclear. Anyway, whatever their real numbers, the SA played an important role not in the seizure of power but in establishing a reign of terror in Germany after power had been achieved.

On 27 February 1933, the Reichstag building burnt down. Officially the fire was blamed on a Dutch Communist, Marinus van der Lubbe. However, there are plenty of good reasons for assuming that the Nazi leadership and the SA (notably *Gruppenführer* Karl Ernst, chief of Group Berlin-Brandenburg) were implicated in the arson as they needed an incident, which would give them the excuse to suppress the opposition for reasons of national security. The Reichstag fire remains a controversial affair and an unsolved mystery. Many questions remain unanswered, but it is certain that it did indeed give the Nazis a marvellously convenient pretext to arrest anyone they chose and silence all criticism in the press. The affair resulted in a major offensive against real and supposed enemies of the new regime. The Communist Party headquarters in Berlin was raided and (probably forged) documents seized there were published, revealing their plans for a revolution. Thousands of opponents were arrested. On 24 March 1933 the *Gesetz zur Erhebung der Not von Volk und Reich* (Law for the protection of People and Empire, or the Enabling Act), was passed. This single act provided the legal foundation for Hitler's dictatorship, as he could now rule by decree.

Hundreds of civil servants were removed and replaced by devoted Nazis. The police was ordered not to take action against the SA and the *Stahlhelm*, but to show no mercy to the 'enemies of the new regime'. A further significant measure was the purging of the national police forces and the formation by Hermann Göring in February 1933 (then Prussian Minister of the Interior) of the *Hilfspolizei* (auxiliary police). The *Hilfspolizei* was a terror police force raised in Berlin and the province of Brandenburg to support the regular police against the remaining opposition. This force was composed of 40,000 hand-picked members of the SA and SS, and 10,000 drawn from the *Stahlhelm*. This was the first of several police formations created by Göring as a means of establishing paramilitary troops under his leadership. At the same time Göring had created a Police Special Duties battalion named after its commanding officer, Major Wecke. This small private police unit later expanded and grew during the Second World War to become the elite Hermann Göring Division.

The auxiliary police played a key role in ruthlessly pursuing, arresting and interrogating all suspects and supposed or real 'enemies' of the newly-established Nazi regime in the Berlin area. At first the auxiliary policemen wore their ordinary SA uniforms with an armband bearing the title *Hilfspolizei*. After two months of existence, this SA auxiliary police force was enlarged. In March 1933, it was re-named *Feldpolizei der Gruppe Berlin-Brandenburg* (Field Police of the district Berlin-Brandenburg). Its members were then issued distinctive police insignia, which set them apart from regular SA men. They wore a silver Prussian police star on their right collar patch, and a blue police greatcoat in place of the brown SA tunic. When on duty, they bore a police silver gorget with the Prussian police star in the middle and a swastika in both corners. In October 1933 the *Feldpolizei der Gruppe Berlin-Brandenburg* was renamed again, becoming the *SA-Feldjägerkorps* (FJK), a kind of military police unit. Its members were issued an olive-brown uniform composed of tunic, breeches, brown top boots, Sam Brown, a greatcoat with dark brown collar, the standard SA armband, SA kepi, and police gorget (only worn on duty). Members were considered legal policemen and allowed to carry a pistol and a

Left: Policeman of the *Feldpolizei der Gruppe Berlin-Brandenburg*, 1933.

dress bayonet, and officers a ceremonial sword on parade. In early April 1935 the FJK ceased to have any connection with the SA. Göring handed his policemen over to the larger Prussian *Schutzpolizei* (Shupo), the uniformed security police headed by *SS-Gruppenführer* Kurt Daluege.

After the Nazis' seizure of power, the ranks of the SA had been increased by numerous opportunists wanting to be on the winning side. All over Germany the large SA organisation served as the instrument of an overt populist insurrection, thereby helping the Nazis bypass the remaining constitutional and legal obstacles to a one-party dictatorship. This was one of the first steps towards *Gleichschaltung*, the co-ordination, total nazification and subordination of the German people to the now all-powerful NSDAP. *Gleichschaltung* meant that everything in

Right: *Obertruppführer* of the *SA-Feldjägerkorps*, 1933 When the SA acted as auxiliary police in 1933, their olive-brown uniform was redesigned to resemble that of the Prussian police. Other features were the brass star worn on the kepi and right collar patch, and the gorget worn on duty.

Germany, from bowling clubs and sports associations to beekeeping, was brought under Nazi control. The result was paradoxical and disastrous. It was a legal rampage directed against political enemies of the Nazi movement, and an officially-sanctioned continuation of previously illegal actions and criminal methods.

All over the country, the SA, whose hour of vengeance had finally arrived, took the law into their own hands. Their gangs roamed the streets, shouting anti-Semitic slogans, singing their *Horst Wessel Lied*, drinking and assaulting people. They also carried out searches, arrests, and interrogations. The persecution of the Jews began with a series of uncoordinated attacks. Jews were taken to a sport stadium and were made to cut the grass with their teeth. SA men forced Jews to clean a street with toothbrushes. It was to humiliate them in public, and to make clear that they were the lowest of the low. Mixed marriages were also targets. For example an 'Aryan' woman married to or dating with a Jew would be paraded in public with a placard reading: 'I am the biggest bitch in the place and cohabit only with Jews'. As for her husband or boyfriend, he would have a placard reading: 'Being a Jewish lout, I take only German girls up to my room'.

The creation of the *Hilfspolizei* and the orders forbidding the police to interfere with Nazi formations all over Germany made possible an upsurge of violence directed against the Left. SA troops were involved in outbreaks of violence soon called the *SA Aufstand* (rising). They made lists of 'enemies of the state', and arrested political opponents such as Communists, Socialists and trade unions leaders, with whom the SA had many bones to pick. The SA wanted blood in revenge for those killed and wounded in its ranks during the time of struggle. But among their victims were also numerous Jews, Democrats, Catholics, Protestants, Conservatives, pacifists, foreigners, Jehovah's Witnesses, Freemasons, homosexuals, modern artists and even ordinary citizens and dissident Nazis. Following the Reichstag fire, the SA arrested many members of the Left and detained them in improvised concentration camps and illegal prisons with thousands of other opponents of the regime. Attempts by the left-wing parties to hold election rallies were broken up. By March 1933, SA violence and police repression had combined effectively to drive the Left out of public life. On 5 March 1933, the SA staged an official parade and procession in Berlin. A bloody night of violence followed, marked by Nazi raids on the meeting places and cafés frequented by the Communists. Brawls broke out in other

German cities notably in Bochum, Breslau, Leipzig, Strassfurt, Danzig and Düsseldorf, where there were several killed and wounded. On 1 April 1933 Julius Streicher organised a nation-wide boycott of Jewish shops. Premises were closed by force, daubed with paints, swastikas, and slogans such as 'Germans! Defend yourself! Don't buy at Jewish shops!' while SA troopers would be stationed outside to intimidate any shoppers still willing to give them their custom. These actions were presented by Göbbels's propaganda as 'spontaneously born from popular anger'. At the same time, the SA raided the headquarters of the Bauhaus in Berlin, the school and research institute founded in 1919 by the architect Walter Gropius. The Bauhaus was part of the modern movement in industrial design. Modernism had been labelled 'degenerate and non-Aryan' by the Nazis. The Bauhaus was closed down and the most important leaders chose emigration. Walter Gropius, Mies van der Rohe, Alberts, Mholy-Nagy, Marcel Breuer and other great names of the modern movement continued their work in the USA. In April 1933, Hermann Göring and his police chief Rudolf Diels created the *Geheime Staatspolizei* (secret state police), soon known as the infamous Gestapo, in order to deal with the enemies of the regime and carry out arrests and interrogations of political suspects.

A highly symbolic *Bücherverbrennung* (book-burning) took place on 10 May 1933. In a public ceremony, Nazi students, SA squads, Hitler Youth groups and other Nazi supporters burnt thousands of books by Jewish authors and others considered as anti-German, Bolshevist, and 'disruptive'. Among the German-speaking authors whose books were burned were Walter Benjamin, Ernst Bloch, Bertolt Brecht, Max Brod, Otto Dix, Alfred Döblin, Albert Einstein, Friedrich Engels, Lion Feuchtwanger, Marieluise Fleißer, Leonhard Frank, Sigmund Freud, Iwan Goll, George Grosz, Jaroslav Hašek, Heinrich Heine, Ödön von Horvath, Heinrich Eduard Jacob, Franz Kafka, Georg Kaiser, Erich Kästner, Alfred Kerr, Egon Kisch, Siegfried Kracauer, Karl Kraus, Theodor Lessing, Alexander Lernet-Holenia, Karl Liebknecht, Georg Lukács, Rosa Luxemburg, Heinrich Mann, Klaus Mann, Ludwig Marcuse, Karl Marx, Robert Musil, Carl von Ossietzky, Erwin Piscator, Alfred Polgar, Erich Maria Remarque, Ludwig Renn, Joachim Ringelnatz, Joseph Roth, Nelly Sachs, Felix Salten, Anna Seghers, Arthur Schnitzler, Carl Sternheim, Bertha von Suttner, Ernst Toller, Kurt Tucholsky, Jakob Wassermann, Frank Wedekind, Franz Werfel, Grete Weiskopf, Arnold Zweig and Stefan Zweig. Not only German-speaking authors were burned but also French authors like

Victor Hugo, André Gide, Romain Rolland, Henri Barbusse; American writers such as Ernest Hemingway, Upton Sinclair, Theodore Dreiser, Jack London, John Dos Passos, and Helen Keller; as well as English authors Joseph Conrad, D. H. Lawrence, H. G. Wells and Aldous Huxley, Irish writer James Joyce; and Russian authors including Fyodor Dostoyevsky, Maxim Gorki, Isaac Babel, Vladimir Lenin, Vladimir Nabokov, Leo Tolstoy, Leon Trotsky, Vladimir Mayakovsky, and Ilya Ehrenburg. The journalist, essayist and significant romantic poet Heinrich Heine had prophetically written in 1828: 'Wherever they burn books, sooner or later they will burn people too.'

The SA collected funds for the benefit of the Party or perhaps simply for themselves and terrorized defenceless peaceable German citizens. Who could stop them? The people of Germany knew that one did not argue with the SA. Power was in their hands, and to resist a gang of SA men was to confront the power of the State. The terror of Röhm's Stormtroopers was 'legal' and all their criminal actions considered 'patriotic'.

On 23 March 1933, Göring had opened the first session of the new Reichstag, and proclaimed a general amnesty for crimes and misdemeanours committed with 'patriotic intentions', in other words crimes perpetrated by the Nazis during the *Kampfzeit*. Only those SA men who made themselves unpopular with their superiors could get into trouble. The senior ranks were almost automatically immune from disciplinary proceedings. The amnesty was complemented on 23 June 1933 by a law annulling the sentences passed against Nazis. The law ordered the immediate release of prisoners, the erasure of their sentences from the police files, and the reimbursement of their fines.

Many of both the new volunteers and the old SA men were more motivated by the desire for self-enrichment than political ideology. The open contempt for law and order shown by the newly created Nazi State encouraged those impulses of cruelty, sadism, envy and revenge, which are normally repressed or controlled in normal society. The SA exploited the power that they were given to plunder and terrorize at random. They became mobsters, except that they did not have to hide their activities or fear retribution from the State, as their 'underworld' was the State and they enjoyed complete impunity. SA teams raided bars, brothels and nightclubs, beating up whores, pimps and homosexuals, ransoming them, arresting and carting them off. Respecting none of the customs or usages of liberal democracy, the SA organised vast raids, searched houses, arrested and kidnapped people, confiscated goods, held interrogations and imprisoned suspects. The SA thugs were greatly helped by another new law promulgated in 1933 by the Nazi government. Habeas corpus was abolished and replaced by the law of *Schutzhaft* ('protective custody'), a euphemism for arbitrary imprisonment without trial. The April 1933 boycott of Jewish shops, the May book-burning and other criminal and violent exactions were (politically speaking) grave errors that did the Nazi government great harm in world opinion. Even staunch supporters of the Nazis (such as Heinrich Hoffman, Hitler's personal photographer) regarded them as serious blunders.

EARLY CONCENTRATION CAMPS

The status and power of SA officers was measured by the number of arrests they made. Each local SA leader had become an arrogant and cruel satrap, a regional potentate, a local *Führer* who abrogated to himself the right of freedom and even of life and death over his fellow citizens. Each of these tyrants organised groups of bodyguards. In certain regions the allies of former days, the right-wing parties, were disturbed by these excesses. In Brunswick, the *Stahlhelm* opposed the SA. As a result the veterans' association was promptly dissolved. The SA, who had been promised a socialist revolution, wanted everything at once. The purge of the civil service, the closing of certain professions and trades to Jews, and the creation of new posts in government and local administration whetted the appetites of the unsuccessful, the ambitious and the envious. There was a race for positions, honours and profits distributed not by reason of merit, capacity or moral value of the individual, but by reason of temporary favour, the momentary supremacy of a faction or the protection and influence of a powerful friend. Within the various Nazi organisations, within each service, even between rival SA groups, a struggle for power evolved between different factions. Each valuable position attracted great envy. At all levels, there was a frenzy of corruption, and odious and loathsome scandals were everywhere. Any opponents arrested or murdered, and also any disgraced colleagues and dismissed rivals, meant a job to be taken over, an apartment or a house to be occupied, and spoils to be distributed to the discontented misfits of the SA. The SA, the fist behind the throne of Hitler, were impatient for jobs and sinecures. >>>

Right: Boycott.
The boycott of April 1933,
which could be repeated at
any time, formed a
permanent threat to the
German Jewish community.
The poster reads:
'Germans! Defend
yourself! Do not buy
at Jewish shops!'

Truckloads of 'enemies of the State' were taken into 'protective custody' and taken to State prisons, Nazi Party jails and illegal SA prisons – known as 'Bunkers' – for detention and interrogation. Each SA *Sturmbann* (battalion) wanted to have its own prison and in Berlin alone there were some fifty improvised 'Bunkers' – cellars, warehouses, sheds, apartments and garages – where prisoners were interrogated, beaten, tortured and sometimes killed. In the provinces, such as Sonnenburg, Oranienburg, Barnim, Königswusterhausen, Wuppertal, Hohnstein, Bredow and Kemma, SA prisons echoed with screams of agony. They were places of utter horror, with prisoners dying of hunger, their bones broken, their faces bruised and swollen, their bodies covered with infected wounds. These horrifying stories were well known but the violence did not shock the Nazi authorities. What bothered them was that their authority was being flouted, and that the atrocities were being not concealed. Göring, by that time Prussian Prime Minister and Minister of the Interior, realised that he had lost control of the SA and that his authority in Germany's largest state was being undermined. He therefore ordered a senior civil servant and police officer, Rudolf Diels (1900–57), the creator of the Gestapo, to enquire into the SA prisons. Diels stuck his nose into the private SA Bunkers, and reported to Göring that they apparently existed everywhere and between 40,000 and 50,000 'enemies of the Fatherland' were languishing in them. Meanwhile, the Ministry of Justice had received countless complaints of the bad treatment meted out to suspects and prisoners. Furthermore the excesses of the SA gave the world the impression of Germany being a chaotic and ill-disciplined nation. The 'ill-mannered' SA had become a liability, their excesses ruining the reputation of the new Nazi rulers. Göring and Diels made many efforts to counter the SA. First of all they made reports and urged Hitler to intervene. Hitler was uneasy about the excesses of the SA, and was well aware that this chaotic situation could not last forever. The 'revolution' had to be replaced by evolution, stabilisation and the reinforcement of his regime. It was no secret that Hitler was unhappy with the SA. Röhm was not the man to follow Hitler slavishly as did so many others, but at the same time Hitler was very glad of the excellent results he delivered. Gradually, measures were taken against the SA and their private prisons were closed – not, of course, for humanitarian reasons or the atrocities committed in them, but because they were run by the SA. However, several of the illegal SA prisons and camps were retained, and 'run more properly' by the SS.

The internal conflict waged between SA and SS went on, but the large number of prisoners was not released. Large numbers of them were transferred into more elaborate *Konzentrationlagern* (KZ, concentration camps) administrated by the dreaded SS and thus outside the jurisdiction of the courts. The first of these camps was Dachau, 12 miles north-west of Munich in Bavaria. KZ Dachau, which was to become tragically notorious, was initially a makeshift holding pen that was set up amid the stone huts of a disused gunpowder factory. Soon the camp overflowed with 2,000 political prisoners subjected to the ruthless rule of the SS commander, Theodor Eicke (1892–1943). The inmates were systematically humiliated, subjected to rollcalls – standing without moving for several hours – and other brutal torments and mistreatment, starved, beaten, worked to exhaustion in pointless hard labour, and not infrequently murdered by the camp guards. KZ Dachau became a place of dread, the prototype of evil, a terrifying example of Nazi ruthlessness toward all opponents. It was the model for the concentration camps that followed: KZ Buchenwald near Weimar in central Germany, and KZ Sachsenhausen near Berlin in the north. Anyone hostile to the barbarous Nazi order disappeared into these camps, which were managed after 1934 by a newly-created SS corps, the *Totenkopfverbände* (Death's Head Detachments), especially formed by Himmler for this purpose. Little was actually known about these camps, and the rumours of the horrors that happened inside them were one of the most effective weapons of Hitler's dictatorship. Many opponents of the regime were too frightened to do anything. Until the end of the Nazi regime in 1945, countless victims, merely on suspicion of having committed crimes or acts against the regime, and without ever being brought to trial, were carted off to concentration camps in accordance with the Nazis' methods of racial, political and social 'purification'.

The SA: a Threat to Hitler's Regime

In September 1933, some 120,000 uniformed SA men participated to the Party Day of Victory at Nuremberg. By January 1934 the number of SA *Obergruppen* (districts) had increased to ten. But the SA had taken into its ranks large numbers of people whose political reliability was, from the Nazis' point of view, highly questionable. The SA had been mainly been recruited from the unemployed and the unemployable. Like the gangsters they were, they were envious and avid for prestige, power and rich pickings. Their motives were as crude as their manners, and they enjoyed their violence, the fun of being feared, their officially-recognised gangsterism and their power. What most of them wanted was sinecures, money, fun and games, the continuation and the increase of their disorganised but nonetheless legal terrorism at the expense of the German community, now that what they considered their Party was in charge. Even Röhm's position within the Nazi movement was questioned and came under pressure from more 'law-abiding' sections of the Nazi Party. His overt homosexual affairs provoked an outraged response from many sources. Elements of the NSDAP were concerned by the growing number of senior SA officers appointed by Röhm from among his homosexual acquaintances. The 'bad company' around Röhm created a potential powder-keg. The SA men caused increasing difficulties for the new regime as they persisted in violent actions, which were condemned by many Nazi leaders. The SA threatened, insulted and molested respectable German citizens. They appeared difficult to control, they caused unease within the Nazi Party itself and were highly unpopular with the population at large. Their violent behaviour was making conservative people wonder if the Nazis were really fit for power. Once the Nazi dictatorship had been established, the SA was less useful to Germany's new leadership. In August 1933 the SA were dismissed from the auxiliary police organised by Göring. Their indiscipline, strength and menacing independence had already set them apart from central authority. The dismissal of his men made Röhm furious.

By a decree issued in December 1933, all members of the *Stahlhelm* were incorporated into the SA. As noted above, the *Stahlhelm* had been formed in December 1918 as an organisation of nationalist ex-servicemen. Headed by vice-president Theodor Düsenberg and its founder Franz Seldte, the association called on veterans to fight against the 'slavery of the Versailles Diktat' and sought to mobilise the spirit of the ex-frontline soldiers against the 'heresy of Internationalism, Pacifism and Marxism'. It became the largest paramilitary group in Weimar Germany, along with Hitler's SA, and played a prominent role in politics in the 1920s and early 1930s. In spite of rivalry with the SA, the *Stahlhelm* consistently undermined the stability of the Weimar Republic. In 1931 it allied with the Nazis to overthrow Chancellor Brüning, but in the presidential elections of March 1932, the association withdrew its support from Hitler. Once in power, the Nazis wanted no opposition of any kind, and the veterans' association was closely controlled. Members up to the age of thirty-five were incorporated into the SA, while older members were formed into SA units called the SA Reserve. This was, however, an unwise decision, for there was antagonism between former *Stahlhelm* veterans and SA men. On occasion, they attacked one another at meetings or in street battles. In February 1934 the associations was renamed the National-Socialist League of Ex-Servicemen. Meanwhile, Hitler had another problem with the SA, as the Nazi Party was in desperate shape financially. Hitler was faced with the tremendous day-to-day cost of maintaining a large political party with thousands of employees in addition to the large SA mob. Debts exceeded contributions and the NSDAP faced bankruptcy.

By early 1934, it was clear that the SA was feared by the German population, a threat to civil order, a rival to the regular Army, an embarrassment for the NSDAP, a challenge to Hitler's own power, and a superfluous financial burden. What was to be done with the SA now that the Nazis were in power? Hitler had climbed the heights and no longer needed the ladder, and Hitler in power was a very different person from Hitler in opposition. In short, the SA had by now become a cumbersome and useless legacy of the *Kampfzeit*. In the shadows, Himmler's SS (then still officially a subordinate part of the SA) was lurking impatiently.

Chapter 16

The Lurking Rivals: the SS

THE CREATION OF THE SS

Throughout the *Kampfzeit*, the SA's attitude was characterised by excesses and lack of discipline, which infuriated Hitler. Although Hitler was in theory the head of the SA, Röhm's own private militia became more and more of an unreliable instrument. In the meantime, Hitler had therefore formed a special and loyal bodyguard unit: the *Schutzstaffeln* (SS). As said before, the origin of the SS was a small squad created in 1923 as a personal bodyguard for Hitler called the *Stabwache* (Staff Guard) and then renamed *Stoßtrupp Adolf Hitler* headed by Lieutenant Berchtold and Julius Schreck. The few men of the *Stoßtrupp* were selected among vigorous young men, aged seventeen to twenty-three, drawn from the SA and the Nazi Party, who were unquestioningly loyal to Hitler. Ulrich Graf, for instance, Hitler's first bodyguard, was a butcher who had made quite a name for himself as an amateur boxer. Emil Maurice, Hitler's bosom companion, was a watchmaker who had been convicted of embezzlement. Christian Weber had been a groom. The bond which held them together was their great task of guarding the lives of Hitler and the other senior Nazi leaders. From this small unit, Hitler demanded *Kadavergehorsam* (blind obedience). He merely had to say the word and they would wade in with their 'indiarubbers' and 'matchboxes', as they called their rubber truncheons and pistols, to protect their leader from tiresome opponents. The *Stoßtrupp* was used to guard the stages from which Hitler spoke to his followers. They would move silently forwards and deliver blows and punches to hecklers, and then frogmarch them out of the hall. They became well known in the streets of Munich in the early days when Hitler was

218

fighting for political power. Originally they did not have a proper uniform but wore a motley garb of kepis, odd tunics, greatcoats and raincoats. Some wore First World War steel helmets with the Reich war flag and NSDAP banners.

After the abortive Beer Hall putsch in November 1923, Hitler was imprisoned, and the *Stoßtrupp* was disbanded. When he was released from Landsberg prison nine months later, the Nazi Party was re-launched and Hitler appointed his trusted chauffeur, Julius Schreck, to form a new permanent bodyguard squad totalling about three dozen, utterly reliable hand-picked men. In early 1925, the unit was reorganised, coming under the SA high command, and took the name *Schutzkommando*, then *Sturmstaffeln* and finally in November 1925 the title *Schutzstaffeln der NSDAP* (protection squads of the Nazi Party), abbreviated to SS, the name under which it would become infamous. The SS was an offshoot of the SA and from small beginnings, the tiny bodyguard was to grow to an elite unit, the *Leibstandarte Adolf Hitler* (Bodyguard Regiment Adolf Hitler). The name *Schutzstaffeln* is generally credited to Hermann

Right: Early *SS-Mann*, 1925.

219

Left: *SS-Mann*, 1929.
Below: Insignia worn on the kepi included an eagle with swastika and death's head.

Göring (who had returned from exile in 1925) as a reference to aircraft that flew escort duties during his period of service with the elite Richthofen squadron. A *Staffel* was a detachment or wing in the *Luftwaffe*. Commanded by a *Staffelkapitän*, it numbered about ten planes of the same type.

Other SS units were created in every region, although they retained their elite status. These were organised into *Zehnerstaffeln*, a ten-man squad commanded by a chief. The idea was to provide in each German city a small group of Nazis of proved toughness who

220

would act in all circumstances out of complete loyalty to Hitler and to protect him during his political campaigning. *Zehnerstaffeln* members were part-timers who had to be on call evenings, weekends and anytime if needed. The *Zehnerstaffeln* were later to become the *Allgemeine-SS* (General SS), the overall body of the organisation composed of full-time, part-time, active and inactive, and honorary members. The *Allgemeine-SS* was placed directly under Hitler's command. Applicants were strictly vetted. They had to be between twenty-five and thirty-five years old, have two SS sponsors, be of 'pure Aryan' stock, sober, disciplined, physically strong and healthy. From the start, the seeds of SS elitism were sown. The dictator came to trust his SS guards absolutely while at the same time the rebellious SA was increasingly falling out of favour. The SS men attended public meetings and political rallies which were affairs staged with great care to impress both themselves and the public. But while the SA men kept order in the hall with their fists or anything else that came to hand if necessary, the small SS squad stood lined up >>>

Right: *SS-Unterscharführer, 1932.*

221

in front of the speaker's podium, their only task being close-quarters protection. In July 1926 some of the first signs of Nazi ritual emerged when Hitler handed over the sacred *Blutfahne* (see Part 3) to the care of the SS. Soon the exclusive SS men were allowed to carry pistols. They were not allowed to argue or brawl in public, their bearing and behaviour had to be exemplary. They were not required to go out into the streets and among the working class attempting to spread Nazism or win recruits and voters, or collect funds. The small SS formation made a virtue of 'honour', and its 'honour' – as its chosen motto declared ('My Honour is Loyalty') – was unquestionable loyalty to Hitler.

By 1929 the SS numbered only 280 selected bodyguards commanded by Erhart Heiden. Hitler had certainly no reason and no intention to let the squad grow in number. On 6 January 1929, Heiden having been found guilty of corruption, the detachment was given a new leader, Heinrich Himmler, and the real history of the SS began.

HEINRICH HIMMLER

Heinrich Himmler (1900–45) was born in Munich into a wealthy Catholic middle-class family. At the end of the First World War, Himmler trained as a cadet but he was too young for active service. After the war, he studied at Munich's technical college where he obtained an agricultural diploma. He worked as a fertiliser salesman and then as a poultry farmer. In 1924 he began his political career. He joined the Nazi Party, became Gregor Strasser's secretary then assistant to Josef Göbbels in the propaganda service, and served as a deputy *Gauleiter*. Although of poor health – he suffered from stomach pains, was short-sighted, feeble in stature and physically rather weak and inadequate – Himmler passed the selection test for the SS and became member No. 168. He became deputy leader of the SS in 1927 and head of the small SS corps in January 1929. Married to Margareta

---

Opposite page left: *SS-Obersturmbannführer.*

Opposite page right: SS black service uniform 1932
For the SS the colour black was deliberately worn as a sign of evil intimidation, useful wickedness, menacing power, and death. The SS was also called *Der Schwarze Korps* (The Black Corps), and the sinister death's head with crossed bones was one of its symbols.

Concerzowo in June 1928 and the father of one daughter, Gutrun, Himmler was mild in appearance and expression, indefinite in feature, modest in habits and manner, insignificant, sober and simple, but at the same time mysterious and secret in personality. He was a man whom it pleased to remain unnoticed. He listened, watching in silence through his rimless spectacles, lurked invisibly, and neatly compiled dossiers of information. He was cut out to be a secret policeman, working efficiently in the shadows. Himmler was a veteran member of the Artaman movement, a group of young fanatics who believed obsessively in the back-to-the-soil movement and the creation of a 'racially pure' Germanic peasant class. Himmler hated hunting, loved nature and had a fervent admiration for military and physical prowess, and a sick enthusiasm for racial purity. He believed obsessively in Nazi values: ultra-nationalism, German racial superiority, eastward expansion and the cult of the 'superman'. He felt a stubborn, absurd and sick hatred for 'Untermenschen' ('sub-human' Jews and Slavs). Himmler was an extravagant mystical dreamer, believing himself to be the reincarnation of Heinrich the Fowler (876–936), Prince of Saxony, Holy Roman Emperor and conqueror of the Slavs. He was a servile clerk rather than a leader, carrying out the most horrifying orders with efficiency and zeal. He kept in the background for most of his astonishing career from 1929 to 1945. But he was a coldly determined, ambitious, evil and fanatical ideologue, an intelligent, hard and scrupulous worker. He was a gifted organiser without a conscience, exercising a ruthless and merciless authority with deadly efficiency, and became Hitler's henchman fulfilling the office of Grand Inquisitor. Himmler obtained one important post after another and by 1945 was the most powerful man in Germany after Hitler. Himmler was a friend of Ernst Röhm, although it is impossible to establish with any accuracy when the two men first met. Their paths had crossed on several occasions, notably in late 1918, and eventually Himmler had served under Röhm's command in the Munich War Ministry during the ill-fated Beer-Hall Putsch of November 1923. Himmler was deeply impressed by Röhm, behaving as the modest barrack-square cadet always unable to forget that Röhm was a heroic veteran, an imposing man of action who stood several rungs higher than he on the military ladder. In his presence, Himmler instinctively tended to stand to attention and click his heels. They were a very ill-assorted pair, yet the much-decorated company commander, frustrated warrior and homosexual freebooter knew how to rouse the naïve enthusiasm of the shy, prim, colourless son of a respectable middle-class family. Before Röhm's return to Germany, Heinrich Himmler corresponded with him in exile in Bolivia, on one occasion writing with pride that the SS was now nearly 2,000 strong. There is no doubt that Himmler admired his chief, but idolized his leader Adolf Hitler even more. Himmler developed a schoolboyish adulation for the *Führer*, and what his friendship and loyalty to Ernst Röhm were worth was soon to be seen.

DIFFERENCES BETWEEN THE SA AND THE SS

The SS was not a logically and rationally planned body but a dynamic and chaotic organisation developing according to circumstances and at the mercy of political events connected with Hitler's accession to power. The SS, like no other institution in the Third Reich, represented the arrogance of Nazi ideology and the criminal nature of Hitler's regime. Although the brutal, odious and inhuman Nazi principles were applied from the start until the end of the regime, the SS was unpredictable. In 1945, the organisation was quite different from what it had been in the *Kampfzeit*. By then, the SS was an autonomous state within the German state, and a private army within the *Wehrmacht*. Although Himmler was able to minimise its subordinate status, the tiny SS squads were, until July 1934, technically and administratively a part of the larger SA organisation. Although Röhm had in practice little power over them, SS-men suffered cavalier treatment by the SA leadership, particularly during the early period before Himmler became chief of the SS. Röhm had the ability to restrict the growth of the SS by manipulating the latter's manpower strength. The SA delighted in finding the most menial tasks for the SS to perform. In spite of the comparative expansion of its membership after 1929, the SS did not play a particularly decisive role and did not look like one of the real winners from the growth of the Nazi Party. But the ambitious Heinrich Himmler was burning to free himself entirely. His first years were a struggle for survival against and then for mastery over the *Sturmabteilung*.

The personalities of the two leaders, Röhm and Himmler, were reflected in the character of the two organisations they commanded. Since their creation, the two bodies diverged. The huge SA was a heterogeneous mass movement with a diverse membership originating from the unemployed, various right-wing formations and ex-*Freikorps* men with their own traditions and loyalty to their own leaders. This resulted in unreliability, a propensity to rebellion and progressively diverging political aims. While the SA men were issued uniforms and equipment, the SS had to purchase theirs at their own expense. This was about 40 Reichsmarks, on top of the much higher membership dues than SA men SS men had to pay. This measure was insisted upon by Himmler himself as a deliberate means to prevent the unemployed from volunteering for his select corps to escape material hardship. From the start the small SS was the hard core of Nazism, a strictly-selected personal bodyguard formation, a brotherhood whose members were blindly faithful and obedient to Hitler. Habitual drunks, gossipmongers, and other delinquents were not admitted. The corps, originally charged to provide Hitler's close-quarters protection, developed into a party police force whose tasks were to maintain the unity of the Nazi Party, oppose to any ideological deviation and crush any internal rebellion. The two organisations were radically different and soon became rivals as eventually became apparent in February 1931 when SS men helped repress Walther Stennes' SA rebellion in Berlin.

In addition, the establishment in 1932 of the *SS-Rasse und Siedlungshauptamt* (RuSHA, Race and Settlement Office) clearly indicated Himmler's ambition to create from of the SS a new, biologically-defined aristocracy to champion the reconstruction of German society along racist lines. Soon the creation of another department, known as the *Ahnenerbe*, the Nazi Ancestral Research Branch, stressed the importance of links with the past – not with the traditions of one's parents and grandparents, but with the rites of one's ancient Germanic ancestors. Himmler wanted the SS to become a brigade of guards, highly disciplined and tightly organised, a perfect instrument rationally suited to its task. Furthermore, he wanted also the SS to be a social elite, a kind of modern puritan knighthood with far-fetched pseudo-religious ceremonial, intended to become the ideological avant-garde of National Socialism. Cunningly Himmler attracted prestigious members of the German and Prussian aristocracy. Prince von Waldeck, Prince von Mecklenburg, Prince Lippe-Biesterfeld, General-Count von Schulenberg, and Prince Hohenzollern-Sigmaringen all joined the SS as honorary members, and their reputation and respectability greatly increased the distance between the elitist SS and the numerous, popular, boisterous, unruly and rough SA. The SS emblem (the *Totenkopf*) was a warning to their enemies, and an indication to Hitler that they were ready to sacrifice themselves. Himmler himself made the comparison: 'The SA' he declared 'is the common infantry. The SS is the Elite Guard!' SS men and SS officers were strictly forbidden to converse with SA men and officers or with civilian members of the NSDAP other than in the performance of their duties.

SS membership grew steadily, albeit slowly as Himmler was determined to be strict and selective. In 1930 the SS numbered about 2,000; in December 1932 it totalled 52,000 members and reached 209,000 by the end of 1933. By that time, to many Germans the SS represented a vision of respectability, loyalty and order sadly lacking in the SA. Few suspected then that the SS would grow into one of the most feared criminal state organisations the world had ever seen.

Himmler also wanted his small corps to be more than a bodyguard unit. An efficient SS police service was formed in 1931. With SS support, Göring created a special intelligence service of its own, the *Sicherheitsdienst* (SD, Security Service). For this job Himmler and Göring found a perfect accomplice, the ex-naval officer Reinhard Heydrich (1904–42), a calculating and dissimulating intelligence expert who watched, controlled and spied on everybody and everything. Brutality, order, and methodical organisation became the hallmarks of the SS, which was organised as a semi-secret order within the Party with the purpose of holding the Nazi movement in an iron grip. The SD became a web of secret police in the service of the ideologue Himmler and the intelligence expert Heydrich. Using informants and spies, and with a total lack of scruples, it service collected intelligence on economic developments and political affairs. The SD also checked over the private lives of prominent political leaders, high-ranking Army officers, senior civil servants, and NSDAP and SA personalities for material that could be used to apply pressure and possibly blackmail.

The 'obligation to be unprecedently brutal' was a fundamental tenet of the SS elite. In their own eyes they were an elite in two ways: elite by birth and blood on the basis of racial selection, and elite in functional sense because of their claims to high achievement, ruthless ability and harsh discipline. From 1931 onwards there was a close collaboration between the Himmler-Heydrich team and Göring, an alliance that in the end was fatal to Röhm. In February 1933 over 15,000 SS policemen were issued firearms, and officially licenced to kill and given power to arrest opponents. By 1934, the SS had evolved from a handful of selected bodyguards into a reliable elite security organisation, which had almost achieved independent status. By that time, many people both inside and outside Germany held the opinion that the SS was a positive force, especially compared to the bad-mannered, unruly, wild and violent SA. The SS were disciplined and polite, they had a serious demeanour, and were on the whole 'acceptable, and respectable', at least on the surface, and thus were respected. By contrast, the undisciplined SA rabble had grown too large to be controlled, and its leadership no longer had any real sense of loyalty to the NSDAP or to Hitler.

Right: SD Policeman
The SS intelligence agency and security service, the *Sicherheitsdienst* (SD), was charged with seeking out and neutralising resistance and opposition to the Nazi Party via arrests, deportations and murders. It was administered as an independent SS office until 1939, after which it was transferred to the authority of the Reich Main Security Office (*Reichssicherheitshauptamt*, RSHA) headed by *SS-Gruppenführer* Reinhard Heydrich.

Chapter 17

The Crisis of 1934

Röhm's 'Second Revolution'

After the *Machtergreifung* of 1933, the SA were helpful in arresting the 'enemies of the state' but after that there was little left for the Brownshirts to do. The SA men had always been turbulent, uncontrollable and in some occasions mutinous. Now they had become an inconvenience. The brutal and scandalous Ernst Röhm stood in Hitler's way as the SA disturbed the three essential elements of his political calculations: economic power, military strength, and foreign relations. Hitler and Röhm had never agreed about the function of the Stormtroopers. The balance of power between both leaders reached breaking-point, and Röhm's SA became a real problem. Röhm had always disliked Hitler's policy of 'legality', and contemptuously called him 'Adolf Légalité'. Röhm had always demanded the primacy of the SA soldier above the NSDAP politician. In one respect Röhm had an important card to play. Unlike the other Nazi bosses such as Ley, Ribbentrop, Rosenberg, Heß and Göring, he did not owe his position solely to Hitler's favour. He was not a man who could be easily removed. Confident of his own strength Röhm did not bother to hide his feelings, and did not take into account Himmler's ambition and rising power. Röhm and his followers, who had done all the dirty work – they said – allowing Hitler to seize power, had political ambitions too. The SA leadership disliked the entire trend followed by 'Adolf' since January 1933. They regarded Hitler's Chancellorship as the signal for the settling of accounts that they had been promised for so long. Röhm saw the SA as the last bastion against Communism. In June 1933 he wrote in a newspaper article: 'A tremendous victory has been won. But not absolute victory! In the new Germany, the disciplined Brown Storm Battalions of the German revolution stand side by side with the armed forces. The SA is the foundation pillar of the coming National-Socialist state –their state for which they have fought and which they will defend. The SA will not tolerate the German revolution to sleep or being betrayed at the halfway stage by non-combatants. The Brown Army is the last levy of the nation, the last bastion against Communism.'

Röhm, together with Gregor Strasser and other early Nazis, formed a 'left-wing' branch within the NSDAP. However, his ambitions were contradictory and paradoxical. Deep in his heart Ernst Röhm was a conservative monarchist who dreamed of restoring the Kaiser to the throne of Germany, but at the same time he was a naïve old-style revolutionary. For him the 'socialist' part of Hitler's National Socialism was what mattered. He wanted the workers, SA men and rank-and-file soldiers to run society, not the self-seeking, privileged politicians of the NSDAP. The confused monarchist intended to lead a workers' revolution against the bourgeoisie, the conservatives, the aristocratic Junkers, the great capitalist and the traditionalist Prussian senior officers. His naivety and misjudgement was to think that Hitler shared his belief in social revolution. Röhm wrongly thought that Hitler wanted the old German privileged society broken by force.

But behind this façade there were also other reasons. As a matter of fact, Röhm and the SA leadership were not more 'Left' or more 'socialist' or less nationalist than Hitler. The truth was that they wanted honours, rewards and power. And they wanted them now. Röhm's dearest ambition was to obtain the post of Minister of War and dreamed of establishing the *Reichswehr* as a traditionalist yet popular army, a force led by his SA political soldiers who would rule Germany. His greedy gang of opportunistic henchmen wanted high posts and important functions in the Nazi state, administration and army. As the SA leadership was largely deprived of high office or significant advancement, and as the long-desired control over the armed forces lay far beyond their reach, anger and discontent increased among them.

The quarrel over the so-called 'Second Revolution' and the establishment of either a revolutionary socialist regime or a conservative nationalist state was be the dominant issue in German domestic politics from mid-1933 to the summer of 1934. The very name of the party –

National Socialist – spelled trouble and placed Hitler in an uncomfortable dilemma. He wanted to retain Röhm's friendship and loyalty, but he also desperately needed financial support from the Rhineland industrialists, all of whom scorned the populist 'socialism' of the Nazi 'left-wingers'. What Röhm did not understand was that Hitler, having come to power by legal means with the support of leading capitalists, wanted to consolidate the new Nazi regime by winning over, not destroying, the conservative and traditional privileged classes in Germany. Eventually Hitler was forced to choose between the two opposing concepts.

The desire for rewards and power was also strongly felt at lower level of the SA. Röhm spoke in the name of thousands of greedy and embittered SA men who had been left out in the cold and wanted no end to the Nazi revolution until they too had been provided for. For years the NSDAP had been instilling revolutionary ardour into the SA, but now it had seized power legally, peacefully and ostensibly constitutionally. In early 1934 in the beer halls frequented by the SA, anti-Hitler sentiment was rife. As before the Stennes putsch of 1931, the word was going round: 'Adolf is betraying us!' The SA men wanted to be rewarded for their contribution, and disapproved of Hitler's move to legality. The ordinary SA men, many of them still unemployed, became increasingly impatient with the new regime for its failure to provide them with any significant material rewards. They remarked bitterly that Hitler was wooing the middle and conservative classes and forgot who his original supporters were. Many grumbled that deserving fighters were being left out on the streets. A wave of revolutionary excitement arose among them. Ignoring all remonstrances, they began to talk of 'clearing out the pigsty and driving the greedy NSDAP swine away'. They nicknamed the PO (Political Organisation of the Nazi Party) the 'P. Zero', and also used the term *Goldfasan* ('golden cock-pheasant') to mock the *höheren Politischen Leiter der NSDAP* (Nazi Party functionaries having important official functions). Many of those administrators were corrupt and the common people and the SA regarded them as ostentatious and filled with a sense of self-importance. The term *Goldfasan* derived from the gold-braid insignia and golden-brown collar patches worn on the gaudily Nazi Party uniform.

The SA-men drank, ridiculed intellectualism, openly mocked the NSDAP leadership, coarsely attacked religion and bawled in the streets obscene and revolutionary songs like this:

Hoist the Hohenzollerns at the lamp post
Let the dogs sway there until they fall,
Hang a black pig in the synagogue
And hurl hand grenades into the churches!

Behind the injured protests lay a barely-concealed threat. If the new masters of Germany had forgotten who had put them in their present lofty position, then there were impatient and embittered SA troopers who could remind them. Hitler was embarrassed. He had always tried to present the Nazis as people who respected institutions, public order, bourgeois morality and religion.

In February 1934, Hitler attempted to solve the SA problem by conciliation and compromise. He gave his radical old SA fighters some attention and passed a law 'Concerning Provision for the Fighters of the National Movement'. Members of the Party and SA-men who had suffered sickness or injury in the political struggle were to receive pensions from the State in the same way as those wounded in the First World War. But this did not silence the complaints of the SA.

The beginning of the fateful year 1934 saw a difficult impasse develop between Röhm and Hitler. The problem of the SA remained and Röhm's attitude now became openly hostile. Recklessly, or with unbelievable naivety, Röhm made barely-veiled threats, and attacked Hitler's conservative allies, including the Army, and senior Nazi Party functionaries in frequent speeches. Public complaints were accompanied by outbursts in private meetings with Hitler himself. Röhm showed increasing contempt for his old friend and did not hesitate to remind him of his humble origins –and by implication of Hitler's immense debt to him. On 6 August 1933, during an SA parade in Berlin, the embittered Röhm declared: 'Anyone who thinks that the tasks of the SA have been accomplished will have to get used to the idea that we are here and intend to stay here, come what may!'

In the struggle for power, Röhm and the SA were becoming increasingly isolated by their more conservative rivals, Hitler and the Nazi Party, the rapidly-expanding SS and the Army. Moreover, the moral record of the SA leadership was a stench in the nostrils of all decent Germans. Corruption, brutality, arrogance, debauchery and perversion were so openly practised as to be impossible to conceal. Röhm and the SA leadership's orgies had long been common knowledge: it was established that they possessed a highly efficient organisation throughout the whole country for the explicit recruiting of a male harem. That these conditions existed could not be, and indeed was not, denied. It was also openly said in Berlin that the greater part of the *Winterhilfe* (a charity fund established by the Nazis for the relief of the unemployed by public collection) went into the pockets of the SA leaders to defray the expenses of their luxurious lifestyles. A large part of the German population complained that the SA was an 'army of occupation'. Several Nazi leaders, including Göring, Göbbels, Heß and Himmler, wanted Röhm removed as an obstacle to their own power and influence. Göring expressed concern that the SA's ambitions threatened to undermine the new state, and the Reich Minister of the Interior, Wilhelm Frick, lost all patience with the SA's subversive nature. One of the leading figures pushing Hitler into taking action against Röhm was Rudolf Heß. The Deputy Leader of the Nazi Party, a petty bourgeois and true believer, was morally outraged about the widespread corruption and homosexuality among SA leaders. Heß was also convinced that Röhm's ambitions to make the SA as the political and military elite of the Third Reich could seriously endanger the position of the Party functionaries. What is more, Hitler's decision to sentence people to death without reference to the law or the courts accorded with Heß's idea of a divine dictator behaving responsibly. Röhm was also hated by many industrialists and right-wing conservatives who gave their grudging support to Hitler, because he wanted to nationalise German industry and much of the privately-owned economy. Abroad, Stalin also wanted Röhm out of the way because the SA Chief favoured an alliance with France rather than the USSR. In short, at all levels everyone wanted Röhm's head.

THE SA AND THE GERMAN ARMY

Hitler had always seen the SA as a political and propaganda instrument subordinate to the NSDAP, not a private army, but by 1934 there were probably more Brownshirts in Germany than regular Army soldiers. Although largely composed of veterans, reservists and 'Sunday' activists, the SA proper represented a challenge to the Army, a serious threat to Hitler's own power and a menace to Nazi Party unity. After Hitler had become Chancellor, and after the SA had helped him firmly establishing his dictatorship, the uneasy alliance between SA and NSDAP was evaporating. The vociferous and radical attitude of Röhm was unbearable to the *Führer*, his party, his capitalist financers, his conservative supporters and the Army. At international level, the new statesman wanted to appease foreign public opinion by giving a reassuring and positive image of Nazi Germany, and to be recognised as an international leader. At the domestic level, Hitler needed the middle-class's goodwill, the total support of industrial capitalism and the regular Army's trust for his long-term policy of territorial expansion by war. Röhm infuriated not only Hitler but also the army commanders. On many occasions Röhm made aggressive public declarations of his determination to turn the SA into the one and only German national armed force with himself as commander-in-chief. Röhm, who had not risen above the rank of *Hauptmann* (Captain), regarded himself as a new Gerhard von Scharnhorst (1755–1813), the talented general who had reformed and re-organised the Prussian army after the Treaty of Tilsit in 1807, by combining traditional military training, Prussian discipline and patriotism. Röhm had also observed with interest the example of Mussolini's Italian Fascist party, which had forced the army to incorporate entire Blackshirt formations as combat units. Taking the historical precedent of the French Revolution of 1789, he argued that all successful revolutions based upon ideological claims must have their own revolutionary armies, which should be the vital expression of their new *Weltanschauung* and their chief means of propaganda. He had a vision of a select Praetorian Guard in Ancient Roman style, a professional patriotic army with verve and élan equal to that of the armies of Carnot and Bonaparte. Alongside this elite force there was to be a mass conscript army. He claimed to be able to create a new style of warfare with political revolutionary soldiers freed of the autocratic discipline that had characterised the Kaiser's army. As a company commander in the trenches of Western Front, Ernst Röhm had seen that the old Prussian barrack-square system was no longer adequate to meet the requirements of modern war. He condemned the generals for being out of date, and regarded them as 'a bunch of old fogeys'. Röhm complained that his men were underpaid, discriminated against by the Party, and inadequately armed. He demanded that the SA should become either a fully-fledged militia or to be integrated into the *Reichswehr*, when he hoped that 'the brown SA flood would submerge the *Reichswehr* grey rock'. To achieve all this, Röhm was prepared to risk a major conflict with the Army, whereas Hitler was not. When Röhm spoke in early 1934 of the SA under him as a people's army, that idea frightened the *Reichswehr* generals whose support Hitler was anxious to keep. The conservative generals, who did not want the Army to be corrupted by the SA bully-boys, were unanimously opposed to Röhm's ambitions. On the whole the Army was split between more or less fervent Nazi supporters and a substantial number of senior officers – usually conservative Prussian – who held the Nazis in barely-concealed contempt. The German regular army looked uneasily upon the ex-*Gefreiter* and dictator Adolf Hitler. The High Command claimed to be neutral and to represent the permanent interest of the German nation independently of the rise and fall of governments and parties. However, they welcomed Hitler's promises to rearm, the increase in spending on modern equipment, and the re-birth of the armed forces' prestigious role. But the Army regarded the SA as a motley bunch of street brawlers, ruffians, bullies, thugs and hooligans who understood nothing of Germany's honour and traditions. Until the summer of 1934, the General Staff was very worried by the rivalry of the *Sturmabteilung*, which had grown to a large force of roughnecks and opportunists. The Army was in danger of total subjugation to the SA. The officer corps was determined never to bow down to the SA as they considered that rearmament and a national army were too important, and a gang of homosexuals, thugs and drunks should not allowed to be part of it. The impatient and threatening Ernst Röhm had clearly gone too far. No matter what his real intentions may have been, the High Command could no longer trust him and could not wait and risk the SA becoming an over-mighty armed force. For as far as the German Army was concerned, the SA was to be disbanded and its leader neutralised. It was Röhm's great misfortune to want the one post to which his accession was opposed by the only entrenched institution Hitler dared not offend: the Army would never tolerate as Minister of Defence the man who wished to swamp the *Reichswehr* with his private SA army. And Hitler needed the German Army for his long-term policy of conquest.

On 28 February 1934, the anniversary of *Feldmarschall* Graf von Schlieffen's birth, the Association of General Staff Officers gathered in Berlin for their annual dinner. Army and SA leaders, including Röhm, were present, as well as Himmler and Göring. Hitler took advantage of their presence to let them know his views on the role of the Army and that of the SA. The Brownshirts were unsuitable for the wars of expansion he intended to launch, therefore the future German national army had to be built on the *Reichswehr*. He clearly expressed the opinion that it was senseless to replace the Army with the SA, and urged the SA leadership not to make difficulties for him at a critical moment. The Army was to be and to remain the only *Waffenträger* (bearer of arms) of the nation. As a compromise, the Army suggested turning the SA into a militia, under its command, that could assist with frontier defence and pre-military training. The huge SA – well-armed, trained and strictly controlled by the Army – could have been indeed a welcome additional to the small *Reichswehr* for the defence of Germany. The SA was not in itself wholly unsuitable for Hitler's long-term aims but Röhm's aggressive leadership made it so. After Hitler's speech, Röhm was beside himself with rage while the Army celebrated.

Hitler's opposition to the expansion of the 'amateur' SA into a regular armed force was entirely logical. He had been a soldier and a politician long enough to know that it was impossible for any political party to fight against the disciplined forces of the Army. With shrewd insight, he saw that he could not consolidate his regime and rebuild German military power with streetfighters but with professional soldiers. Hitler saw the situation perfectly. On one side the Generals, both powerful and respected by public opinion; on the other, the SA feared and despised by the German people. The Army, which had weapons and professional skills, the support of conservative circles and the respect of the majority of the German people, had to be reckoned with in any calculations concerning the maintenance of his power, and for his future policy of conquest. Obviously there was no question of handing the control of the mechanised warfare of the future to the turbulent, undisciplined, drunken and debauched SA.

As it became clear that Hitler placed greater reliance upon the professional skill of the *Reichswehr* than upon the political élan of the Brownshirts, Röhm's discontent resulted in reckless behaviour. The relations between the SA chief and General Werner von Blomberg (the Minister of Defence) grew strained and at all levels there was hostility and mistrust. The *Reichswehr* began to take military precautions, which were reciprocated by the SA. Throughout Germany tension visibly mounted and there were an increasing number of incidents and direct clashes ranging from verbal insults to physical blows, such as an Army officer being slapped by SA men when he refused to salute their flag.

Röhm was furious that Hitler should turn to the reactionary, conservative generals, and not to his own loyal SA troops. As he saw it, he was responsible for the Nazi's power, but rewards and power were denied him. He gave no ground, but on the contrary increased his demands. He pressed on toward his goal with, without or against the *Führer*, and refused to accept the judgement of the 'ignorant corporal', as he now called Hitler. But Röhm was no providential Scharnhorst, he was only a man of low intelligence, a noisy, self-indulgent and scandalous pervert only obsessed with his own importance, who wanted to give good jobs and high ranks to his pervert friends 'in the recognition of the success of their work'. For all his personal bravery and organisational talents, Röhm lacked guile in his political dealings. His hatred of accommodation with civilian society and ordered bourgeois life made him blind to reason. As an experienced conspirator and military man Röhm should have realised that the SA did not have the means to rebel against the new Nazi regime and the Army. He should not have underestimated the combined power of his enemies – the Nazi Party, the ambitious SS, the armed forces and public opinion – which represented a formidable opposition. He should have realised that he could never overcome them and that everybody's patience was beginning to wear thin. He failed to see that given the unity of Army and Party there was no room for a third player, and he could not say that he had not been warned.

As frequently happens in the history of revolutions, the old friends, the comrades of the first hour, the more or less naïve idealists became troublesome rivals. A clash became inevitable. The *Führer*, tired of being sandwiched between the SA and the conservatives, decided to purge the regime of the dangerous elements in the SA leadership.

HITLER'S HESITATION

Tensions between the SA leadership and Hitler, heightened by rumours and speculation, came to a head in the spring of 1934. Hitler had seen the massive SA rallies and parades staged by Röhm as a provocative show of force, and heard the hot-headed and aggressive speeches he made. In addition he had learned that Röhm was secretly arming his Staff Guards, something he had expressly forbidden. In early 1934, the issue of how far Röhm could adapt to Hitler's views, or whether he was capable of defying him successfully became all-important. The *Führer* was caught between his warm friendship for Röhm and his pragmatic sense of political reality. He said of Röhm '… to thank Heaven for having given me right to call you my friend and comrade-in-arms'. On New Year's

Day 1934, Hitler had written him thanking him for his 'immeasurable services rendered to the National Socialist movement and to the German people' but at the same time he warned him against any rash act. It is difficult to known Hitler's feelings by that time. Hitler probably had a vague fear of opposing Röhm openly, maybe he had some gratitude for what he owed him. Perhaps he had a confused feeling of inferiority and a memory of the military respect of the former *Gefreiter* (Corporal) for the *Hauptmann* (Captain). Moreover, Röhm was an *Alte Kämpfer*, a man who had been at his side, risking his life during the failed Beer Hall Putsch of 1923, and a loyal organiser to whom he owed so much. All this prevented him from sacrificing his old friend. To this must be added that by removing Röhm, Hitler was well aware that a dangerous power-vacuum would be created. Anyone, Göring or Himmler for example, stepping into such a gap might become a dangerously powerful rival. Besides an independent and powerful SA made a useful counterweight to the *Reichswehr*, which might on their removal feel less obliged to come to terms with Hitler.

As a last resort Hitler tried to reason with Röhm. The two leaders had a five-hour man-to-man conversation on 4 June 1934. Hitler begged his good old friend to keep in line. '… I implored him for the last time to oppose this madness of his own accord, to use his authority to stop a development which in any event could only end in a catastrophe,' Hitler declared in July 1934 in a speech to the Reichstag. But Hitler failed to persuade Röhm to moderate his attitude. Driven at last to make a decision, Hitler came to the conclusion that Röhm and the SA leadership had to be eliminated for the good of the Nazi cause.

It is also said that right after his rise to power, the superstitious Hitler once called on the philosopher, historian and 'oracle' Oswald Spengler (1880–1936) in Munich. Although ostracised by the Nazis in 1933 for his pessimism about the future of Germany and Europe, his refusal to support Nazi ideas of racial superiority, and his critical work *The Hour of Decision*, Spengler was regarded by some Nazis as their intellectual precursor. The rumour goes that Sprengler would have warned Hitler. 'Beware of your Praetorian Guards!'

Hitler had long tolerated Röhm's scandalous private life because the man's talents and connections were useful to him. But Hitler was nothing if not a ruthless, egocentric pragmatist. As soon as it seemed opportune, for reasons of power politics, he decided to dump his old comrade and posed as the great exponent of moral purity. Subjected to pressure from the Army, from Göring, from Heß, from Himmler and many others, it was evident that the idea of eliminating Röhm had made great progress in Hitler's mind. Hitler was well known for hesitating when faced with grave decisions, sometimes with almost disastrous effects. Indeed before taking any decision Hitler hesitated always for some time, and after a period of wavering he made up his mind.

Pressure on Hitler increased. Röhm's attitude also left no choice as he undermined Hitler's prestige and authority. Some senior Nazi officials whispered that the *Führer* was not able to keep order in his own house. Within the NSDAP itself there was a ferocious struggle between the Nazi bosses, each seeking to carve out his own private domain. These plots and quarrels were if anything encouraged by Hitler, as they made his position as the ultimate arbiter the more assured. By that time, old President Hindenburg was clearly dying and without him the traditionalists and the Army might call for the return of the monarchy. The leading candidate for the throne was the Kaiser's fourth son August Wilhelm (1887–1949). The Prince had been allowed to return to Germany from exile in the Netherlands as a private citizen promising not to intervene in politics. However, he broke that promise, joining the *Stahlhelm* which in 1931 merged into the Harzburg Front, a right-wing organisation opposed to the democratic Weimar Republic. The Prince was reportedly interested in the idea of running for *Reichspräsident* as the right-wing candidate against Hindenburg in 1932. He was also a honorary SA *Gruppenführer*. It was well known that deep in his heart, Röhm was a monarchist. Would he not support the restoration of monarchy in Germany? At the same time the Deputy Chancellor, von Papen, made a speech at Marburg University denouncing the methods of National Socialism, the violation of human rights and the anti-Christianity of the Nazis. A purge of the SA would make them responsible by implication for all the illegal brutalities of the Nazi past. The time had come for Hitler to show where the real power lay in Nazi Germany. The time had come to remove the threat to internal stability and international respectability posed by the SA. The time had come to reassure the armed forces, the industrialist and financial magnates, and the German people as a whole.

The crucial period preceding the bloody SA purge of late June 1934 is rather difficult to reconstruct. The outline of the situation are clear enough, but not all the parts played by individuals. No part is more difficult to trace in this confused story than that played by Hitler himself. It is indeed difficult, if not impossible, to penetrate his state of mind and feelings in the period from April to June 1934. Göring recognised the wisdom of allying with Himmler, and many secret bargains and arrangements were made between Hitler's entourage and the Army High Command.

In early April 1934, Hitler went aboard the pocket battleship *Deutschland* at Kiel accompanied by Admiral Räeder and Generals von Blomberg and von Frisch. Naval manoeuvres were held and Hitler was deeply impressed by the techniques of modern warfare, executed with perfect skill and scientific precision. No one actually knows what Hitler and Blomberg said to each other but everything supports the thesis that the two men made a secret arrangement. It is a very plausible hypothesis that Hitler agreed to sacrifice his old SA comrades in exchange for the Army's support. There seems little doubt that Hitler had made up his mind to break with Röhm, and it is clear that the Army was ready to accept a consolidation of Hitler's political power so long as Röhm was removed and the SA neutralised.

The signs of this fruitful bargain were soon to be observed. On 1 May 1934, to honour National Labour Day, regular troops of the *Reichswehr* marched for the first time beneath Nazi colours. At the same time, by order from the War Ministry, officers and men had to wear the eagle and swastika emblem. A few of the older officers protested against this, as it violated the political neutrality of the Army, but everywhere young officers and troops accepted it. It was assumed that the High Command of the *Reichswehr* knew what it was doing. On 25 May, von Frisch issued a new version of the 'Duties of a German Soldier', intended for use of every member of the *Reichswehr*. It was the Army's breviary, its code of honour, which soldiers had to swear to respect. General Blomberg, speaking on behalf the High Command, declared in a speech at Ulm: 'We give our full confidence, our unreserved adherence, our unshakable devotion to our profession, and it is our determination to live, to work, and if necessary to die in this new Reich which had been animated with new blood.' In less than three weeks the secret pact almost certainly sealed aboard the *Deutschland* had borne fruit.

THE PURGE OF 29–30 JUNE 1934

The massacres of June 1934, known as *Nacht der langen Messer* ('the Night of the Long Knives'), offer a good example of Hitler's supreme ability to proceed by a series of carefully planned moves and improvisations to intermediate ends which themselves became the means that compelled him to take the next steps and so all the way to the attainment of unlimited power. In this progression he seemed to be helped by good luck, but on closer inspection it turned out that the only thing he was gambling on was the gullibility of his allies, the corruption and 'sense of honour' of his opponents, and the incompetence of both. The way he played this bloody game of leapfrog at this time was a model for the tactics that led to the outbreak of the Second World War in September 1939. The same tactics were used with equal cynicism in the discrimination against, persecution and then extermination of the Jews.

In the second half of June 1934, events moved swiftly. For the execution of the plan, Hitler found a convenient ally in Himmler, as his secret ambitions were for independence from the SA, and the building-up of a SS police empire within the Nazi state. The time for vacillation was over and the unscrupulous *Führer* and his loyal SS chief organised a cunning trap. The SS was the perfect instrument to solve the problem of the SA by force once and for all. The SS leadership masterfully and skilfully executed a plot to eliminate the SA. The pretext given for this purge, which involved the killing of Röhm and many other SA leaders, was the claimed existence of a plot against Hitler. The conspiracy, invented by Himmler's subordinate Heydrich, was called the 'Röhm Putsch'. The whole story of an imminent SA *coup d'état* was a lie, either invented later by Hitler as a pretext for his own actions, or possibly at the time by Göring and Himmler to force him to move against Röhm. So great was Hitler's capacity for self-dramatisation and duplicity, however, and so convenient the pretext, that it would be wiser, on the available evidence, to keep an open mind. Röhm certainly had many ambitions for himself and his SA and made no secret of them, but no preparations for a coup were ever made, and none of Röhm's plans had gone so far as to merit the name of a conspiracy. The conspirators of June 1934 were not Röhm and the SA but their enemies, Göring, Himmler and Heydrich, who had no problems forging evidence. Using false documents, paid informants, threats, rumours, lies and whispers, the operation was carefully prepared in total secrecy. A fake dossier created by Heydrich suggested that Röhm had received secret funds from the French to carry out a coup. The 'counter-plot' was an entanglement of Machiavellian intrigues, a dark web of struggle for power, laying bare the Nazi's ugly mixture of brutal fanaticism, insane ambition and cold cynicism. The aims of the 'counterplot' were simple: eliminate the SA leadership by force; terrorise the bulk of SA men into subservience; profit from the opportunity to get rid of unreliable rivals; cast the blame for all previous Nazi excesses onto the Stormtroopers; and as the end result have Hitler appear as the saviour of Germany. The men close to Hitler (Himmler, Heydrich, Göring, Lutze and others) had compiled secret lists of those to be eliminated. The SD provided 'irrefutable evidence', the Gestapo provided the police personnel for arrests, and the LSSAH, headed by Jozef 'Sepp' Dietrich, provided the firing squads, assisted in this task by the recently-created *SS Totenkoftverbände* (Death's Head Detachments, concentration camps guards) headed by Theodor Eicke (chief of Dachau concentration camp). No *Reichswehr* firing squad would have been legally permitted to execute SA leaders and German citizens without due process. So the whole operation had to be carried out outside the law. For the SS there already existed only Hitler's will as sole law above and beyond all regulations and principles. At that time there was no reason to believe that the SS would ever refuse to carry out any order from Himmler and Hitler. All members swore total obedience on joining.

Although officially uninvolved, the military authorities tacitly agreed to stand aside from the massacre but it provided transport, weapons and ammunition for the SS executioners. During the weekend of 29–30 June 1934 the *Reichswehr* was secretly put on low-level alert, with troops confined to barracks, and put in state of readiness because of 'a serious threat of a putsch by the SA or by the Communists elements which have infiltrated the SA'.

On 28 June, Röhm had agreed to Hitler's request for a conference with the main SA leaders in Pension Hanselbauer at Bad Wiessee, a quiet summer resort at the edge of Tegern Lake near Munich, where the future of the SA would be discussed. Far away from the tensions and rumours, totally unaware of what was secretly being prepared in Berlin, the SA leaders were relaxed, confident and optimistic that Hitler and Röhm would work out things between them. Röhm himself was so unaware and confident that he had left his special *Stabwache* (staff guards) in Munich. In fact, the meeting was a trap to have all top SA leaders gathered in one place. By means of forged handbills several units of the SA were called out on a parade through the streets of Munich on 29 June. Although the marching men were neither armed nor led by their officers (who were relaxing at Bad Wiessee), they were accused of plotting to overthrow Hitler's regime. This was the pretext for the start of the 'counter-insurrection operation'. Hitler, in the company of Göbbels and a group of the faithful, flew to Munich where they landed at 4 a.m. on Saturday 30 June. Berating the SA officers Scheinhuber and Schmidt who had come to welcome him, Hitler stripped them of their rank badges, medals and honours and had them arrested by the local civil police and then shot by his SS guards. A cavalcade of cars and trucks loaded with SS guards raced in a hurry to Bad Wiessee, as the *Führer* insisted on being in at the kill. The accounts of what actually happened at the hotel are contradictory. By 8 a.m. it seemed that the hotel was brutally stormed. Hitler drew a pistol in an outburst of hysterical rage, and personally arrested Röhm. At the same time, a detachment of SS kicked in the doors of the neighbouring rooms and homosexual members of Röhm's circle, some with their catamites, were either shot or dragged from their beds, mostly without offering any resistance. Together with a furiously protesting Röhm, they were taken to Stadelheim Prison in Munich. All the victims of the purge, beginning with Röhm himself, were taken completely by surprise, which supports the thesis that no SA plot ever existed. Of the thirteen senior SA commanders present at Bad Wiessee several were shot immediately, including Edmund Heines, Schmidt, von Spreti-Weilbach, von Heydebreck, and Hayn, as according to eyewitnesses, Hitler ordered the 'ruthless extermination of this pestilential tumour'.

Simultaneously, the round-up and slaughter of senior SA officers spread all across Germany. In Berlin, Göring and Himmler ordered the SA headquarters to be searched. Here weapons were found which served to support the existence of the Röhm's 'putsch', and the bewildered Berlin SA leaders were arrested. After a perfunctory and farcical court martial, they were executed by firing squads on the parade ground of the Lichterfelde Cadet School. During the weekend of the 'Long Knives' the Brownshirt organisation was summarily decapitated without trial.

All over Germany the liquidations began on the night of 29/30 June and continued throughout the Saturday and Sunday. SA senior officers and leaders were arrested, some summarily executed by SS death squads. *Obergruppenführer* Karl Ernst, a man deeply involved in the mysterious burning of the Reichstag, drove to Bremen with his bride to board a ship for a honeymoon in Madeira. Near the port a gang of SS killers fired on his car, wounding his bride and chauffeur; Ernst was knocked unconscious, flown back to Berlin and executed.

Incredibly, despite the number of people involved in the 'counterplot', the secret had not leaked, and all SA victims had no idea why they were arrested and why they were being arrested, assaulted and executed. Still wearing their uniforms with badges of rank and Nazi insignia, they could not believe what had happened to them when the last words they heard were: 'You have been condemned to death by the *Führer* for high treason. *Heil Hitler*! Ready! Aim! Fire!' Some SA officers believed that they, along with Hitler, were the victims of a plot by the 'reactionaries', Göring and Göbbels. They believed the *Führer* could do no wrong and some died saying '*Heil Hitler!*'

After his arrest, Röhm was stripped of his rank and positions for high treason, and was detained in Munich prison for a few days. His sister tried to save him, swearing to Hitler that her brother would never have

Right: *SS-Sturmmann Totenkopf* unit.
Totenkopf (Death's Head) detachments were special SS units which ran the concentration camps.

attempted to overthrow him. But Hitler remained silent. The leader of the SA, who had known Hitler for such a long time, was totally unimpressed by the *Führer*'s Byzantine attitude, to which all other *Alte Kämpfer* and Nazi leaders capitulated, including the cynical Göring and Göbbels. Like Gregor Strasser, Röhm did not believe in Hitler's infallibility, mocked his megalomania, and, above all, knew too many of Hitler's secrets to be pardoned or be allowed to go into exile. He was given a pistol with one bullet. The furious Röhm, who had often disagreed and quarrelled with Hitler but who had never been disloyal, refused to commit suicide. Instead he loudly demanded to meet Hitler immediately. It was Theodore Eicke, head of the *Totenkoftverbänd*, who was entrusted with the task of disposing of the SA leader. Ernst Röhm was shot in his prison cell on 1 July 1934. While Eicke executed Röhm, Hitler was giving a garden party in the Reich Chancellery for members of his cabinet. Eicke was soon promoted to the rank of *SS-Gruppenführer* and later appointed General-Inspector of Concentration Camps.

OTHER VICTIMS OF THE PURGE

The 'Night of the Long Knives' was not limited to the liquidation of the SA leadership. The purge also included the elimination of rivals and offered an opportunity to gain power. A number of old scores were settled. Some troublesome individuals, not at all connected to the SA, fell victim to private quarrels. Hitler and the other Nazi leaders had long memories. They needed to blot out their troubled pasts, and were eager to see any embarrassing witnesses disappear. Göbbels, Himmler, Göring, Heydrich and other lesser-known figures had all made lists of victims. Private reckonings of the most sordid and lowly kind took place alongside elaborately-conceived state assassinations. Arrests and executions went on throughout Germany until 2 July 1934.

Hermann Göring, jealous of the influence of the master of intrigue, General Kurt von Schleicher, ordered him and his wife to be executed. Von Schleicher's assassination was described as 'accidental'. Hitler's rival, the dissident Gregor Strasser – one of the original founders of the Nazi movement, a talented man to whom Hitler owed everything as the organiser of the Party, and who had withdrawn from politics – was arrested and 'committed suicide' (actually he was shot in his cell). Hitler, who apparently had not agreed to his execution, gave orders that provision should be made for Strasser's widow. Two SS officers, Toifl and Sempach, who had quarrelled with Himmler were killed. The ambitious *SS-Oberabschnittführer* Erich von dem Bach Zelewski arranged the murder of his rival, Anton Freiherr von Hoberg und Buchwald, just to take over his post. The journalist Walther Schotte (who had opposed the Nazis in the election of 1932), Gehrt (a First World War flying ace), Ramshorn (chief of police in Gleiwitz), Schagmüller (Magdeburg chief of police), Edgar Jung (a lawyer and conservative philosopher) and many others were among the victims.

The Catholic Centre Party, the only other party still in the Reichstag, was viciously bludgeoned into acceptance of the Nazi order. Therefore, on the list of enemies to be abducted and shot were several outspoken Catholics like Erich Klausener, the chairman of Catholic Action. Klausener's execution caused a great stir but the Nazis insisted that he had committed suicide and the Vatican finally preferred to keep quiet about it. Father Bernhart Stempfle was dragged to KZ Dachau where he quickly died from ill-treatment. He was a faithful Nazi but knew too much. He had corrected grammatical errors, rewritten certain passages and improved the style on the proofs of Hitler's *Mein Kampf*. He also knew some secrets about Hitler's amorous passion for his niece, Geli Raubal. The Catholic editor Fritz Gerlich and the head of the Catholic Youth movement in Munich, Adalbert Probst, were arrested and murdered in prison. Göbbels, who had many links with the SA, ordered the murder of the non-political owner and headwaiter of the Bratwurst-Glöckle tavern, only because they had been witnesses to numerous meetings which he wanted to keep secret at all costs. Gustav Ritter von Kahr (who had ordered the crushing of Hitler's putsch in November 1923) was dragged from his home, beaten to death, and his body dumped in a swamp.

An error was considered better than an oversight, and a useless death preferred to an enemy who escaped. A certain Wilhelm Eduard Schmidt (a respected music critic) was mistaken for the opposition leader Dr Ludwig Schmitt. He was arrested and killed. His wife received his dead body in a coffin a few days later from KZ Dachau. The SS eventually offered a pension tor Frau Schmidt to redress the error and found her refusal difficult to understand. What did one life more or less mean to them? Many people died in whom Hitler had little interest, and it was not the sort of affair that could be subjected to any official enquiry. A group of Jews were murdered, for no other apparent reason than for the amusement of the local SS at Hirschberg in Silesia. Jews were also massacred at Goglan, Gunzenhauzen and in Franconia where the paranoiac sadist Julius Streicher reigned.

Victims were murdered without any explanation at their homes by icy, dispassionate and methodical gangs of SS killers who did not ask questions, simply obeyed orders and liquidated those whose names were on their lists. Sometimes a wife or a relative, too, paid with their lives for a hasty gesture. Some victims were shot in front of witnesses, but these looked away, knowing it was better not to see anything. Others 'committed suicide'. The bodies were left where they fell –at home, in the entry of an office, on the street, by the side of a road, half sunk in the mud of some woodland swamp or floating in a river.

Only a few people miraculously managed to escape the assassins. The SS intended to murder Prince/*SA-Gruppenführer* August Wilhelm, but the Kaiser's son was protected by Göring. The notorious and flamboyant Gerhard Roßbach, SA commander in Munich, the man who had introduced the brown uniform in the SA, miraculously survived the purge and lived on as a businessman in Frankfurt, dying in 1967. Franz von Papen (Reich Chancellor in 1932 and Hitler's Deputy Chancellor in 1933–4) had been warned of the purge. Advised not to leave his home, he was kept under surveillance, his office was looted, and two of his advisers, Bose and Jung, were shot, but he and his wife narrowly escaped death. Von Papen – gladly enough – soon resigned the Vice-Chancellorship, and became Ambassador to Vienna in 1936. Hermann Ehrhardt (1881–1971), the ex-*Freikorps* leader who had led the Kapp Putsch in Berlin in March 1920, was considered by Hitler to be a potential rival. Although listed as undesirable and under SD surveillance, he managed to escape to Austria. Gottfried Reinhold Treviranus, the leader of a faction of the Nationalist Party who, way back in 1929, had opposed Hitler, was in the middle of a game at the Wannsee Tennis Club when he saw SS men at the entrance. Understanding immediately that they had come to arrest him, he jumped over the fence, managed to get out of Berlin and later escaped to England. Lieutenant-Colonel Düsterberg narrowly escaped death because of his family's close ties with President Hindenburg. The former SA commander from 1926 to 1930, Franz Felix Pfeffer von Salomon, was saved at the last moment when Hitler erased his name from the death list.

The number of victims of the Night of the Long Knives, both SA leaders and 'troublesome' individuals, has never been clearly settled as all records and documents related to it were destroyed immediately afterwards. In an effort to prevent too much becoming known, Göbbels forbade newspapers to carry obituary notices of those who had been executed or had 'committed suicide'. The ban on any mention of what had really happened only led to exaggerated rumours and to the intensification of the feeling of horror, terror and fear. The Nazis spoke later of seventy-seven seniors SA officers killed. Other Nazis sources mentioned between 250 and 300 victims. The Nuremberg tribunal refrained from establishing the exact number, but the figure has been given as possibly 1,076.

HITLER'S TRIUMPH

On the evening of 1 July 1934, the bloody events of the weekend were publicly announced to the German people and to the world via a radio broadcast by Göbbels. The Propaganda Minister described in dramatic terms how the *Führer* had saved Germany by himself arresting perverted traitors and corrupt conspirators.

The massacre of the Night of the Long Knives was more than the hideous outcome of a struggle between two rival groups of thugs, both equally criminal, one rather more stupid and credulous than the other. The purge in fact unmasked the true face of Hitler's National Socialism. The bloodbath clearly showed that the Nazis were determined to operate well outside the bounds of the law, and that violence in the Third Reich had reached new levels. The fact that men had been arrested and assassinated without trial not for plotting or rebellion, but merely for representing sectors of society outside the Nazi movement, left no one safe. The one thing that emerged with startling clarity was the wholly personal character of Hitler's rule, manifest in his will for a permanent revolution on his own terms. Only Hitler himself was the law. His wish was sufficient reason for arresting and killing any one, at any time, in any way. No investigations into the circumstances of the murders were ever made and, on Hitler's personal orders, all records related to the purge were destroyed. Rumours ran rife, and it was with great eagerness that the public awaited Hitler's own account of events, which was finally delivered at considerable length in a speech before the Reichstag on 13 July 1934. The speech was broadcast to all of Germany to justify the 'clean-up' operation. Immediately afterwards the text was published in the national and international press. Hitler's speech was a masterpiece of misrepresentation and falsification of the facts. The principal witnesses all being dead, the story was told so near to what might well have happened that it was impossible for anyone to positively contradict it. Hitler revealed only part of the story and gave a formal and rosy explanation of the events. After a lengthy recital of the past and future achievements of his regime, he took responsibility upon himself but did it in such a way that the German people believed he was covering up for the misdeeds of the SA leadership. He disguised the ruthless criminal purge as an action forced on him by circumstances, disloyalty and conspiracy. He presented the massacre not as illegal and barbaric but as an action of 'higher justice'. He threw the whole blame on Ernst Röhm, who was accused of being unable to assist the Nazis with the vital work of reconstructing Germany, and gave prominence to the charges of corruption and favouritism against the depraved and unscrupulous SA leadership. Professing to be scandalised by the homosexual goings-on in the SA (which he had tolerated for years without any problem), he could set himself up as the guardian of the nation's moral health, and formally assumed the function of Supreme Judiciar. Hitler's own undeniably puritanical mode of life stood in healthy contrast, and the brutal elimination of his rival Röhm took on the appearance of a crusade against corruption, obscenity, filth and immorality. The image of the almighty *Führer* personally rousting out the traitors and degenerate perverts began to be engraved in the popular imagination, supporting the idea of a virtuous regime, a defender of the family and traditional values. However, Röhm's homosexuality had only been a pretext. Hitler's whole account tallied with the truth except for the one factor that the whole massacre hinged upon: the existence of the SA plot. Carefully Hitler did not mention those victims unconnected with the 'conspiracy'. The speech also came as a deadly threat towards anyone who dared oppose the Nazi dictatorship. Hitler was now clearly ready to stamp out opposition from any quarter, and anyone who in the future raised his hand against the regime would be ruthlessly eliminated.

An extraordinary retrospective law had been drawn up by Reich Minister of the Interior Wilhelm Frick, and quickly passed by the puppet deputies in the Reichstag on 3 July 1934. This entirely unconstitutional law was accepted without adverse comment – even in some cases with fulsome praise – by virtually all of Germany's judges and legal associations. The law declared Hitler's purge to be legal and statesmanlike, carried out against the threat of high treason, which endangered national security. In a single sentence all acts committed between 30 June and 2 July were exempted from prosecution, and retrospectively justified the murders as lawful measures taken in defence of the State.

The SA leadership (and other 'troublemakers') had been physically eliminated but not all the men arrested during the purge died in front of firing squads. Hundreds of prisoners languished for months in prison and camps. About 2,000 trials were held to terrorise the SA membership into submission, not for of course for political dissent, but for criminal acts: molestation of innocent citizens, alcoholism, homosexuality and sexual perversion, adultery, favouritism, misuse of official funds and corruption.

It is worth noting that the SA was a large and formidable organisation but that it only took the elimination of a few hundred leaders to cause the supposedly powerful corps to collapse. Probably one of the reasons for this apathy was the fact that the SA leaders never succeeded in giving their troops a real soul and a feeling of pride. The absence of reaction of the ranks proved that the SA was indeed a huge but heterogeneous group with little cohesion and no *esprit de corps*. It must also be said that Hitler presented the purge as directed against the degenerated, depraved and unscrupulous SA leaders who had betrayed the German people, the Nazi Party and the bulk of the ordinary 'decent' SA men. Röhm and the SA leaders were certainly guilty of many evil crimes, but they were not guilty of the crime of treason imputed to them by Hitler and his henchmen, as all indications are that there was no plot.

Once dead, Röhm and his SA senior officers became 'party comrades who were wrong and had turned dangerous'. The majority of the SA rank-and-file believed this lie and remained loyal to Hitler while the officers and leaders who had survived the purge hastily reaffirmed their blind obedience and reassured him of their loyalty. As a token of submission, all weapons accumulated by the SA were handed over to the *Reichswehr*. On 5 July 1934, after inspecting the SA's arsenal, General Liese, head of the army's Weapons Agency, declared: 'I won't need to buy any more guns for a long time!' In an attempt to reassure the German establishment and to lessen the anxiety among civil servants who had been frightened by the SA purge, on 7 August 1934 Hitler granted a limited but highly publicised amnesty, benefiting a few prisoners but leaving the vast majority in the new concentration camps which were soon to spring up all over Germany.

The ruthless massacre of members of his own movement was a great triumph for Hitler. On the whole, the Night of the Long Knives was greeted with enthusiasm throughout Germany, although some people had difficulty to digest the uneasy and stunning events. Many people could not conceal their satisfaction but few of them realised that the real purpose of the purge was the crushing of a destabilising element within the new regime, notably Röhm's plan to incorporate the Army and the SA in a single armed force with himself as Minister of Defence. The average German was glad and grateful to Hitler for getting rid of the brutal SA whose continuing politically counterproductive violence in 1933 and early 1934 had made them highly unpopular. The elimination without trial of the SA was presented to the unpolitical German people as an act of 'popular justice', eradicating immorality, arrogance, greed, blind violence and corruption in an emergency. For many people Hitler became the sacred saviour of the German nation. With such arguments consciences were soothed as the majority eagerly grasped at any excuse. Crimes that would have offended or concerned 'normal' people a few years before were now accepted as normal in this new environment. Bloodshed had become the norm and the law. Now that the threat of arrest or simple assassination hung daily over their heads, an over-obsequious attitude was adopted by many notable dignitaries, functionaries and senior civil servants. A leading Protestant bishop sent Hitler a telegram expressing 'warmest thanks for firm rescue operation, along with best wishes and renewed promises of unalterable loyalty'. For most people, the triumph of the nationalist conservative branch of the Nazi movement was seen as a constituent part of bourgeois normality, the restoration of public order, the revival of the greatness of the fatherland and the return of economic prosperity. No one asked questions, the crisis had been solved, the abscess had been drained, life continued and the Nazi machine was running smoothly again.

BUSINESS AS USUAL

In September 1934, the Nazi Party celebrated its sixth national rally in Nuremberg including speeches, festivities and mass meetings of 500,000 enthusiastic participants. Only a minority of honest people were appalled at the realisation that they had but exchanged one tyranny for another. Only a few people, both at home and abroad, realised that the Night of the Long Knives carried against erstwhile comrades only proved the ruthlessness of Hitler's regime, and was a foretaste of terrors to come.

At international level the massacres of late June 1934 caused a stir, some anxiety and a few protests, but soon the carnage was forgotten and regarded as a regretful domestic German incident. The June 1934 bloodbath did not prevent Hitler's Reich being chosen to host the 1936 Olympic Games in Berlin, nor its participation in the Paris Exhibition of 1937. Those two successful major international events brought the Nazi regime what it most needed: good publicity, respectability, recognition of Hitler as a serious statesman, and the return of Germany to active participation in international affairs as a great nation.

Hitler had eliminated men who had fought for him since the beginning, men without whom he would probably never have succeeded in attaining power. Shrewdly, Mussolini, the Italian Fascist dictator, had already observed that 'it takes one set of men to make a revolution, but another sort to maintain the new order'. After the bloody purge of June 1934, Hitler – until then a rather healthy man without important physical problems, who abstained from alcohol, tobacco and meat, began to suffer from ringing in the ears, eczema and stomach cramps which caused him considerable pain and disturbance of sleep.

In the Soviet Union, another tyrant, as ruthless and cunning as Hitler himself, had followed with keen interest the events of June 1934 in Nazi Germany. Joseph Stalin made no official comment but welcomed the suppression of the SA, which he thought was the signal that Hitler was now master in his own house, which made him a more useful ally for the USSR. Stalin seemed to have learned much from Hitler's brutal reaction. In three years' time he was to apply to the leadership of the Red Army the same merciless repression that the *Führer* had inflicted on the SA. In 1937 the paranoid Soviet dictator ordered the murder of some 40,000 officers (accused to plot against him), which left the Soviet armed forces leaderless and in a complete shambles.

Chapter 18

The SA Until 1945

Viktor Lutze

In July 1934 Hitler appointed the loyal and colourless *SA-Obergruppenführer* Victor Lutze to replace Röhm. Born on 28 December 1890, Lutze had served as an officer in the First World War, joined the Nazi Party in 1922 and had risen rapidly in the SA hierarchy. He was SA leader and deputy *Gauleiter* in 1924 and subsequently promoted to the rank of *SA-Oberführer* in 1928. In 1930 he became a Nazi member of the Reichstag representing the electoral district of South Hanover-Braunschweig. Appointed Police President of Hannover in March 1933, Lutze became a member of the Prussian State Council in the same year. He had never forgiven Röhm for usurping the leadership of SA, which he considered his by right after Pfeffer's departure. The jealous and embittered Lutze had secretly reported to Hitler on Röhm's alleged plans. He had helped the SS intelligence service to forge evidence and draw up death lists for the Night of the Long Knives. He had accompanied Hitler to Munich to arrest Röhm. So, when Hitler officially appointed the despicable traitor Lutze as SA Chief of Staff, he made a good choice. Lutze was not only an insignificant and contemptible man, self-effacing with the dull personality of a well-disciplined follower, he had now become an accomplice soiled with blood, thus a faithful Nazi. Lutze was a capable and conscientious executive, without any special abilities and ambition. Hitler made clear to him that henceforth the role and influence of the SA would be drastically reduced. The *Führer* dictated to Lutze the new course of the *Sturmabteilung*. He demanded blind obedience from the SA, from its top leaders down to the most humble ranks. He gave him a special twelve-point order directed against drinking bouts, parties, automobile trips and unnatural lewdness among SA members, and declared: 'I expect all SA leaders to help to preserve and strengthen the corps in its capacity as a pure and cleanly institution. In particular, I should like every mother to be able to allow her son to join the SA without fear that he may become morally corrupted in their ranks. I want to see men as SA commanders, not ludicrous monkeys!'

RE-ORGANISATION OF THE SA

Ernst Röhm's name disappeared rapidly from standard reference books, as well as from the vocabulary and the consciousness of Nazi Germany. His name was removed from all SA swords and daggers of honour, and all portraits and photographs of him were disposed of. Because Ernst Röhm and his henchmen were filmed next to Hitler in the 1933 propaganda film *Der Sieg des Glauben* ('The Victory of Faith'), the embarrassed Nazi Party and *Führer* ordered the destruction of all copies, leaving only one known to have survived in Britain. Hitler commissioned the production of another film as a replacement. The result was *Triumph des Willens* ('Triumph of the Will'), directed by Leni Riefenstahl that chronicled the Nazi Party rally of autumn 1934 at Nuremberg, this time without the now hated, disgraced and dead SA leadership.

After the June 1934 purge, the Nazi authorities had no clear answer to the question of what the function of the SA was to be in their new state. The Brownshirts, who had believed in Hitler as the leader of a social revolution, were disinherited by Germany, despite having marched, fought, suffered, and in many cases died for so many years in the hope of becoming the cream of the new Nazi society. After the bloody purge the SA remained a social problem in Germany. Just as 1933 had been the year of SA expansion and zenith, so 1934 was the year of decline and fall. The Nazi administration could do nothing else but maintain the permanent members within its structure. Therefore the SA was never abolished. The organisation did not disappear, but it never recovered. Many SA men were dismissed and tried to get back into civil life. Many remained unemployed and several thousand were directed to emergency work camps. Many went into the SA Reserve. Some SA men were transferred to police units and to various Nazi organisations such as the *Organisation Todt* (OT, public works building company), the

Deutsche Arbeitsfront (DAF, the National Labour Front), or the *Reicharbeitsdienst* (RAD, National Labour Service). A very few were taken by the Army. The *Kyffhauserbund* veterans league was reformed independent of the SA and continued in its former role as an organisation for ex-servicemen. The *SA Brigade Ehrhardt* was purged and the remaining element, the few judged loyal enough, were detached to form part of Himmler's SS. The SA did remain a *Gliederung* of the NSDAP, and although the title of *Obergruppenführer* was retained, the ten SA *Obergruppen* (districts) were abolished. The largest SA formation was now the *Gruppe* (division). As a reward for the role it had played in the June 1934 purge, the SS was made an independent corps, becoming a *Gliederung* of the NSDAP in its own right.

The *Sondereinheiten* (special military units) were disbanded. The MSA was hived off and all its vehicles and some of its members were incorporated into the NSKK, which was then raised to the status of an independent Nazi Party formation. The *Flieger-SA* was integrated into Hermann Göring's newly-created DLV, which became the clandestine forerunner of the *Luftwaffe*. Later, in 1936, the *Reiter-SA* became the semi-military *Nationalsozialistische Reiter Korps* (NSRK, Nazi Cavalry Corps) headed by its commander Litzmann. The *SA-Marine* was not disbanded. It served as an auxiliary to the *Kriegsmarine* and performed search-and-rescue operations as well as harbour defence.

The SA Starnbergersee school survived the purge but in February 1936, control passed from the SA to the Nazi Party although the principal remained an SA officer, *SA-Obergruppenführer* Julius Görlitz. The title of the establishment was now *NS Deutsche Oberschule Starnbergersee* (National-Socialist German High School Starnbergersee). In 1941 all connection with the SA was severed. Pupils were enrolled in the *Hitler Jugend*, and the staff in the NSDAP.

The permanent *SA-Stabswachten* (bodyguards) were disbanded in mid-1934, and some units were regrouped into a single ceremonial formation called the *Wachstandarte* (guard regiment). This was renamed in September 1936 *Standarte Feldherrnhalle* (after the building in Munich which housed a shrine to the fallen Nazis of the failed putsch of November 1923). The *Standarte Feldherrnhalle* became a small elite regiment of armed volunteers employed to guard SA senior officers, State and Nazi Party buildings and offices. To celebrate Göring's birthday in 1936, Lutze appointed him Honorary Commander of this elite formation, which he accepted gratefully. By that time, *Luftwaffe*

General Kurt Student was creating a paratrooper force, but found little response from the reluctant German Army. As a result Kurt Student was forced to scrounge troopers wherever he could to bring up his strength. In desperation he turned to Göring who, in a move for power, ordered that the *SA Feldherrnhalle* unit be incorporated into his air force. Lutze and the SA leadership were not pleased, but did not dare oppose his decision. Student was, of course, delighted, and in January 1937 the fittest members of the SA *Feldherrnhalle* regiment underwent training as parachutists. The unit became the embryo from which developed the *Luftwaffe* paratrooper force, and later a *Luftwaffe* infantry division. The remaining part of the *SA Feldherrnhalle* Regiment was transferred to the German army to form a battalion within Infantry Regiment 271. This formation expanded to regimental size in 1940, and to a fully-fledged armoured corps, named *Panzerkorps Feldherrnhalle* in 1945. A small detachment of *SA Feldherrnhalle* continued to serve under the SA as ceremonial unit until the end of the Second World War.

All this considerably reduced the size of the SA from supposedly 4.5 million to about 500,000. But here again, the exact number of SA men after the reconstruction is quite unclear. Despite the reductions, the number of SA formations continued to grow, but obviously the newly created units were far below regulation strength. Thirty-six new *Standarten* were created in 1935, a further twenty-five in 1936, thirty in 1937 and forty-two in 1938. Many new members joined up probably because job prospects or advancement often depended on evidence of Nazi affiliation.

The once feared and powerful SA organisation was completely deprived of political power. The men were relegated to a backseat role, assigned mundane tasks, and the corps turned into a veterans' association. The days of the radical political bullies had ended with the death of Ernst Röhm and the purging of the radical elements. Never again would the SA be in a position to challenge the German Army, the supremacy of the SS or Hitler's leadership. The SA, now chastened and disarmed, provided a physical manifestation of the power and authority of the Nazi state in public demonstrations such as the Nuremberg Party Day held in September each year. Until the end of the war in, the SA continued to exist as Nazi propagandists, as a sports organisation and as street fund collectors, but it had been deprived of any real strength.

The SA continued to be an active component of the *Winterhilfswerk* (WHW, Winter Help League). This was the official German winter >>>

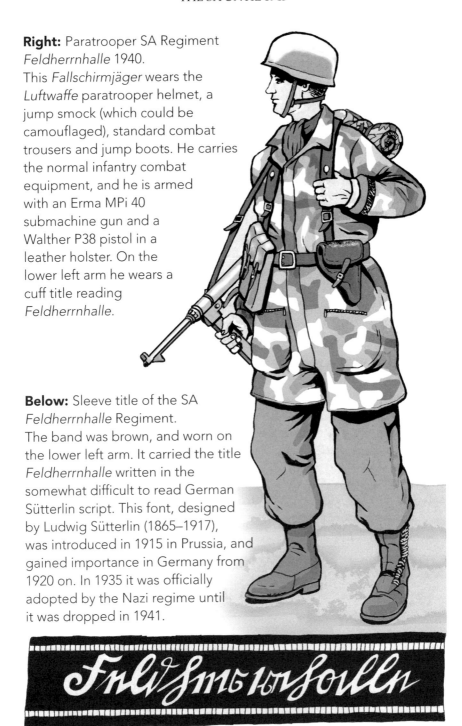

Right: Paratrooper SA Regiment *Feldherrnhalle* 1940.
This *Fallschirmjäger* wears the *Luftwaffe* paratrooper helmet, a jump smock (which could be camouflaged), standard combat trousers and jump boots. He carries the normal infantry combat equipment, and he is armed with an Erma MPi 40 submachine gun and a Walther P38 pistol in a leather holster. On the lower left arm he wears a cuff title reading *Feldherrnhalle*.

Below: Sleeve title of the SA *Feldherrnhalle* Regiment.
The band was brown, and worn on the lower left arm. It carried the title *Feldherrnhalle* written in the somewhat difficult to read German Sütterlin script. This font, designed by Ludwig Sütterlin (1865–1917), was introduced in 1915 in Prussia, and gained importance in Germany from 1920 on. In 1935 it was officially adopted by the Nazi regime until it was dropped in 1941.

relief organisation, the 'socialist' aspect of Hitler's image, which struck a chord among many of the poorer Germans who were recipient of the charity campaign. The WHW, launched in the winter of 1933/34, was organised on an annual basis by the *Nationalsozialistische Volkswohlfahrte* (NSV, National Socialist People's Welfare Organisation). The NSV, headed by *SS-Gruppenführer* Erich Hilgenfeldt, was devoted to the welfare of party members and their families especially mothers and children. The WHW was supported by members of the SA and NSDAP, *Hitler Jugend* boys and girls, prominent artists, civil servants or sportsmen with the aim of collecting money, food, shoes, blankets, warm clothing and other items for the poorest Germans. With the help of voluntary contributions, the Nazis provided hot meals, warm clothes and comfort for the needy. The Jews were of course excluded from benefiting from the organisation. In the winter of 1935/36, the WHW organisation collected some 31 million Reichsmarks. In 1937 helping the WHW was made compulsory. Every worker had to pay a special winter tax (10 to 15 per cent of their salary) from October to March. During the Second World War, the *Kriegwinterhilfswerk* (KWHK, Wartime Winter Relief Organisation) continued the activities of the WHW, and collected for the front-line soldiers, for the widows, and for the civilian victims and homeless due to the Allied air raids. Failure to give generously could bring private threats of violence or public shame.

After the 1934 purge, the SA continued to engage in the dissemination of Nazi racist propaganda and violence at a domestic level including harassing opponents and smashing Jewish shop windows. Some SA units participated to the so-called *Kristallnacht* (Night of Broken Glass), the anti-Jewish riots of 9 November 1938 when synagogues were wrecked and destroyed by fire, Jewish-owned stores and business premises were damaged and pillaged, Jewish homes raided and looted, Jews arrested, severely maltreated, wounded and about thirty-six of them murdered.

The SA was also charged of the pre-military training units of the SA Reserve and the boys of the *Hitler Jugend* They also trained Nazi paramilitary militias, namely the DAF *Werkscharen* (Work squads of the German Labour Front) and the Organisation Todt *Schützkommando* (OT-SK, armed protection squads of the Organisation Todt). The DAF *Werkscharen* were formations intended to act as the political shock troops of the DAF, which had replaced the banned trade unions. It was a huge organisation that brought all aspect of labour in Germany under

Nazi control. The DAF squads saw to it that discipline, command and instruction, and Nazi order were respected in all workshops, plants and factories.

The Organisation Todt (OT) was a conglomerate of public building companies developed by the Nazi regime. The OT was charged to carry out civilian public works (for instance highways), but also military projects (for instance concrete fortifications), and obviously the Organisation needed an armed police force for protection, and the OT-SK were created in 1942. The role of the OT-SK included guarding building sites against theft and sabotage, to be prepared for any surprise attack on building sites, escorting and protecting German workers, leaders, engineers and high-ranking OT officers, and the supervision and control of forced workers and slave-labourers on and off building sites.

For these various training purposes, a new branch of the SA, known as *SA-Wehrmannschaften* (defence teams), was created in January 1939. The *SA Wehrmannschaften* were composed of all able-bodied males other than those who were already members of the SS, NSKK or NSFK, and who had completed their two years' military service. These units were also assigned as auxiliary military police and some of them, in 1942, were organised as anti-partisan forces in Yugoslavia. By that time, the *SA-Werhmannschaften* were also responsible for overseeing the allocation of men and support to the *Heimatflak* (Home anti-aircraft artillery), *Stadwacht* (Auxiliary Urban Police) and *Landwacht* (Auxiliary Rural Police).

SA units were among the first in the occupation of Austria in March 1938. The SA supplied many of the men and a large part of the equipment, which composed the Sudeten *Freikorps* of Konrad Henlein (the Czechoslovak pro-Nazi, pan-Germanic nationalist leader), although it appears that the corps was under the jurisdiction of SS during its operations in Czechoslovakia.

A very little known unit deriving from the SA was the *Verstärkter Grenzaufsichtsdienst* (VGAD, Reinforced Border Surveillance Service) created in 1939 at Danzig (today Gdansk in Poland) from the SA Brigade VI. As the title implies, the VGAD was intended as a paramilitary unit for patrolling the frontiers around the Free City of Danzig and as an extra defence against the Poles. Members of the VGAD usually wore standard German army uniform with a black collar displaying the SA collar patch and a sleeve title reading *Grenzwacht* (Border Guard).

Right: VGAD Guard.

During the invasion of Poland in September 1939 members of the VGAD fought as part of the *Sonderverband Danzig* (Special Detachment Danzig), also named *Brigade Eberhardt* after its commanding officer *Generalmajor* Friedrich Eberhardt. This unit is principally remembered for capturing the central post office of Danzig after heavy fighting.

When war II broke out in September 1939, the strength of the SA was greatly depleted, as many of its younger and fitter members were drafted into the *Wehrmacht*. Unlike the SS, the SA did not establish itself in the occupied territories, once several European nations were defeated and occupied. From then on the SA was composed in majority of partially disabled men or those deemed unfit for regular military service, as well as older senior members of the Hitler Youth, and older

Right: Militiaman of the OT-SK. Personnel of the OT and OT-SK wore several kinds of uniform ranging from working and fatigue suits to foreign captured uniforms dyed to match the standards of the German forces. They were only lightly armed and often wore an armband bearing the abbreviation 'ORG. TODT'.

men not serving in the army reserve. After the occupation of Poland, the SA Group Sudeten was used for escorting prisoners of war. Units of the SA were employed in the guarding of prisoners in Danzig, Posen, Silesia, and the Baltic States. Groups of the SA were involved in the ill-treatment of Jews in the ghettos of Vilna and Kaunas.

On 26 May 1943 SA commander-in-chief *Obergruppenführer* Viktor Lutze, always a minor figure in the Nazi hierarchy, was killed in a car crash while on a food-foraging expedition outside Berlin. Other source asserts that he was murdered in a partisan ambush. Whatever happened, he was replaced with the even more colourless and obedient *SA-Obergruppenführer* Wilhelm Schepmann (1894–1970).

SA Resentment

The survivors of the Night of the Long Knives were relegated to the status of an old comrades' association. But the SA still seethed with resentment against the SS murderers, and until the end of the Nazi regime, the SA's hatred for them and for the NSDAP was never to diminish.

According to the French historian Jacques Delarue (1919–2014) in his book *The Gestapo: A History of Horror* published in 1962, right after the purge, in the second half of 1934 and in early 1935 unknown killers murdered SS men. On the dead bodies were pinned little cards bearing the initials *RR* meaning *Rächer Röhm* ('Röhm's Avengers'). They would

have been a secret group of SA men who had remained faithful to their former leader and who had dedicated themselves to avenging the execution of their chief. At least 150 SS-men were murdered in retaliation by the unknown avengers. The Gestapo made serious enquiries but was never

Above: SA Day medal.
After the purge the SA continued to organise and take part in Nazi meetings, ceremonies and events, like this one commemorating a rally of SA Gruppe North Sea in Bremen on 6 and 7 June 1936.

Right: SA Gruppe North Sea Sport Badge, 1938.

Left: SA Headgear. Italian-style forage cap of a *Sturmführer* in the SA *Wehrmannschaft*, 1943.

Below: SA Rally Badge 1937 Darmstadt.

able to identify the mysterious 'Röhm's Avengers'. At least the author claimed. Jacques Delarue is regarded as a serious historian, but as he was the only source for these actions, this story has to be taken with extreme caution. It is possible that the mysterious 'Röhm's Avengers' never existed.

Nevertheless, the truth is that until the end of Hitler's regime in 1945, the SA authorities always tried to sabotage the development of the SS. Lutze and his successor Schepmann always had an uneasy relationship with the NSDAP leader Martin Bormann, and harboured a long-lived hatred against Himmler. The SA always remained a centre of opposition to the SS to whom anyone involved in a conflict with the SS turned for assistance. In May 1938, after the fall of Generals von Blomberg and von Fritsch, the well-known anti-Nazi General Ulex secretly asked what the attitude of the SA would be in the event of *Wehrmacht* action against the SS. Lutze's answer was: 'Unconditionally at your side.' Alfred Rosenberg, the Minister for the East, together with SA leaders took up the cudgels against excessive SS influence in occupied eastern territories. Ribbentrop, the Minister of Foreign Affairs, often stood in the way of Himmler's foreign-policy ambitions by filling embassy and

Right: *SA-Mann Wehrmannschaft*, Styria 1945. This SA Private wears the olive-brown uniform and distinctive Italian forage cap. The collar patches are raspberry-red. On the left arm he wears the special white and green brassard with the black griffin of Steiermark (Styria, a province in south-eastern Austria) in a white circle. He is armed with a Mauser carbine.

legation posts in the Balkans with SA leaders, deliberately selecting survivors of the Röhm purge. For example *SA-Obergruppenführer* Siegfried Kasche was posted to Zagreb, SA-*Obergruppenführer* Dietrich von Jagow to Budapest, and SA-*Obergruppenführer* Adolf-Heinz Beckerle to Sofia. None of these men had forgotten that they were once close to death at the hands of the SS.

Only a few SA men ever enlisted in the SS and *Waffen-SS*. Despite its name and its SA emblem, the 18th *Waffen-SS Freiwilligen Panzergrenadier Division Horst Wessel* had little to do with the SA. For the purpose of improving the poor relations between SS and SA, Hitler encouraged the constitution of *Waffen-SS* divisions with SA volunteers, but as very few SA

men in fact enlisted, he insisted that at least one *Waffen-SS* division would bear the name of the SA's great martyr and hero Horst Wessel. Himmler was somewhat less than enthusiastic about the idea, but yielded. The 18th Division of *Waffen-SS* Grenadier Volunteers 'Horst Wessel' was formed during the winter of 1943/44. It counted very few SA men, as most of the physically-fit SA members of appropriate age for military service had already been drafted by or had volunteered for the armed forces. Also due to the >>>

Left: *SA-Truppführer Wehrmannschaft*, Niederrhein 1944. This *SA-Truppführer* (Staff Sergeant) of the Gruppe Niederrhein (Lower Rhine) wears the olive-brown SA uniform with black collar patches piped in yellow. On the left arm he wears a swastika armband and a black cuff title reading *Sturmbann z. b.V* (*zur besonderen Verwendung*, Regiment for special duty) indicating a unit available for active duty in an emergency. He is armed with an MPi 40 submachine gun with ammunition pouches on the service belt.

Right: *SA-Mann* drafted into the *Volkssturm*, 1945.

He wears the typical German Army peaked cap and the *Mantel* (overcoat) with an orange armband carrying the title *Deutscher Volkssturm*. He is armed with a *Panzerfaust*. The *Panzerfaust* ('armour fist'), designed by Dr Heinrich Langweiler, was a genuine breakthrough in hollow-charge weaponry and anti-tank warfare. It was a one-man disposable missile launcher. It was compact, light and effective at short distance and thus ideal in defensive ambush warfare, which the Germans found themselves in during the last two years of the war. The Panzerfaust was cheap to produce and simple to operate; it consisted of a disposable steel discharge tube (which interestingly was manufactured by the Volkswagen Company), a blow-off cardboard cap and a percussion igniter fitted near the top and incorporating a basic sight. The warhead was conical in shape, stabilised by four spring steel fins, and was held in place by a safety pin which was removed before use.

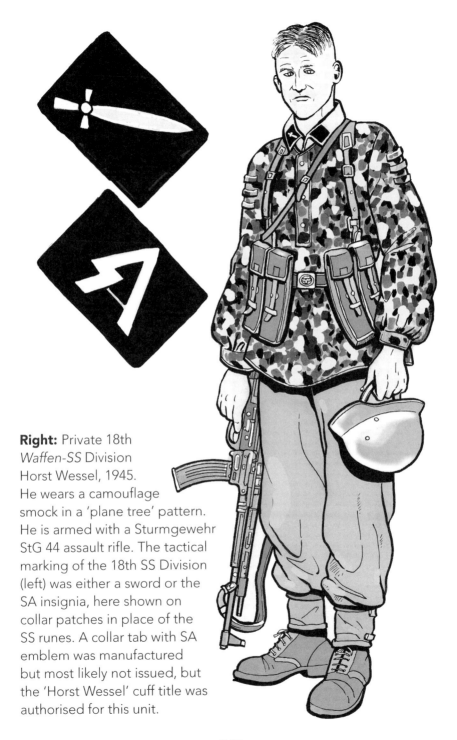

Right: Private 18th *Waffen-SS* Division Horst Wessel, 1945. He wears a camouflage smock in a 'plane tree' pattern. He is armed with a Sturmgewehr StG 44 assault rifle. The tactical marking of the 18th SS Division (left) was either a sword or the SA insignia, here shown on collar patches in place of the SS runes. A collar tab with SA emblem was manufactured but most likely not issued, but the 'Horst Wessel' cuff title was authorised for this unit.

Horst Wessel

Above: 18th *Waffen-SS* Division Horst Wessel cuffband.

general hostility between the SA and the SS, not enough of them were available. As a result the planned SA *Waffen-SS* unit was constituted of cadres from the 1st *SS Infanterie-Brigade (motorisiert)*, while the rank and file were for the most part *Volksdeutsche* (ethnic Germans), many of whom were drafted members of pro-Nazi Hungarian political parties. The 18th Division totalled some 8,530 men in June 1944 and 11,000 in December 1944. It fought in Hungary (January 1944–July 1944), on the Eastern Front, central sector (July 1944–October 1944), and in Poland and Czechoslovakia (October 1944–May 1945). The survivors surrendered to Czech and Soviet forces at the end of the war.

The mutual hostility between the SA and the SS was still inveterate as late as August 1944 -ten years after the purge- when Hitler decided the creation of the *Volkssturm* (Home Guard). By the end of the war, in October 1944, some *SA Wehrmannschaften* were transferred to the *Volkssturm*. The SA were still then considered unreliable, and Bormann lobbied to have the control of the *Volkssturm* handed to the *Gauleiter*, and not to the despised SA command. The *SA Wehrmannschaften* units were drafted into the *Volkssturm*, they did not volunteer. In October 1944, SA Chief of Staff Scheppmann was appointed Director of Rifle Training of the *Volkssturm*. Franz Pfeffer Salomon re-emerged from obscurity to take command of a *Volkssturm* brigade on the quiet Swiss border.

THE ARMY AFTER JUNE 1934

The purge of June 1934 was one of Hitler's most cunning operations as it freed him of his dependence on both the Army and the SA at one and the same time.

Only a few senior officers were shocked by the murder of the former Minister of Defence and Chancellor, General von Schleicher, the man who had virtually controlled the destiny of the *Reichswehr* a decade. The bulk of the German Army was grateful for the murderous action taken by Hitler during the Night of the Long Knives and, on the death of Hindenburg in August 1934, backed his claim to the Presidency. For the Army leadership the Night of the Long Knives simply represented the victory of General von Blomberg over Röhm. They soon forgot the part played by the SS, executors of an ugly necessity. They believed they had skilfully managed to overcome the dangerous SA, and that they had kept their integrity and remained faithful to their code of honour. By the autumn of 1934 the Army was in the process of increasing its size 240,000 men. Meanwhile, secret plans were made for the reintroduction of conscription, and a further expansion to twelve corps each of three divisions. In addition Hitler and the Generals made plans for the creation of a new *Panzerwaffe* (armoured force) and a new *Luftwaffe* (air force). The re-organisation and increase of the German Army were announced in March 1935. The limitations imposed by the Treaty of Versailles were then completely abolished, and Hitler could carry out the aggressive programme he had set out in *Mein Kampf* more than ten years earlier. Blomberg decided that the Army had to demonstrate loyalty to the *Führer*, and ordered that 'non-Aryans' – that is Jews – were to be dismissed from the armed forces immediately. Hitler skilfully manipulated and exploited the traditional Prussian military code of honour, duty, loyalty and patriotism. The support of the Army was institutionalised to an unprecedented degree in an oath of allegiance, making any future opposition an act akin to treason. In August 1934, all officers and soldiers had to take the *Eid* (oath of allegiance) on their regiment flag: '*Ich schwöre bei Gott diesen heiligen Eid daß ich dem Führer des Deutschen Reiches und Volkes, Adolf Hitler, dem obersten Befehlshaber der Wehrmacht, unbedingten gehorsamheiten und als tapferer Soldat bereit sein will, jederzeit für diesen Eid mein Leben einzusetzen*' ('I swear before God this sacred oath, that I will render unconditional obedience to Adolf Hitler, the *Führer* of the German Reich and people, Supreme Commander of the Armed Forces, and will be ready as a brave soldier to risk my life at any time for this oath.').

The oath was totally illegal but Hitler could legalise anything he wanted. For the Army the oath was an act of folly. Sworn personally to Hitler, it was taken very seriously by soldiers and officers. The oath was to affect profoundly all attempts to remove Hitler as the war turned unmistakably against Germany and kept most of the army obedient till the end of the war. The Nazi influence within the Army went even further. Every attempt was made to Nazify the armed forces through the adoption of the *Hoheitsabzeichen* (eagle/swastika insignia) on uniforms and through a prolonged process of indoctrination.

In preparation for the forceful action he was planning, on 4 February 1938, Hitler abolished the War Ministry, dismissed the generals at the head of the Armies (von Fritsch and von Blomberg), created the *Oberkommando der Wehrmacht* (OKW, Supreme Command of the German Armed Forces), and took command personally.

During the Second World War, the oath, the Nazi indoctrination, the propaganda and the traditional German discipline resulted in war crimes and atrocities on all fronts but particularly in Russia, Poland, Yugoslavia and the Balkans. Exactions were committed by some members of the *Wehrmacht*, either by active participation or by passive attitude. The atrocities, shooting of prisoners out of hand as well as the mass killing, displacing of civilian populations, destruction, burning and looting of villages and towns effected by the SS *Einsatzgruppen* (SS murder squads) and the *Waffen-SS* were regarded with disgust by the army soldiers and commanders, but a large number of ordinary German service personnel were involved in supply and administrative roles. The question of the innocence or guilt of the regular German Army during the Second World War is still a controversial question but evidences shows that atrocities, on and off the battlefields, were not only committed by the SS. Some units of the Army played an central part in the shooting of civilians in Poland and in Russia. Many German soldiers of the regular Army were transformed into 'brutalised and fanaticised fighters'. Such was the straightjacket in which Hitler had bound his regular Army that, on the whole, little complaint and no serious obstruction were made against war crimes, exactions, atrocities and genocide.

It must, however, be pointed out that the most serious attempts to remove Hitler from power came from the Army. As early as 1937 plans were made by Admiral Canaris to oust Hitler before war broke out. In 1938 Generals Beck and Halder unsuccessfully conspired with senior army officers to arrest Hitler. In March 1943 a conspiracy involving Generals von Tresckow, Görgeler, Olbricht and Schlabrendorff unsuccessfully attempted to murder Hitler during a visit to Army headquarters in Smolensk. The most famous attempt to remove Hitler, and take over power in order to stop the war happened in July 1944 when Count von Stauffenberg and a core of conspirators failed to kill the *Führer* by placing a bomb in his bunker at Rastenburg. >>>

Above: *Sturmabteilung, the Iron Cohort of the German Revolution,* 1929. A woodcut by Mjölnir (Hans Schweitzer).

Ironically the top leadership of the Nazi Party, notably the *Gauleiters*, the men who had helped to eradicate the SA in 1934, had adopted a totally different view ten years later. When it became evident that the German Army could not win the war, and when *Wehrmacht* generals plotted against Hitler, they now regarded Röhm's bygone efforts to form a large popular Nazi army as a missed opportunity. Such an army would have bred an officer corps and troops imbued with the National Socialist spirit, they argued, and it was especially the lack of that peculiar spirit that had produced setbacks, disintegration, plots and ultimately defeat of Nazi Germany.

Chapter 19

Aftermath

Hitler had always been wholly indifferent to the homosexual leanings, scandals and intrigues of his erstwhile friend and associate. As long as he had a use for Röhm he shielded him from attack with every ounce of authority he had. He only became worried when Röhm became a threat to his leadership and an obstacle to his plans. Only then he took the decision to jettison him.

The elimination of the SA marked a turning-point in the path followed by Nazi Germany. At last the menace of the 'left-wing' SA was broken and the long dispute between Hitler and Röhm was ended. At last Hitler got what he always had wanted: absolute independence and unquestioned power. The period of struggle for power was over and, with the subjugation of the Army, active preparations for war could begin. For many in the NSDAP and Army leadership, the Night of the Long Knives appeared to be their victory over Röhm, but they were very wrong.

Without its leaders the SA were impotent, the corps limped on, but its place was usurped by a more powerful and terrible body. Although nobody could foresee it, the purge of June 1934 marked the breakthrough of the SS, and the beginning of its monopoly. Indeed it marked the start of the rise of the much more dangerous SS, which provided Hitler with an instrument allowing him to exercise his domination over the party and eventually over the whole German nation. Himmler, far more than the *Wehrmacht* generals, was the ultimate beneficiary of the humbling of the rival SA. The day of the ultimate criminal bureaucrats had dawned.

As a reward, Himmler's loyal and devoted SS were given their independence from the SA. The SS corps became a fully autonomous

Gliederung der NSDAP (branch of the Nazi Party). After 1934, the bureaucratised violence and systematised terror of Himmler's SS replaced the more spontaneous hooliganism of the SA. By the time of the Night of the Long Knives, Himmler was happy with the elimination of Röhm and the SA, which he regarded as fundamentally dangerous to the Nazi regime. As Hitler had anticipated, the elimination of the SA leadership created a vacuum into which Himmler moved as he started to expand the numbers and power of the SS. Himmler, with Hitler's backing, could now deploy his skill to develop the SS corps, which indeed became the largest murder-machine in history and grew into several major branches.

The first main groups of the SS included the *Leibstandarte* (Hitler's bodyguards), and the *Totenkopfverbände* (concentration camps guards). Bodyguards, prisons and camps warden were later integrated with the so-called *SS-Verfügungstruppen* (SS-VT, military formations) allowing Himmler to develop his own armed force better known as the *Waffen-SS*. During the war, the *Waffen-SS* grew to a strong military force composed of ethnic Germans and later opened to volunteers from all over Europe. Contrary to Hitler's promise that the *Wehrmacht* would be the only official national armed force, Himmler's *Waffen-SS* actually succeeded in achieving Ernst Röhm's aim: the creation of an independent private Nazi army. The views of Himmler and Röhm in regard to the German army and its future role in Hitler's Third Reich were not widely divergent after all. Both aimed at the subjection of the professional soldiers to the revolutionary armies of the Nazi Party, and indeed Himmler was destined to succeed where Röhm had failed. The establishment of the *Waffen-SS*, the position which it subsequently enjoyed and the appointment of Himmler to the command of the Home Army in July 1944 were in many respects the realisation of those dazzling visions which had stirred Röhm's imagination.

The second major branch of the SS corps was a huge bureaucratic organisation. Among many other sub-branches- this corps included the *Reichssicherheitshauptamt* (RSHA, the State Central Security Office) created in 1939 including the dreaded Gestapo (secret state police) and the *Sicherheitsdienst* (security service), charged with police duties and repression of real or supposed enemies of the regime. The *Rasse-und Siedlungshauptamt* (RuSHA, Central Office for Race and Settlement) was the service controlling racial purity and the organising of the settlement of German colonists in the conquered eastern territories. The *Wirtschafts-*

und Verwaltungshauptamt (WuVHA, the Economic and Administrative Office) ran the various economic activities of the organisation including many profitable businesses using slave labour, and the managing of concentration and extermination camps. All SS branches, and their numerous agencies, offices and sub-offices participated in the crimes of Hitler's regime particularly those against the Jewish people. By identifying, repressing, arresting, killing on the spot, or transporting to extermination camps, the SS were responsible for industrial-scale genocide after 1942.

After the defeat of Germany in May 1945, the Allied launched a process of *Entnazifizierung* (denazification). In October 1946 the Allied Control Council determined five categories of Nazis.

1) Major offenders: to be sentenced to death, twenty years or life imprisonment.
2) Activists, militarists and profiteers: to be sentenced to a maximum of ten years of prison.
3) Lesser offenders deserving leniency: placed on probation for two or three years.
4) Followers and supporters of the regime: to be placed under police surveillance and obliged to pay a fine.
5) Exonerated individuals.

The process of denazification was a complex task, which proceeded slowly and with difficulty. All surviving SA men were interrogated about their past, and ex-SA officers holding the rank of *Sturmbannführer* (Major) or higher were arrested for investigation. Many sought to disassociate and distance themselves from the guilt for the excesses and crimes of Nazism. Many minimised their role in Hitler's regime, and some of those deserving punishment were able to escape.

The International Military Tribunal at Nuremberg, which sat from November 1945 to October 1946, considered the SA a criminal organisation together with the NSDAP and government leadership; the German General Staff and High Command (OKW); the SS including the SD, the *Waffen-SS* and the Gestapo, and several other related Nazi organisations.

Service in the SA did not generate the bonds of pride, mutual trust and camaraderie that was relived, renewed and celebrated after the war in veterans' associations. The SA had always had a very bad reputation.

The corps never developed military traditions, it had too many stained records, and too tumultuous and chaotic a history. After the war, SA members of the pre-1934 period were on the whole of relatively advanced age, and had absolutely nothing to be proud of. Created by the Nazis purely as an instrument for the conquest and consolidation of power, rejected and destroyed when they were no longer needed, the SA was ultimately a corps that most men who had served in it simply wanted to forget. SA veterans never showed any inclination to organise themselves, and associations of ex-SA men never became a feature of post-war Germany. For the same reasons, today the SA is not a favourite subject for re-enactment.

SA men were prominent in Nazi propaganda newsreels of the late 1920s and early 1930s. As said above they were the subjects of two 1933 Nazi propaganda films: *SA-Mann Brand* and *Hans Westmar*. In the post-war period, the SA only made a few appearances in films. A member of the industrialist Essenbeck family is a member of the SA in the 1969 Luchino Visconti film *The Damned* (starring Dirk Bogarde and Ingrid Thulin). Scenes in the 1972 film *Cabaret* (directed by Bob Fosse and starring Liza Minnelli, Michael York and Joel Grey) depict the savage actions of SA men in Germany right before the seizure of power by the Nazis. Fictionalised American Brownshirts are one of a group of 'villains' who oppose Jake and Elwood (Dan Aykroyd and John Belushi) in *The Blues Brothers* directed by John Landis in 1980. SA activists also appear in *Bent*, a 1997 British/Japanese drama film directed by Sean Mathias, based on the 1979 play of the same name by Martin Sherman.

Chronology

1889
April 20: Birth of Adolf Hitler in Braunau-am-Inn, Austria.

1914–1918
First World War.

1918
November 9: Kaiser Wilhelm II abdicated after revolts and mutinies. Republic proclaimed by the social-democrat Philip Scheidemann and a new government formed.
November 11: Armistice signed between Germany and the Allied.

1919
January 5: Founding of the DAP.
January 11–15: Spartacist revolt in Berlin crushed.
February 6: Weimar Republic created.
May 2: Communist revolt in Munich crushed.
June 28: Treaty of Versailles signed. Germany lost territories, her military forces were drastically reduced and she had to pay enormous reparations.
September 10: Austria-Hungarian Empire broken up.
September: Hitler joined the DAP.

1920
January 10: The Treaty of Versailles came into effect. League of Nations formed in Geneva.
February 24: First meeting of the DAP and publication of the Nazi programme.

March 12-17: The unsuccessful Kapp Putsch in Berlin.
April 1: Hitler renamed the DAP the *Nationalsozialistische Deutsche Arbeiterpartei* (NSDAP).
August 7: Official creation of the NSDAP by Adolf Hitler.

1921

February 3: First Nazi mass meeting in Munich.
July 29: Hitler appointed first chairman of the NSDAP.
November 4: Creation of the SA.
November 12–February 1922: Disarmament conference in Washington (USA, Britain, Japan, France and Italy).

1922

March 8: Hitler formed the first NSDAP youth group.
September 30: Official creation of the USSR.
October 31: Fascist march on Rome. Mussolini appointed prime minister.

1923

January 11: France occupied the Ruhr (until July 1925).
January 28: First Nazi Party day, held in Munich.
July: Inflation in Germany ($1 =1 million marks).
September 30: Kampfbund formed by NSDAP and other Bavarian right-wing parties.
November 8–9: The Munich Beer Hall Putsch.
November 11: Hitler arrested.

1924

February 24: Nazi Party proscribed: Hitler's treason trial began.
April 1: Hitler sentenced to five years' imprisonment (of which he only served nine months, during which he wrote *Mein Kampf*).
December 20: Hitler released from prison.

1925

February 24: Nazi Party re-established.
April 27: Hindenburg elected President of the Weimar Republic.
July 18: Publication of *Mein Kampf*.
October 5–16: Locarno Treaty (Germany, Belgium, France, Britain and Italy) guaranteeing European borders.

November 9: Creation of the SS.

1926
July 3: Nazi Party Day held in Weimar. Hitler Youth established.
September 8: Germany admitted to the League of Nations.
December 1: Göbbels appointed *Gauleiter* of Berlin.

1927
March 10: Lifting of public speaking ban on Hitler.
August 19–20: Nazi Party rally in Nuremberg. Parade of 30,000 SA men.

1929
January 6: Heinrich Himmler appointed *Reichsführer-SS*.
August 2: Nazi Party rally in Nuremberg with 150,000 participants.
October 24: Wall Street Crash.

1930
June 30: French troops withdraw from the Rhineland.
February 23: Death of Horst Wessel.
September 2: Hitler made supreme leader of the SA.
September 14: Nazi electoral breakthrough.
October 30: Baldur von Schirach appointed Nazi youth leader.
December 31: SS Central Office for Race and Settlement (RuSHA) set up by Walther Darré.

1931
January 31: Röhm reappointed as SA chief of staff.
July 13: Germany stopped paying reparations.
October 11: Harzburg Conference of right-wing parties (including the NSDAP) against the Weimar Republic.
October 16: Large SA demonstration and riots in Brunswick.

1932
January 27: Meeting between Hitler and Rhineland industrialists in Düsseldorf.
February 25: German citizenship granted to Hitler.
March 13: Hitler received 13.7 million votes in presidential election.
April 10: Hindenburg re-elected President.
April 14: The SA, the Nazi Party and Hitler Youth temporarily banned.

June 16: Ban on the SA and SS lifted.

July 31: Nazi election success; 230 out of 608 seats.

December 6: Hermann Göring elected president of Reichstag.

1933

January 4: Secret meeting between Hitler and von Papen.

January 30: *Machtergreifung*: Hitler appointed Chancellor.

February 2: Nazi programme laid out in the *Völkischer Beobachter*.

February 27: Reichstag fire.

February 28: Laws to 'protect' the German people and the State.

March 1: Official Army support for the Nazis.

March 9: Himmler made Munich police chief.

March 13: Göbbels made Minister of Propaganda.

March 24: Hitler given full powers by the Enabling Act.

March 17: Creation of the SS *Leibstandarte*.

March 21: Special courts established for the prosecution of political enemies.

April 1: Nazis boycott of Jewish shops and professionals.

April 21: Rudolf Heß made deputy *Führer* of the NSDAP.

April 26: Formation of the Gestapo.

May 2: Dissolution of the trade unions.

May 10: Book-burning throughout Germany.

May 17: Right to strike abolished.

July 14: NSDAP the only political party allowed in Germany. Creation of the first concentration camps.

July 20: Concordat between Hitler and Pope Pius XI.

October 14: Germany withdrew from the League of Nations.

1934

January 30: Re-organisation of the Reich.

February 7: The *Reichsverteididungsrat* decided the economical preparation for war.

April 20: Himmler made chief of the Prussian Gestapo.

June 30: Night of the Long Knives: Röhm and main SA leaders liquidated.

July 13: Hitler's speech in the Reichstag justifying the purge.

July 20: The SS made independent of the SA.

July 25: Failed Nazi putsch to take power in Austrian; Chancellor Dollfuss killed.

August 2: Death of Hindenburg, Hitler declared himself *Führer* of the Third Reich. The *Reichswehr* required to swear oath of loyalty to Hitler.
October 7: The Reich Land Service was introduced, sending city youths to work on farms.

1935

January 13: Saarland rejoined to Germany by plebiscite.
March 16: Creation of the *SS-Verfügungstruppen* (future *Waffen-SS*). Reintroduction of conscription and the beginning of re-armament. Official creation of the *Luftwaffe*.
June 18: Anglo-German Naval Agreement.
June 26: Law creating Labour Service.
September 15: Anti-Jewish Nuremberg laws to 'protect German blood and honour'.
November 3: Italian invasion of Abyssinia.

1936

March 7: The demilitarised Rhineland re-occupied by Germany.
March 29: The SS totalled 3,500 members.
June 17: Himmler appointed head of all German police services.
July 18: Outbreak of the Spanish Civil War (to March 1939).
August: Olympic Games in Berlin.
September 9: Economic Four-Year Plan launched, directed by Göring.
October 25: Italo-German Axis Pact signed.
October 25: Anti-Comintern pact signed between Germany and Japan.

1937

April 27: Guernica in Spain bombed by the *Luftwaffe*.
May 28: Neville Chamberlain appointed British prime minister).
November 5: Hoßbach conference (outlined Hitler's plans for aggression and European domination).
November 6: Italy joined Anti-Comintern Pact.
December 11: Italy withdrew from the League of Nations.

1938

February 2–4: Purge of the High Command; Blomberg, Fritsch and several others dismissed, Hitler became head of the OKW with Keitel appointed chief of High Command.
February 12: Beginning of the Austrian crisis.

March 12 and 13: 'Anschluß', Austria annexed to the German Reich to form *Großdeutschland* (Great-Germany).

April 24: Beginning of Sudetenland crisis.

September 15, 22 and 24: Chamberlain and Hitler meet.

September 29–30: Munich Agreement signed by France, Britain, Italy and Germany: Czechoslovakia dismembered.

November 9–10: *'Kristallnacht'* (Night of Broken Glass or Crystal Night): anti-Jewish violence and burning of shops, property and synagogues throughout Germany.

December 3: Nazi law for the confiscation of Jewish property.

1939

March 15: Bohemia-Moravia (Czechoslovakian provinces) annexed by Germany as Protectorate.

March 23: Memel occupied by German troops.

March 25: Membership of Hitler Youth made compulsory for all boys aged over ten.

April 7: Albania conquered by Italians.

May 22: Pact of Steel between Italy and Germany.

August 22: After month of secret negotiations, Nazi-Soviet Non-Aggression Pact signed.

September 1: Invasion of Poland by Germany.

September 3: France and Britain declare war on Germany.

September 4: Australia, New Zealand, South Africa and Canada declared war on Germany.

September 5: US proclaimed neutrality.

September 17: Russian invasion of Poland.

September 27–28: German occupation of Warsaw. Poland divided between USSR and Germany.

October 7: Nazis began forcing Polish farmers off their land.

November 8: Attempted assassination of Hitler in Munich.

November 30: Beginning of the 'Winter War' between Finland and Russia.

December 17: German 'pocket battleship' *Graf Spee* scuttled off Montevideo.

1940

March 12: End of the war between Finland and Russia.

April 9: Operation *Weserübung*: German invasion of Denmark and Norway.

May 10: German invasion of the Netherlands. Begin of the western campaign against Belgium and France. Winston Churchill appointed British prime minister.

May 14: Destruction of Rotterdam by *Luftwaffe* and capitulation of the Netherlands the next day.

May 17: Brussels captured by the Germans.

May 28: Capitulation of Belgium.

May 26–June 4: Evacuation of British troops from Dunkirk (Operation Dynamo).

June 10: Italy declared war on France and attacked Nice and the Alps.

June 14: Open city of Paris occupied by Nazis.

June 17: Surrender of France.

June 18: General De Gaulle in London called for resistance.

June 22: Signature of armistice between Germany and France at Compiègne.

June 24: Signature of armistice between Italy and France in Rome.

June: Outbreak of war in Libya.

July 11: Pétain head of (Vichy) French State.

July 3: French fleet destroyed by Britain at Mers-el-Kebir.

August–October: Battle of Britain.

September 13: Egypt attacked by Italians, repulsed in December.

September 17: Invasion of Britain (Operation Sealion) postponed.

September 27: Signature of military pact between Germany, Italy and Japan.

October 24: Meeting between Pétain and Hitler in Montoire.

October 28: Italian invasion of Greece repulsed.

1941

January 22: Fall of Tobruk to the British.

February 12: Arrival of General Rommel in North Africa.

March 2: German invasion of Bulgaria.

March 24: German offensive in North Africa.

April 6: German invasion of Yugoslavia and Greece.

April 17: Capitulation of Yugoslavia.

April 23: Capitulation of Greece.

May 10: Rudolf Heß's flight to England to negotiate peace; replaced as vice-president of the NSDAP by Martin Bormann.

May 20–June 1: German airborne invasion of Crete (Operation *Merkur*).

May 27: Sinking of the battleship *Bismarck* in the North Atlantic.

June 1: Crete taken by Germans.

June 22: German invasion of Soviet Union (Operation *Barbarossa*).

June 27: Finland entered war on German side.

June 27: Hungary entered war on German side.

July 20–5 August: battle for Smolensk.

August 24: Novgorod seized by Germans.

September 8-19: Kiev taken by Germans.

September: Beginning of SS *Einsatzgruppen* mass murders.

October 24: Kharkov taken by Germans.

November 3: Kursk taken by Germans.

November 18: British counter-offensive in Northern Africa.

December 5: The Germans reached the outskirts of Moscow.

December 7: Japanese attack on Pearl Harbor, USA entered the war.

December 7: Germany and Italy declared war on the USA.

December 19: Hitler assumed command of the *Wehrmacht*.

1942

January 20: Wannsee Conference: plans for the 'Final Solution' formalised.

January 21–31: Rommel advanced in North Africa.

February 9: Albert Speer appointed Armaments Minister to succeed Fritz Todt.

February 8-May 1: German troops encircled in Demjansk.

February 23: Russian counter-offensive in central front begins.

April 20: The German Army allowed the formation of foreign volunteer units.

May 6-June 30: Germans troops encircled in Cholm.

May 12: First record of mass murder with gas in Auschwitz.

May 17–28: Battle for Kharkov.

May 30-31: Massive RAF air raid on Cologne.

June 4: Reinhard Heydrich died after attack by British-trained Czech agents in Prague.

July 22–October 3: Uprising in the Warsaw ghetto crushed.

August 19: Canadian landing in Dieppe repulsed.

August 21: Germans troops climb Mount Elbrus in the Caucasus.

October 23: Battle of El Alamein began.

October 25: German Stalingrad offensive began.

November 5: German/Italian retreat to Tunisia began.

November 7-8: Allied landings in North Africa (Operation Torch).

November 11: Occupation of Vichy France and Corsica by Germans.

November 19: Russian counter-offensive on the south-west front (Stalingrad) began.

November 27: French fleet scuttled at Toulon.

December 28: German withdrawal from the Caucasus.

1943

January 14: Casablanca Conference, demanding unconditional German surrender.

January 19: The Russians recaptured Leningrad.

January 30: Ernst Kaltenbrunner made chief of SD and RSHA.

January 31–February 2: Von Paulus's Sixth Army surrendered in Stalingrad.

February 18: 'Total War' proclaimed by Göbbels.

March 13: Failed attempt to kill Hitler by von Tresckow in Smolensk.

March 21: Failed attempt to kill Hitler in Berlin.

March 25: Begin Allied 'round the clock' air attacks on Germany.

April 8: Russian offensive in Crimea.

April 19–May 16: Second revolt of the Jews in the Warsaw ghetto.

May 2: SA commander Viktor Lutze, killed in a car crash and replaced by Wilhelm Schepmann.

May 7–11: Axis forces in North Africa surrendered.

June 12: Soviet summer offensive in Orel began.

July 4–August 23: Battles for Kursk (Operation *Zitadelle*).

July 10–August 17: Allied landings in and battle for Sicily.

July 25: Mussolini deposed and arrested; replaced by General Badoglio.

August 11–23: Battle of Kharkov.

August 24: German withdrawal from Smolensk.

August 25: Himmler appointed Minister of the Interior 'to combat defeatism'.

September 3: Allied landings in southern Italy.

September 8: Italy's unconditional surrender.

September 9: Allied landings at Salerno.

September 12: Mussolini rescued by German paratrooper commando from Gran Sasso.

September 15: Fascist Salo Republic formed in northern Italy.

October 13: Italy joined the Allies against Germany.

November 6: Kiev recaptured by the Russians.

November 28–December 1: Stalin, Roosevelt and Churchill met in Teheran.

December 22: Hitler ordered the presence of *Nazi-Führungsoffiziere* in the Army.

December 24: General Eisenhower made supreme commander of Allied forces for the invasion of Europe.

December 24: Soviet winter offensive began.

December 26: German battleship *Scharnhorst* sunk off North Cape.

1944

January 3: Soviet troops reach former Polish border.

January 12– May 18: Battles for Monte Cassino.

January 19: Twenty-nine-month siege of Leningrad relieved.

January 22: Allied landing at Anzio.

February 1: Soviet forces reached Narva.

February 4–7: Battle on the Dnieper.

March 4: Soviet spring offensives began.

May 9: Sevastopol re-taken by Soviets.

June 4: Rome liberated by US forces.

June 6: Allied landings in Normandy (D-Day).

June 12: First V1 launched at London.

June–August: Battle of Normandy.

July 13: Soviet offensive in Ukraine began.

July 20: Failed attempt to kill Hitler at Rastenburg . Himmler appointed head of Home Army.

July 25: Allied breakthrough at Avranches (operation Cobra).

July 28: Brest-Litovsk retaken by Russians.

August 1–September 16: Warsaw uprising.

August 7–8: Trial of the 20 July conspirators.

August 15: Allied landings in Southern France (Operation Dragoon).

August 16–19: German forces encircled at Falaise.

August 25: Paris liberated. Romania declared war on Germany.

August 26: German withdrawal from Greece.

September 3: Brussels liberated.

September 8: First V2 rockets on London.

September 11: The first Allied troops reached the border of the Reich.

September 17–27: German forces repulsed Allied airborne attack (Operation Market-Garden) at Arnhem (Netherlands).

September 25: Hitler created the *Volkssturm*.

October 5: German troops encircled in Kurland.

October 10: Soviet troops reached East Prussia.

October–November: Belgrade and Budapest taken by Russians: Germans withdrew from Greece and the Balkans.

November 21: German withdrawal from Finland.

December 3: The Western Allies reached the Ruhr.

December 8: Bulgaria declared war on Germany.

December 16: German counter-offensive in the Ardennes (Battle of the Bulge).

1945

January 12: Soviet offensives in East Prussia being.

January 14: Russian offensives on northern front begin.

January 17: Warsaw taken by Soviets.

January 18: Krakow and Lodz taken by Soviets.

February 4–11: Allied conference at Yalta.

February 7: Ardennes offensive halted.

February 19: Himmler's contacts with Count Bernadotte of Sweden.

March 7: The Western Allies took Cologne and crossed the Rhine at Remagen.

March 11: The Western Allies took Koblenz.

March 19: Hitler ordered the '*Nerobefehl*', the total destruction of all military, industrial and economic property in Germany.

April 1: The Western Allies reduced the Ruhr pocket.

April 11: The Western Allies reached the Elbe: Germans collapsed on all fronts.

April 16: Beginning of the battle of Berlin.

April 21: Collapse of German resistance in Italy.

April 20: Hitler's 56th birthday.

April 25: Western Allies and Soviet forces met in Torgau.

April 28: Mussolini, his mistress and several senior fascists executed by Italian partisans near Lake Como.

April 29: Marriage of Hitler and his mistress Eva Braun.

April 30: Suicide of Hitler and Göbbels in the Berlin bunker.

May 1: Admiral Karl Dönitz appointed *Führer*.

May 2: Surrender of the last defenders of Berlin to Soviet troops.

May 7: Unconditional surrender of German armed forces signed by General Alfred Jodl at Reims. End of the war in Europe: Germany occupied and divided in four sectors (USA, Great Britain, France and Soviet Union).

May 8: Amsterdam liberated.

May 9: Göring arrested.

May 23: Suicide of Himmler.

July 16: First US atom bomb test at Los Alamos.

August 2: Allied conference in Potsdam.

August 6: Atomic bomb on Hiroshima.

August 8: Soviet Union declared war on Japan.

August 9: Atomic bomb on Nagasaki.

September 2: Capitulation of Japan signed on the US warship *Missouri*. End of the Second World War.

November 20: Opening of the Nuremberg International Military Tribunal.

1946

October 1: Nuremberg trials end.

October 16: Execution of Nazi criminals at Nuremberg.

1949

May: Partition of Germany. In the west, the Federal Republic of Germany (BRD) was created with its capital in Bonn. It was a sovereign state intended to create a rampart against the eastern communist Democratic Republic of Germany (DDR, with its capital in Berlin), which was a Soviet satellite. The 'Cold War' culminated in the construction of the Berlin Wall in August 1961 and the Cuba missile crisis in October 1962. The reunion of both Germanies on 3 February 1990 and the collapse of the Soviet Union in December 1991 marked the end of the Cold War and the post-Second World War era.

Bibliography

Arend, Hannah, *The Origins of Totalitarianism* (New York, 1951).

Ayçoberry, P., *La Société Allemande sous le IIIe Reich* (Paris, 1998).

Benoist-Méchin, J. *Histoire de l'Armée Allemande* (Paris, 1938).

Bennecke, H., *Hitler und die SA* (Munich, 1982).

Bessel, R., *Political Violence and the Rise of Nazism* (New Haven, 1984).

_____, *Life in the Third Reich* (Oxford, 1987).

Blandford, L. E., *Hitler's Second Army, the Waffen-SS* (Shrewsbury, 1994).

Bloch, C., *Die SA und die Krise des NS-Regime 1934* (Frankfurt-am-Main, 1970).

Bracher, Karl Dietrich, *Die Auflösung der Weimarer Republik* (Stuttgart, 1955).

Bullock, Alan, *Hitler: A Study in Tyranny* (London and New York, 1952).

Castellan, Georges, *L'Allemagne de Weimar 1918-1933* (Paris, 1969).

Childers, T. *The Nazi Voter* (Chapel Hill, NC, 1983).

Craig, Gordon, *Germany 1866-1945* (Oxford, 1978).

Davis, B. L., and McGregor, M., *Flags of the Third Reich (3): Party & Police Units* (London, 1994).

Eschenburg, Theodor, *Der Weg in die Diktatur 1918-1933* (Munich, 1962).

Evan, Richard, *The Coming of the Third Reich* (London, 2003).

Eyck, Erich, *Geschichte der Weimarer Republik,* two volumes (Stuttgart, 1956).

Faure, Edgar, *La condition humaine sous la domination nazie* (Paris, 1946).

Favez, J., *Hitler et la Reichswehr* (Paris, 1970).

Fest, J., *The Face of the Third Reich* (London, 1970).

Fischer, C., *Stormtroopers. A Social, Economic and Ideological Analysis* (London, 1983).

Gallo, Max, *La Nuit des Longs Couteaux; 30 juin 1934* (Paris, 1970).

Gisselbrecht, André, *Le fascisme hitlérien* (Paris, 1972).

Goldhagen, Daniel, *Hitler's Willing Executioners* (London, 1996).

Grebing, Helga, *Der Nationalsozialismus* (Munich, 1959).

Guyot, A., and Restellini, P., *L'Art Nazi* (Brussels, 1987).

Hanfstängl, Ernst, *The Missing Years* (London, 1957).

Höhne, H., *Mordsache Röhm: Hitler's Durchbruch zur Alleinherrschaft* (Reinbek, 1984).

_____, *Der Orden unter dem Totenkopf* (Gütersloh, 1967).

Kammer, Hilde, and Bartsche, Elisabet, *Jugend-lexikon National-Sozialismus* (Hamburg, 1985).

Lattimer, John, *Hitler and the Nazi Leaders: A Unique Insight into Evil* (London, 1999).

Layton, Geoff, *The Third Reich 1933-1945* (London, 2000).

Lee, S. E., *Hitler and Nazi Germany* (London, 1998).

Lepage, Jean-Denis, *An Illustrated Dictionary of the Third Reich* (Jefferson, 2014).

Littlejohn, David, and Volstad, Ronald, *The SA 1921-45: Hitler's Stormtroopers* (Oxford, 1990).

Longerich, P., *Die braunen Bataillone. Geschichte der SA* (Munich, 1989).

Lukacs John, *The Hitler of History* (New York, 1997).

Lynch, Michael, *Nazi Germany* (London, 2004).

Mabire, Jean, *Röhm, l'homme qui inventa Hitler* (Paris, 1983).

Mann, Chris and Hughes, Matthew, *Inside Hitler's Germany, Life under the Third Reich* (Lincoln, 2000).

Mann, Erika, *Zehn Millionen Kinder, Die Erziehung der Jugend im Dritten Reich* (Munich, 1986).

Mollo, A., *German Uniforms of World War II* (London, 1976).

Orlow, Dietrich, *The Nazi Party 1919-1945* (New York, 2013).

Overy, R. J., *The Penguin Historical Dictionary of the Third Reich* (London, 1996).

Poidevin, Raymond, *L'Allemagne de Guillaume II à Hindenburg 1900-1933* (Paris, 1972).

Richard, Lionel, *La vie quotidienne sous la République de Weimar* (Paris, 1983).

Röhm, E. J., *Die Geschichte eines Hochverräters* (autobiography) (Munich, 1928).

Rosenberg, Arthur, *Geschichte der Weimarer Republik* (Frankfurt-am-Main, 1969).

Ruge, Wolfgang, *Deutschland 1917-1933* (Berlin-Est, 1967).

Rühle, Gerd, *Das Dritte Reich* (Berlin, 1936).

Shirer, William, *The Rise and Fall of the Third Reich* (London, 1960).

Sklar, Dusty, *The Nazis and the Occult* (New York, 1977).

Snyder, Louis L., *Encyclopedia of the Third Reich* (London, 1976).

Sontheimer, Kurt, *Antidemokratisches Denken in der Weimarer Republik* (Munich, 1968).

Speer, Albert, *Inside the Third Reich* (New York, 1970).

Stibbe, Matthew, *Women in the Third Reich* (London, 2003).

Stoffel, G., *La Dictature du Fascisme Allemand* (Paris, 1936).

Stern, J. P., *Hitler, the Führer and the People* (New York, 1975).

Tolstoy, Nikolai, *Night of the Long Knives* (New York, 1972).

Trevor-Roper H. R. (ed.), *Hitler's Table Talk 1941-1944* (London, 1953).

Weale, Adrian, *The SS: A New History* (London, 2010).

Williamson, G., *The SS: Hitler's Instrument of Terror* (Osceola, 1994).

Index

Action Française, xv, 187, 188

Adolf Hitler Spende, 143

Adolf Légalité, 229

Ahnenerbe, 226

All for Germany, 51, 155

Allgemeine-SS, 221

All Quiet on the Western Front (film),
   118

Alte Kämpfer, 28, 39, 53, 56, 238

Althing, 37, 38

Arbeit adelt, 51

Arrow Cross Party, 201

Arbeitskommando, 66

Artaman, 224

Aryan, 13, 14, 16, 31, 47, 51, 108, 116,
   187, 209, 221

Autobahn, 165

Barbarossa, 180

Bauhaus, 210

Beefsteak Nazi, 29

Beer Hall Putsch, 4-6, 12, 23-26, 28, 37,
   57, 90, 91, 96, 101, 102, 106, 112, 114,
   116, 134, 136, 138, 145, 147, 156

Bekenntniskirche, 22

Bent (film), 276

Black Front, 20, 111

Black Reichswehr, 66, 86

Black Shirts, 184

Blum, Léon, 188

Blutfahne, 160, 161, 223

Blut und Boden, 23, 37

Blut und Ehre, 51

Buch, Walter 32, 40

Bullock, Alan, 9

Burgondia, 199

Bolshevism, 65, 66, 132

Book burning, 210-2

Boxheimer Papers, 125, 126

Boycott, 212, 213, 280

British Union of Fascists, 185, 186

Brown shirts, 96

Brown House, 110

Bucard, Marcel, 189

Bunker, 214

Burgondia, 199

Cabaret (film), 276

Cagoule, 190-2

Camelots du Roi, 188

Caporale Onorario, 185

Chang Kai-shek, 112

Chaplin, Charles, 17

Christus Rex Party, 199

Clausen, Fritz, 195

Confessional Church, 23

Conti, Leonardo, 106, 110, 176

Cornelius, Peter, 57

Coty, François, 189

Dachau, 215, 242, 246

Dagger, vi, 46, 49, 50, 51, 57, 155, 156

Dalügue, Kurt, 208
Danzig, xi
Darré, Walther, 3, 13, 23, 24, 39
Davis, Brian L., 53, 135
Déat, Marcel, 193, 194
De Clerq, Staf, 198
De Gaulle, Charles, 192
Degrelles, Léon, 199
Delarue, Jacques, 262, 263
Deloncle, Eugène, 190
Denazification, 275
Deutschland erwache, 18
Die Fahne hoch, see Horst Wessel Lied
Diels, Rudolf, 210, 214
Dietrich, Josef 'Sepp', 242
Dispos, 189
Divide and rule, 43
Dolchstoss, see Stab in the back
Doriot, Jacques, 193
Drexler, Anton, 1-3, 28, 85, 87, 114
Duce, 185 (see also Mussolini, Benito)

Eckhart, Dietrich, 86, 87, 105
Edelweiss, 169, 170
Eicke, Theodor, 215, 242, 245
Emsland, 174
Enabling Act, 206
Ernst, Karl 119, 206, 243, 244

Feder, Gottfried, 2, 29, 39
Feldpolizei, 207
Ford, Henry, 142
First Holy Roman Empire, 27
Fock-Kantzow, Karin von, 79
Françisme, 189, 190
Frontbann, 5, 92-5

Gardenstern, 158, 160
German American Bund, 187
German Labour Front (DAF), 5, 21, 27, 39, 42, 44
Germanic SS, 199
Gestapo, 30, 274, 275
Gleichschaltung, 21, 22, 30, 78, 80, 208

Gobineau, Joseph Arthur, 14
Göbbels, Josef, 9, 17, 24, 25, 27, 28, 29, 39, 40, 43, 44, 101, 111, 106, 109, 121, 124, 129, 130, 132, 186, 246, 248
Goldfasan, 231
Gömbös, Julius, 201
Gorget, 158, 159
Göring, Hermann, 28, 43, 44, 78-82, 88, 90, 91, 92, 102, 107, 144 117, 122, 136, 140, 173, 206, 211, 214, 220, 227, 238, 241, 243, 245, 247
Granninger, Peter, 108
Grimminger, Jakob, 160, 161
Grossdeutschland, 12, 19
Gruber, Kurt, 174

Hakenkreuz, 47, 56, 57, 158
Hammer League, 47
Hans Westmar (film), 131
Heil Hitler!, 33, 34, 80, 244,
Heine, Heinrich, 211
Heines, Edmund, 108, 124
Heinrich the Fowler, 224
Herrenvolk, 15, 16, 19
Herzl, Theodor, 17
Hess, Rudolf, 5, 17, 27, 28, 40, 41, 43, 75, 87, 110, 120, 125, 140, 233
Heydebreck, Hans-Peter, 109
Heydrich, Reinhard, 24, 44, 78, 227, 228, 241
Hierl, Konstantin, 2, 39
High School of the NSDAP, 32
Hilfspolizei, 207, 209
Hilgenfeldt, Erich, 258
Himmler, Heinrich, viii, 17, 24, 40, 43, 112, 199, 215, 217, 223-225, 227, 229, 238, 240, 241, 243, 263, 273, 274
Hindenburg, Paul von Beneckendorff und von, xii, 10, 70, 129, 239
Hird, 195, 196
Hitler, Adolf, xi, xii, xiii, 2, 3, 4 et seq
Hitler salute, 33, 34
Hitler Youth, xv, 27, 30, 35, 37, 42, 51, 99, 129, 121, 122, 131-132, 136, 177-

179, 210, 255, 258
Hoffmann, Heinrich, 28, 44
Hohenzollern, August Wilhelm von,
    Prince of Prussia, 108, 239, 247
Homosexuality, 96, 97, 108
Honorary Aryans, xvi, 16
Horst Wessel Lied, 57, 58, 130, 209
Höss, Rudolf, 132
Hungary, 201

Japanese, 16
Jehovah Witnesses, 22, 31
Jews, 15-8, 20, 21, 31, 32, 64, 118, 119,
    120, 129, 187, 209, 210, 212, 241,
    246, 261, 275
Joyce, William, 186
Jung, Edgar, 246

Kampfbund, 4, 90-2
Kampfzeit, 28, 43, 114, 115, 116, 125,
    211, 218
Kapp Putsch, 70, 71, 247
Kirchenkampf, 23
Klausener, Erich, 246
Kristallnacht, 258
Kuhn, Julius, 187
Kyffhausen, 180, 255

Leader's Principle, 25, 26, 43
Landsberg Prison, 5, 6
Lebensraum, iii, 12, 15, 19
Lee, Stephan J., 103
Légion des Volontaires Français contre
    le Bolchévisme (LVF), 193, 194, 195
Lenk, Gustav, 177
Ley, Robert, 17, 24, 27, 28, 43, 44, 109,
    119
Lie, Jonas, 195
Liebknecht, Karl, 66
Lilienthal, Otto, 172
Lüdecke, Kurt, 76, 77, 91
Ludendorff, Erich Friedrich Wilhelm,
    xi, 4, 65, 97
Lutze, Viktor, 253, 261

Luxemburg, Rosa, 66

Main Bleue, 190
March Violets, 29
Maurice, Emil, 75, 82, 120, 218
Maurras, Charles, 187, 188, 198
May, Karl, 105
Mein Kampf, v, 5, 11, 20, 22, 25, 95
Might is Right, 21
Milch, Erhart, 143
Milizia Volontaria, 185
Mitlaufen, 29
Mjölnir, *see* Schweitzer, Hans
Mosley, Oswald, 185-7
Muchow, Reinhold, 39
Mussert, Anton, 197
Mussolini, Benito, 13, 19, 27, 33, 40, 77,
    127, 164, 184, 188, 189, 191

Nasjonal Samling, 195
Nationaal-Socialistische Bewering
    (NSB), 197
Nazi Party programme, 2, 3, 11-5, 19,
    24, 35
Norkus, Herbert, 35
November Criminals, 7, 8, 62, 71, 91
Nuremberg Trials, 275

Organisation Consul, vii, 71, 86, 96, 109
Organisation Todt, 17, 24, 43, 254, 258,
    259, 261
Organised chaos, 26, 42, 43
Our Leader-our Faith, 154, 155

Panzerfaust, 266
Papen, Franz von, 239, 245, 247, 246,
    280
Paratroopers, 256, 257
Parteigenosse, 28, 29
Parti Populaire Français, 193
Party Courts, 32
Party School for Orators, 32
Personality cult, 26
Pfeffer von Salomon, Franz-Felix, vi,

82, 98, 99, 100, 101, 102, 106, 112, 247, 268
Polycratic system, 26
Pope Pius XI, 22
Porsche, Ferdinand, 165
Prussia, xi, 1, 4, 7, 17, 27, 61, 71, 72, 80, 87, 90, 100, 122, 124

Quisling, Vidkun, 195

Rassemblement National Populaire, 194
Ratti, Achille, 22
Red Front, 72, 120, 122
Reichstag, xii, 82, 96, 101, 108, 129
Reichstag Fire, 206
Religious freedom, 22
Remarque, Erich Maria, 118
Riefenstahl, Leni, 35, 254
Röhm, Ernst, xiii, 4, 82-8, *et seq*
Röhm's Avengers, 262, 263
Rosenberg, Alfred, 13, 22, 23, 24, 29, 32, 40, 87
Rossbach, Gerhard, 145, 247
Ruhr, xi, 3, 91, 98, 100, 132

SA-Flieger, 172, 173
SA-Gebirgsjäger, 168, 169, 170
SA-Leibstandarte, 174, 175
SA-Marine, 170, 171, 172
SA Motor, 164, 165
SA-Musik, 175, 176
SA-Nachrichten, 167, 168, 169
SA-novels, 105
SA-Pioniere, 173, 174
SA-Reiters, 166, 167
SA-Reserve, 179, 180, 181, 254
SA-Sanität, 176, 177
SA-Streifendienst, 174
Scharnhorst, Gerhard von, 234, 237
Schaumburg-Lippe, Friedrich, Christian, Prince of, 104
Schenk von Stauffenberg, Claus, 270
Schepmann, Wilhelm, 261

Schirach, Baldur von, 27, 39, 43
Schlageter, Leo, 69, 131, 132
Schleicher, Kurt von, 64, 101, 129, 245, 268
Schutzhaft, 212
Schutzpolizei, 127, 128
Schweitzer, Hans, 116, 271
Second Reich, 27
Seeckt, Hans von, 70
Sieg! Heil!, 34, 78, 115
Speer, Albert, 23, 24
Sport, 163
Sprengler, Oswald, 238
Squadristi, 164, 183
Stab in the back, xi, 18, 62
Stahlhelm, 70, 71, 99, 122, 135, 180, 205, 206, 216, 217, 239
Stalin, Joseph, 120, 252
Stempfle, Bernhart, 246
Stennes, Walther, 100, 106, 110-2, 226
Stephen J., 103
Storm Afdelinger, 195
Strasser, Gregor, 20, 24, 28, 39, 80, 121, 223, 230, 245
Strasser, Otto, 20, 24, 28, 101, 111, 112, 121, 122
Streicher, Julius, 17, 45, 112, 125, 210, 247
Stresemann, Gustav, 118
Student, Kurt, 256
Struggle for Life, 21
Szalasi, Ferenc, 201

The Blues Brothers (film), 276
The Damned (film), 276
The Great Dictator (film), 17
Third Reich, 27, *et seq*
Thule Gesellschaft, 87
Thyssen, Fritz, 9, 205

Ubermensch, 15, 16
Untermensch, 15
Up with the Flag, *see* Horst Wessel Lied

Valois, Georges, 188, 189

Versailles, Treaty of, xi, 1, 3, 7, 10, 22, 28, 29, 64, 65, 67, 69, 70, 78, 90-92, 109, 129, 200, 216, 269

Vexillum, 156, 157

Volksgemeinschaft, 15, 19

Volkssturm, 266, 268

Waffen-SS, 7, 42, 43, 121, 126, 136, 179, 195, 197, 198, 199, 264, 265, 267, 268, 270, 274, 275

Waffenträger, 236

Wall Street Crash, xii, 7, 103, 182

Weber, Christian, 164

Weidemann, Alfred, 57

Weimar, Republic of, xi, xii, 3, 4, 6, 10 *et seq*

Weltanschauung, 12, 234

Wessel, Horst, 57, 264, 267

Westmar, Hans (film), 131, 276

White Man's Burden, 14

Wiele, Jef van de, 198

Winterhilfe, 233, 256, 258

Zionism, 17, 18